The Day of the Lord…

Unveiling the Mysteries in the Book of Revelation

PATRICK R. BASAL

ISBN 978-1-0980-2701-8 (paperback)
ISBN 978-1-0980-2702-5 (digital)

Christian Faith Publishing, Inc.
832 Park Avenue
Meadville, PA 16335
www.christianfaithpublishing.com

Unless otherwise indicated, all Scripture quotations are taken from the New American Standard Bible (NASB) Version, Copyright © 1960, 1962, 1963, 1968, 1971, 1972, 1973, 1975, 1977, 1995 by The Lockman Foundation. King James Version (KJV) Public Domain.

Printed in the United States of America

TO MY WIFE & CHILDREN

Your dedication, selflessness, and love has been my sustaining comfort over the many years as I have toiled on this work. My God continue to bless you and hold you in His hand.

Contents

Foreword

What follows in the pages of this book will amount to heresy in the Prophecy Buff's world because I have upset their preconceived ideas and entrenched positions. Instead of people looking at this dispassionately and with open eyes and ears, it becomes a political hot potato because I am debunking many Prophecy Buffs' sacred ground or, in their eyes, established church doctrine. They have earned a living spreading their false teaching concerning eschatology and to have them recant or confess that they had it wrong would mean that their revenue from their many books may cease.

By shattering their false eschatology idol, I and those who choose to see the truth will get a lot of pushback and angry emails in the middle of the night. For it's not easy being a reformer and challenging set doctrines of the church, if they are such. I am reminded of Dr. Martin Luther who, at the Diet of Worms having made his argument to the leading theologians of his day, proclaimed *"Here I stand, I can do no other, so help me God."* Yet instead of embracing his teachings, they were condemned and he was excommunicated; however, time and the printing press proved he was right and correct in his theology.

Introduction

The only certain barrier to truth is the presumption that you already have the truth and there can be no other. These presumptions bar us from grasping the truth about the Word of God, specifically in the Book of Revelation. It is essential from time to time to step back and reestablish a fresh perspective and let God's Word do the speaking through His Scriptures to us by putting aside our preconceived ideas and discarding the teachings of our modern-day Prophecy Buffs. So as we approach the Book of Revelation anew, with a blank slate, we discover that where once the passages were confusing (due to bad exegetical and hermeneutical work) they are now revealing new insight into the book.

Where once we thought that the seals, trumpets, and bowls were a progression of separate events leading up to the situation going from bad to worse; however, now we discover that they are the same event looked at through different lenses. This insight is revealed to us in two parallel, but separate set of interwoven visions, which take place both in heaven and on Earth. Both sets of visions start with a broad overall picture of what will take place, then the picture is refined with more detail, and finally the picture is brought into focus.

The first set of visions is depicted in the Seven Seals, Seven Trumpets, and the Seven Bowls, which culminates the focus on the Wrath of God depicted in the vision of the Seven Bowls. The second set of visions, which I call the First, Second, and Third Previews, depict the struggle between the forces of God and Satan and finally focuses with the Third Preview on the Victorious Christ.

We also gain unique insight about the two Beasts. We once thought, per our Prophecy Buffs, that the two Beasts are the

Antichrist and the False Prophet, both of who will assist Satan in deceiving mankind; thus we have been looking for two evil people to appear on the scene. However, now through proper exegetical and hermeneutical work, we discover that the first beast is the governmental religious entity which gives the second beast (the Antichrist/ False Prophet, they are one and the same) the power and authority to carry out the evil intentions of Satan in order to get man to bow down to him.

The Prophet Daniel reveals to us that Antiochus IV Epiphanes will be the forerunner or archetype of the end-times Antichrist who will, just like Antiochus, cause the temple to be desecrated and claim that he is god. The Antichrist will emerge from the region of the north which comprised the Seleucid Empire from which Antiochus came from and is in line with the "kings of the north," rather than from the "revived Rome Empire" or Russia as commonly assumed and taught by most Prophecy Buffs. Remember "My people perish for lack of knowledge" and by the false teachings of our Prophecy Buffs who presume they know it all.

Thus, by letting go of our presuppositions and preconceived ideas, we discover God's truth through His Word and the Book of Revelation no longer becomes a mystery which has made us look at the future with fear and trepidation. So now let's begin our new discoveries.

Outline to the Book of Revelation

I. The Revelation (Rev. 1:1–8)

II. The Glorified Christ (Rev. 1:9–20)
(Key Verse: "Write, therefore, what you have seen, what is now and what will take place after these things," *meta tauta*)

III. The Seven Churches (Rev. 2:1–3:22)
(Prophetic look at the Church Age through history)

IV. The Throne Room of God (Rev. 4:1–11)
(Key Verse: "I will show you what must take place after these things," *meta tauta*)

V. The Scroll/Deed to the Planet Earth (Rev. 5:1–14)
  A. The Seven Seals (Rev. 6:1–17 and 8:1): Overall Picture
  (Interlude: The Sealing and Tribulation Saints, Rev. 7:1–17)

  B. The Seven Trumpets (Rev. 8:2–9:21 and 11:15–19): Refined Picture
  (Interlude: The Little Scroll and Two Witness, Rev. 10:1–11:19)

Outline to the Book of Revelation

First Set of Parallel Visions	Second Set of Parallel Visions
The Seven Seals (Rev 6:1-17 & 8:1)—Overall Picture (*Then I saw, kai horao*)	**The First Preview (Rev 12-14)**—Overall Picture (*Then I saw, kai horao*)
The Seven Trumpets (Rev 8:2-9:21 & 11:15-19)—Refined Picture (*And I saw, kai eidon*)	**The Second Preview (Rev 17-19)**—Refined Picture (*After these things, meta tauta*)
The Seven Bowls (Rev 15:1-16:12 & 17-21)—Focus on Wrath of God (*And I heard, kai akouo*)	**The Third Preview (Rev 19-21)**—Focus on Victorious Christ (*And I saw, kai eidon*)

Revelation

CHAPTER 1

The Revelation of Jesus Christ

¹ The Revelation of Jesus Christ, which God gave Him to show to His bond-servants, the things which must soon take place; and He sent and communicated it by His angel to His bond-servant John, ² who testified to the word of God and to the testimony of Jesus Christ, even to all that he saw. ³ Blessed is he who reads and those who hear the words of the prophecy, and heed the things which are written in it; for the time is near.
(New American Standard Bible, NASB)

Message to the Seven Churches

⁴ John to the seven churches that are in Asia: Grace to you and peace, from Him who is and who was and who is to come, and from the seven Spirits who are before His throne, ⁵ and from Jesus Christ, the faithful witness, the firstborn of the dead, and the ruler of the kings of the earth. To Him who loves us and released us from our sins by His blood—⁶ and He has made us to be a kingdom, priests to His God and Father—to Him be the glory and the dominion forever and ever. Amen. ⁷ BEHOLD, HE IS COMING WITH THE CLOUDS, and every eye will see Him, even those who pierced Him; and all the tribes of the earth will mourn over Him. So it is to be. Amen.
⁸ "I am the Alpha and the Omega," says the Lord God, "who is and who was and who is to come, the Almighty."

The Patmos Vision

⁹ I, John, your brother and fellow partaker in the tribulation and kingdom and perseverance which are in Jesus, was on the island called Patmos because of the word of God and the testimony of Jesus. ¹⁰ I was in the Spirit on the Lord's day, and I heard behind me a loud voice like the sound of a trumpet, ¹¹ saying, "Write in a book what you see, and send it to the seven churches: to Ephesus and to Smyrna and to Pergamum and to Thyatira and to Sardis and to Philadelphia and to Laodicea."

¹² Then I turned to see the voice that was speaking with me. And having turned I saw seven golden lampstands; ¹³ and in the middle of the lampstands I saw one like a son of man, clothed in a robe reaching to the feet, and girded across His chest with a golden sash. ¹⁴ His head and His hair were white like white wool, like snow; and His eyes were like a flame of fire. ¹⁵ His feet were like burnished bronze, when it has been made to glow in a furnace, and His voice was like the sound of many waters. ¹⁶ In His right hand He held seven stars, and out of His mouth came a sharp two-edged sword; and His face was like the sun shining in its strength.

¹⁷ When I saw Him, I fell at His feet like a dead man. And He placed His right hand on me, saying, "Do not be afraid; I am the first and the last, ¹⁸ and the living One; and I was dead, and behold, I am alive forevermore, and I have the keys of death and of Hades. ¹⁹ Therefore write the things which you have seen, and the things which are, and the things which will take place after these things. ²⁰ As for the mystery of the seven stars which you saw in My right hand, and the seven golden lampstands: the seven stars are the angels of the seven churches, and the seven lampstands are the seven churches.

Notes on Revelation 1

The Key to Unveiling the Revelation

From the very beginning of this prophecy, the Disciple John informs the reader that the Book of Revelation is all about Jesus Christ returning in all His Glory. For it is *"the Revelation of Jesus Christ, which God* (Yahweh) *gave Him* (Jesus) *to show to His* (Jesus's) *bond-servants* (us Christians)*, the things which must soon take place."* This glory is revealed in the things that will soon take place, which will establish Jesus as *"the King of kings and the Lord of lords"* allowing His full glory to be revealed. In other words, the Book is all about the Victorious Christ, for He wins in the end. There is nothing to fear and nothing to dread, for every knee shall bow and every tongue confess that Jesus Christ is Lord.

Even though John was a prisoner on the Isle of Patmos, having been banished and exiled there around 92 AD, he identifies with the reader as a *"fellow partaker in the tribulation and kingdom and perseverance which are in Jesus."* John lets us the reader know that there will be persecution in the believer's Christian walk, like he and his fellow disciples experienced. (For a better understanding on the martyrdom of the Disciples read *Foxe's Book of Martyrs.*)

Now according to the early Church Father, Tertullian, in the second century, John had been sentenced to death by Emperor Domitian and had been thrown or plunged into a pot of boiling oil for political offenses to Rome (prophecy was perceived as a threat to Roman political power and order). John, however, miraculously survived unscathed and was than exiled to the Island of Patmos. So he knows something about the tribulation that we will experience as we read the prophecy; he also knows something about perseverance and steadfastness in the faith. The kingdom part on the other hand is what the whole revelation is all about. Yes, the Kingdom of God is within us, but it is also something we will experience once Christ returns, and that is what John will reveal through this prophecy, the *"Kingdom of the Victorious Christ."*

Now the main key to unveiling the whole revelation is found in chapter 1 verse 19: "Therefore write the things which you have seen (past), and the things which are (present), and the things which will take place after these things (future)," so the prophecy covers past, present and future all at the same time. However, in order to assist the reader through the prophetical narrative which can become quite scary at times and confusing, we are given several clues or key phrases, which will help in our understanding of this prophecy.

Like most of John's revelation, the scenes are not in sequential or chronological order and do not follow one another as many Prophecy Buffs teach, so it is important to watch for these key phrases (i.e., after these things, *meta tauta*; and I saw, *kai eidon*; and I heard, *kai nkousa*; then I saw, *kai hŏraŏ*, etc....). These phrases denote scene changes and assist the reader in following the prophetical narrative for they will move the reader either forward or backwards throughout the prophecy: past, present or future within the prophecy itself which is repeated throughout the revelation, as well shall see.

So if you are paying attention to verse 19, you should be asking the question; what things will take place after these things? What future event will take place after some future event which has already taken place? Well, the keys to understanding how the *prophetic application of the phrase meta tauta, "After these things,"* fits into the revelation can be found in chapters 4, 7, 18, and 19. Where they all point the reader back to chapters 2 and 3, which deals with the epistles (letters) to the seven churches whom prophetically become *"the Church age"* (which is the unfolding of all subsequent church history). This will become clear when we get to chapters 2 and 3.

However, the phrase applied here means that *"after"* the *"end of the church age"* and *"the great falling away" "these things"* will take place. What things will take place you ask again? Well, the *"Destruction of*

Babylon" and then the *"Reign of the Victorious Christ"*! These things are the focus of John's prophecy.

So now, let us look closer at the prophetic application of this key phrase which I have stated is also found in other chapters throughout the book. In Revelation 4:1 there is a dual emphasis of the phrase *meta tauta*, which states *"After these things I looked...and the voice... said...I will show you what must take place after these things."* Thus *"these things"* in the present (*"the church age"* which John had just witnessed) become *"these things"* in the future (prophetic) which must happen before Christ is seated on the throne with His Father in the throne room of heaven.

Skip ahead to chapter 7, where the breaking of the seven seals gives the reader the overall big picture of what will take place at the end of days. Again we find the phrase *meta tauta*, found in Revelation 7:9, *"After these things I looked...standing before the throne and the Lamb,"* pointing us back to *"the end of the church age"* where the martyred saints who are the ones *"who come out of the great tribulation, and they have washed their robes and made them white in the blood of the Lamb,"* by what they had to endure, are now before the throne of God and the Lamb.

Going on further, at the opening of Revelation 18:1 we find the reader being drawn back to the narrowly focused refined picture of the seven bowls for the phrase *"After these things,"* does not follow chronologically after Revelation 17:18, but moves the reader back to the beginning of the book where Christ himself tells the Disciple John to write down what he see in the past, the present, and in the future. *"Write, therefore, what you have seen* (past), *what is now* (present) *and what will take place after these things* (future)" (Rev. 1:19). This scene now describes the fall of Babylon and completes the victory over Satan. Chapters 17 and 18 mark this second preview of the refined picture displaying God's triumph over Babylon and the Harlot. However, the term *meta tauta,* *"After these things,"* points us back to the seven churches and the *"end of the church age"* and not to the preceding chapter where the harlot is revealed.

Finally in Revelation 19:1 we have the last of the *meta tauta,* phrases. *"After these things I heard something like a loud voice of a great* *multitude in heaven, saying…"*This scene again takes the reader back to the *"end of the church age"* where the multitudes who have been crying out for God's justice are now rejoicing over the fresh victory just won. The *"end of the Church Age"* thus becomes the catalyst which John's prophecy revolves around. Everything hinges upon *"the great falling away,"* which is revealed in the last epistle (letter) to the last church, the church in Laodicea.

This church which is "neither cold nor hot" but "lukewarm," Christ says that He will spit you out of His mouth, thus ending "the church age" and beginning the final conflict in which He will be Victorious. So the entire prophetical narrative is all about what will happen after the unfolding of all church history as revealed in the seven epistles (letters) to the seven churches which is revealed here in the key verse of the first chapter, Revelation 1:19.

Revelation

CHAPTER 2

New American Standard Bible (NASB)

Message to Ephesus

2 "To the angel of the church in Ephesus write:

The One who holds the seven stars in His right hand, the One who walks among the seven golden lampstands, says this:

2 'I know your deeds and your toil and perseverance, and that you cannot tolerate evil men, and you put to the test those who call themselves apostles, and they are not, and you found them to be false; 3 and you have perseverance and have endured for My name's sake, and have not grown weary. 4 But I have this against you, that you have left your first love. 5 Therefore remember from where you have fallen, and repent and do the deeds you did at first; or else I am coming to you and will remove your lampstand out of its place—unless you repent. 6 Yet this you do have, that you hate the deeds of the Nicolaitans, which I also hate. 7 He who has an ear, let him hear what the Spirit says to the churches. To him who overcomes, I will grant to eat of the tree of life which is in the Paradise of God.'

Message to Smyrna

[8] *"And to the angel of the church in Smyrna write:*

The first and the last, who was dead, and has come to life, says this:

[9] *'I know your tribulation and your poverty (but you are rich), and the blasphemy by those who say they are Jews and are not, but are a synagogue of Satan.* [10] *Do not fear what you are about to suffer. Behold, the devil is about to cast some of you into prison, so that you will be tested, and you will have tribulation for ten days. Be faithful until death, and I will give you the crown of life.* [11] *He who has an ear, let him hear what the Spirit says to the churches. He who overcomes will not be hurt by the second death.'*

Message to Pergamum

[12] *"And to the angel of the church in Pergamum write:*

The One who has the sharp two-edged sword says this:

[13] *'I know where you dwell, where Satan's throne is; and you hold fast My name, and did not deny My faith even in the days of Antipas, My witness, My faithful one, who was killed among you, where Satan dwells.* [14] *But I have a few things against you, because you have there some who hold the teaching of Balaam, who kept teaching Balak to put a stumbling block before the sons of Israel, to eat things sacrificed to idols and to commit acts of immorality.* [15] *So you also have some who in the same way hold the teaching of the Nicolaitans.* [16] *Therefore repent; or else I am coming to you quickly, and I will make war against them with the sword of My mouth.* [17] *He who has an ear, let him hear what the Spirit says to the churches. To him who overcomes, to him I will give some of the hidden manna, and I will give him a white stone, and a new name written on the stone which no one knows but he who receives it.'*

Message to Thyatira

¹⁸ *"And to the angel of the church in Thyatira write:*

The Son of God, who has eyes like a flame of fire, and His feet are like burnished bronze, says this:

¹⁹ *'I know your deeds, and your love and faith and service and perseverance, and that your deeds of late are greater than at first.* ²⁰ *But I have this against you, that you tolerate the woman Jezebel, who calls herself a prophetess, and she teaches and leads My bond-servants astray so that they commit acts of immorality and eat things sacrificed to idols.* ²¹ *I gave her time to repent, and she does not want to repent of her immorality.* ²² *Behold, I will throw her on a bed of sickness, and those who commit adultery with her into great tribulation, unless they repent of her deeds.* ²³ *And I will kill her children with pestilence, and all the churches will know that I am He who searches the minds and hearts; and I will give to each one of you according to your deeds.* ²⁴ *But I say to you, the rest who are in Thyatira, who do not hold this teaching, who have not known the deep things of Satan, as they call them—I place no other burden on you.* ²⁵ *Nevertheless what you have, hold fast until I come.* ²⁶ *He who overcomes, and he who keeps My deeds until the end,* TO HIM I WILL GIVE AUTHORITY OVER THE NATIONS; ²⁷ AND HE SHALL RULE THEM WITH A ROD OF IRON, AS THE VESSELS OF THE POTTER ARE BROKEN TO PIECES, *as I also have received authority from My Father;* ²⁸ *and I will give him the morning star.* ²⁹ *He who has an ear, let him hear what the Spirit says to the churches.'*

Notes on Revelation 2

The Heptadic Structure

Throughout the Book of Revelation, there are numerous *heptadic* (sevenfold) structures that are found. Many of them are rather obvious, many of them are quite subtle, and many of them are rather well "hidden," and as we will see. This heptadic structure is reflected continually throughout the book (i.e., the Seven Titles of Christ, Seven Spirits, Seven Churches, Seven Golden Lamp Stands, Seven Blessings, Seven Seals, Seven Trumpets, Seven Bowls, Seven Crowns, etc....). Even though the number Seven is God's perfect number, it does not always mean God's perfection—i.e., Satan counterfeits what God has created and subverts things for evil (i.e., the Seven Kings, Seven Heads, and the Seven Horns). So the heptadic structures can be either something from God or it can be something evil.

Now the message to the Seven Churches: Ephesus, Smyrna, Pergamum, Thyatira, Sardis, Philadelphia, and Laodicea, are often overlooked as the seven most important epistles of all scripture. For these seven epistles (letters) comprising chapters 2 and 3 were authored by Jesus Himself personally and gives us a look into *"the Church Age."* It is also very interesting that Jesus Himself incorporated this heptadic structure into each epistle. A key aspect to understanding the significance of the letters as Dr. Chuck Missler[1] suggest is to understand and grasp the internal structure of their design, for revealed within the letters is a heptadic structure all its own.

[1.] Chuck Missler, "Personal Update News Journal," *Seven Mysterious Letters, A Timely Challenge:* (Coeur d'Alene: Koinonia House Inc, 1993), http://khouse.org/articles/1993/32/.

So now, if we carefully examine the epistles (letters), we find seven key parts or components revealed within each letter itself, which is as follows:

- The meaning of the name of the church being addressed.
- The title of Jesus, each chosen relevant to the message to that particular church.
- A commendation of things that have been done well.
- A criticism of things that need attention.
- The exhortation which is specific to the condition of each particular church.
- The key phrase, *"He that has an ear, let him hear what the Spirit say to the churches."*
- A promise to the *"overcomer"* included with each letter.

What is interesting that this key phrase *"He that has an ear, let him hear what the Spirit say to the churches"* (component 6), is the final part in the last four letters, but appears *before* the "Promise to the overcomer" (component 7) in the first three. Leaving the promises to the overcomers as a kind of post script after the body of the letters themselves. When we look at the letters the design may suggest that the first three letters and the last four may share some particular characteristic. Also, only the last four letters include explicit references to the *parousia*, the Second Coming of Christ.

It is also interesting that once the basic structure is evident, we notices that two of the letters, Smyrna and Philadelphia, have "N*o Criticism"* (component 4), which is rather encouraging to the reader. However, two of the letters, Sardis and Laodicea, have "N*o Commendation"* (component 3), which is rather disparaging and should give us pause. It is also something we should pay close attention to.[2]

[2.] Chuck Missler, "Personal Update News Journal," *Seven Mysterious Letters, A Timely Challenge:* (Coeur d'Alene: Koinonia House Inc, 1993), http://khouse. org/articles/1993/32/.

Now that we understand the internal structure and components of each letter, we need to look at the four levels of application to these letters as Dr. Missler states,

1. *Local*: These were actual, historic churches, with valid needs. Many archaeological discoveries have confirmed this fact.

2. *Admonitory*: In each of the letters there appears the key phrase, *"Hear what the Spirit says to the churches."* Note the plural, *churches.* It turns out that each of the letters applies to *all churches* throughout history. As we understand the sevenfold internal structure, the uniquely tailored messages, and the specific admonitions in each of the letters, we discover that any church can be "mapped" in terms of these seven composite profiles.

3. *Homiletically*: Each of the letters also contains the phrase, *"He that has an ear let him hear..."* Each letter applies to every one of *us because we all have ears*. There are some elements of each of these seven "churches" in each of us. Thus, this may be the most practical application of the entire Book of Revelation.

4. *Prophetically*: The most amazing discovery, however, of these seven letters is their apparent prophetic application. These letters describe, with remarkable precision, the unfolding of all subsequent church history. If these letters were in any other *order*, this would not be true!

If these seven letters really do include a *preview* of all church history, then where are we now? Are we, indeed, in the period suggested by the letter to Laodicea? I will also, submit to you that there is an intended parallel between these seven letters of Jesus Christ and His seven "Kingdom Parables" found in Matthew 13:3–52.

Dr. Chuck Missler also underscores this distinction and suggest that the Apostle Paul wrote thirteen epistles; however three of these had "duplicate" addressees: Corinthians, Thessalonians, and Timothy. My question is, were each of these three letters really two separate letters or where they considered one. For example, the Book of Samuel found in the Jewish scriptures is one book, not two as we find in our Bibles today. Thus if we look at Paul's epistles we find that 13—3 = 10 addressees. But three addressees were written to individuals: Timothy, Titus, and Philemon, so now 10—3 = 7. It is now apparent that Paul wrote to Seven Specific Churches (Romans, Corinthians, Galatians, Ephesians, Philippians, Colossian, and Thessalonians). So is there a possible parallel between these seven churches Paul wrote to and the seven churches that Jesus addressed in Revelation 2 and 3? Food for thought!

Now the message to the Seven Churches—Ephesus, Smyrna, Pergamum, Thyatira, Sardis, Philadelphia, and Laodicea—are often overlooked or even dismissed as not having any relative barring on the prophecies, which take place later on in the Book of Revelation.[3] This presumption can lead to a false or erroneous interpretation of the Book as a whole. It is thus imperative to seek out the truth (*veritas*) in all matters of scripture and let God be our guide through His written Word.

When we come to the Bible we need to view it, not in our western American-centric worldview based on Greek philosophic thought, but with an eastern Jerusalem-centric Hebraic worldview. The Hebraic view does not ask how or why things happen (Greek mind-set), but what is God's ultimate purpose in the midst of what is happening (Hebrew mind-set—the answer to all the questions ultimately is to show God's redemptive history, how man fell from grace and how man can return and have fellowship with God once again).

The other key component in understanding Hebraic thought is realizing that a scripture passage can be past, present, and future all at the same time or any combination thereof, especially if it is part of Jewish prophetic literature. A careful examination of the epistles (letters) comprising chapters 2 and 3 reveals this Hebraic thought within the application of the passage. For example, all seven churches were

---

[3.] Chuck Missler, "Personal Update News Journal," *Seven Mysterious Letters, A Timely Challenge:* (Coeur d'Alene: Koinonia House Inc, 1993), http://khouse. org/articles/1993/32/.

actual, historic churches, with valid needs. All seven churches have characteristic that apply to our own churches today and as it turns out, and each of the epistles (letters) applies to all churches throughout history. So we have past, present, and future captured within all these seven letters.

Now many archaeological discoveries have confirmed that these were actual historic churches. The most amazing discovery, however, of these seven churches is their apparent prophetic application. These letters to the seven churches describe, with remarkable precision, the unfolding of all subsequent church history.[4] Dr. Missler suggests we label the positions according to the following criteria: Name and meaning of each Church followed by the prophetical name and place in history for each Church as we see in the following chart.

The Church Age

Ephesus	*The Desired One*	The Apostolic Church	34–150 AD
Smyrna	*Death*	The Persecuted Church	150–325 AD
Pergamos	*Mixed Marriage*	The Married Church	325–1000 AD
Thyatira	*Daughter/ the Prostitute*	The Medieval Church	1000–1517 AD
Sardis	*Remnant*	The Denominational Church	1517–1788 AD
Philadelphia	*Brotherly Love*	The Missionary Church	1788–1918 AD
Laodicea	*People Rule*	The Apostate Church	1918–2244? AD

These seven epistles prophetically represent *"the Church Age."* From the beginning of church history we have the Apostolic Church which then becomes the Persecuted Church, out of the persecutions arises the Married Church where we have a mixing of those who suffered under the persecutions with those who did not, which then leads to unfaithfulness and becomes the Medieval Church. The Denominational Church rises out of this unfaithful church and

---

[4.] Ibid.

moves toward their love for mankind and becomes the Missionary Church. However, like most organizations, people tend to dominate them and they become apathetic in their daily practices, which leads them to leave the church thereby becoming the Apostate Church. If these churches were in any other order, this would not be true, but because they are, we have a prophetic picture of the church age! The question which arises now is, where do we fit in, if we are truly in the last days wouldn't that put us in the Apostate Church?

The last key component in understanding Hebraic thought is realizing that a scripture passage can interpret the text literally, spiritually, and prophetically. Literally, these churches were actual churches in the location/city specified. Spiritually, the message of each of these churches can be applied to every church past and present as well as future who are contending with problems of false teaching, heresy, immorality, and apathy. Prophetically, we can view these seven churches as representing the *"Church Age,"* as I have just stated. However, this would not be true if these letters were in any other order. Which Missler states, and I which agree with, "Just move one church letter around to a different position in the passage and the prophetic goes right out the window; yet in the order they are found in our scriptures, the apparent prophetic application becomes remarkably precise."[5]

Now as I have stated in chapter 1, the key to understanding how the prophetic application of the Church Age fits into the Book of Revelation can be found in verses 1:19, 4:1, 7:9, 18:1, and 19:1. In Revelation 1:19 Jesus Himself tells the Apostle John to write down what he is about to behold, *"Write, therefore, what you have seen* (past), *what is now* (present) *and what will take place after these things* (future). "After these things, denotes that these letters are significant events which John is instructed to record which will take place both now and afterward.

---

[5] Chuck Missler, "Personal Update News Journal," *Seven Mysterious Letters, A Timely Challenge* (Coeur d'Alene: Koinonia House Inc, 1993), http://khouse. org/articles/1993/32/.

Thus after the seven letters found in chapters 2 and 3 about the churches, chapter 4:1 continues with a dual emphasis of *meta tauta,* by stating *"After these things I looked...and the voice...said...I will show you what must take place after these things."* Thus *"these things"* in the present become *"these things"* in the future (prophetic Church Age) which must happen before the scroll in heaven is revealed and the seven seals are broken.

These seven letters representing all of church history, tie in with and fill the interval between the sixty-ninth and seventieth week described in chapter 9 of the Book of Daniel. Hence, *"these things"* must take place first in the future before the Antichrist comes, culminating with the *"Day of the Lord"* and the *"Marriage of the Lamb."* Remember that the coming *"apostasy"* or *"the falling away"* in 2 Thessalonians 2:3 is in reference to the apathy of the Laodicean Church which must take place first before *"the man of lawlessness"* (the Antichrist) is revealed.

The question that I raised earlier is, if these seven letters really do include a preview of all church history, then where are we now? Are we, indeed, in the period suggested by the letter to Laodicea? And if that is the case doesn't that mean the rest of the Revelation is about to unfold before our eyes?

Notes on Revelation 2

Hard Questions about Predestination and Salvation

As we read the letters to the seven churches we discover several things; first, that three letters (Ephesus, Pergamum, and Thyatira) are dealing with heresy, false doctrine (teachings) among the church. These false doctrines have lead many in the church astray, both then and now.

The second thing we discover about the seven churches is that two of the letters (Sardis and Laodicea) have *"No Commendation"* (element 3), which is rather discouraging and should give us pause. It is also something we should pay close attention to as I have stated earlier. God is not happy with these two churches for he makes some astonishing remarks about them:

> *"Therefore if you do not wake up, I will come like a thief, and you will not know at what hour I will come to you,"* and *"because you are lukewarm, and neither hot nor cold, I will spit you out of My mouth."*

Both of these statements deal with believer's salvation. With the church of Sardis, if they do not wake up than they may find it's too late to repent. With the church of Laodicea because they are apathetic, God will have nothing to do with them, thus there salvation is in jeopardy. Both of these statements have raised concern about the believer's state of grace when it comes to their salvation. Will they, or won't they be saved?

Now before we look at the hard questions about predestination and salvation, we have to answer some basic questions about who are the elect and who are the saints. The misunderstanding to who we are has led to some misinterpretations of scripture and many theological errors.

So Who Are the Elect?

God's "elect" is just another name for the faithful members of Jewish believers, a.k.a. "the remnant" (those who are of the root of the vine of Judaism). God has predestined all the tribes of the sons of Israel to be saved, but each individual decides (through free will) whether or not they will be among the faithful. Hence, the elect will be saved, but this is conditional (not unconditional) because we all have a choice.

> *"God did not reject his people* (the Jews), *whom he foreknew...So too, at the present time there is a remnant* (the Jewish believers) *chosen by grace... What then? Israel has not obtained what it seeks; but the elect* (the remnant) *have obtained it, and the rest were blinded..."* (Romans 11:2, 5–7)

> *"Therefore I endure all things for the sake of the elect* (God's chosen people, the Jews), *that they also may obtain the salvation which is in Christ Jesus with eternal glory."* (2 Timothy 2:10)

> *"Paul, a bond-servant of God and an apostle of Jesus Christ, according to the faith of God's elect* (the Jewish believers) *and the acknowledgment of the truth which accords with godliness, a faith and knowledge resting on the hope of eternal life, which God, who does not lie, promised before the beginning of time..."* (Titus 1:1)

"Peter, an apostle of Jesus Christ, To God's elect (the remnant) of the Dispersion in Pontus, Galatia, Cappadocia, Asia, and Bithynia, who have been chosen according to the foreknowledge of God the Father, through the sanctifying work of the Spirit, for obedience to Jesus..." (1 Peter 1:1)

The Greek word used here is *eklektois*, which means elect, and it is in reference to the believing Jews who were dispersed with all the other nonbelieving Jews throughout the known world by the Romans after Jerusalem fell in 70 AD.

When we read Romans 11:11–24, we find that Christians have been grafted into the vine of Judaism, not the other way around as many of our Prophecy Buffs teach, which is Replacement Theology and is a heresy:

"I say then, they did not stumble so as to fall, did they? May it never be! But by their (the Jews) transgression salvation has come to the Gentiles (those who are not Jewish), to make them (the Jews) jealous. Now if their (the Jews) transgression is riches for the world and their failure is riches for the Gentiles (those who are not Jewish), how much more will their (the Jews) fulfillment be! But I am speaking to you who are Gentiles (those who are not Jewish). Inasmuch then as I am an apostle of Gentiles (those who are not Jewish), I magnify my ministry, if somehow I might move to jealousy my fellow countrymen (Israel) and save some of them. For if their (Israel's) rejection is the reconciliation of the world, what will their acceptance be but life from the dead? If the first piece of dough (Judaism) is holy, the lump is also; and if the root (Judaism) is holy, the branches are too.

But if some of the branches (unfaithful Jews) were broken off, and you (those who are not

Jewish), *being a wild olive, were grafted in among them* (the Jews) *and became partaker with them of the rich root* (Judaism) *of the olive tree, do not be arrogant toward the branches* (the Jews)*; but if you are arrogant, remember that it is not you who supports the root* (Judaism)*, but the root* (Judaism) *supports you.*

You will say then, "Branches (unfaithful Jews) *were broken off so that I* (those who are not Jewish) *might be grafted in." Quite right, they* (unfaithful Jews) *were broken off for their unbelief, but you stand by your faith. Do not be conceited, but fear; for if God did not spare the natural branches* (unfaithful Jews)*, He will not spare you, either.*

Behold then the kindness and severity of God; to those (unfaithful Jews) *who fell, severity, but to you* (those who are not Jewish)*, God's kindness, if you continue in His kindness; otherwise you* (those who are not Jewish) *also will be cut off. And they* (unfaithful Jews) *also, if they do not continue in their unbelief, will be grafted in, for God is able to graft them* (now faithful Jews) *in again. For if you* (those who are not Jewish) *were cut off from what is by nature a wild olive tree, and were grafted contrary to nature into a cultivated olive tree* (Judaism)*, how much more will these who are the natural branches* (the Jews) *be grafted into their own* (Judaism) *olive tree?"*

Now the Apostle Paul assures us: *"All Israel will be saved; just as it is written, "The Deliverer will come from Zion, He will remove ungodliness from Jacob. This is My covenant with them, When I take away their sins." But from the standpoint of God's choice they are beloved for the sake of the fathers; for the gifts and the calling of God are irrevocable."* (Romans 11:26–29)

It is thus reassuring to know that all the tribes of ancient Israel to include those who fell away to idolatry will be saved like us on account of their faith in God, if and only if they believe.

So Who Are the Saints?

The saints then are us Christians (former Gentiles, who now are Believers) who believe that the Messiah/Christ Jesus is their Lord and Savior. We are distinct and separate from the Elect in the fact that we are not Jewish, but we have been grafted into the vine of Judaism whereby we become "one new man" in Jesus.

> *"To the church of God which is at Corinth, to those who are sanctified in Christ Jesus, called to be saints* (former Gentiles now Believers), *with all who in every place call on the name of Jesus Christ our Lord..."* (1 Corinthians 1:2)

> *"To all who are in Rome, beloved of God, called to be saints* (former Gentiles now Believers): *Grace to you and peace from God our Father and the Lord Jesus Christ."* (Romans 1:7)

> *"Dare any of you, having a matter against another, go to law before the unrighteous, and not before the saints* (Christians or former Gentiles)? *Do you not know that the saints* (Believers in Jesus) *will judge the world? And if the world will be judged by you, are you unworthy to judge the smallest matters?"* (1 Corinthians 6:1–2)

> *"Now He who searches the hearts knows what the mind of the Spirit is, because He makes intercession for the saints* (Believers) *according to the will of God."* (Romans 8:27)

"I commend to you Phoebe our sister, who is a servant of the church in Cenchrea, that you may receive her in the Lord in a manner worthy of the saints (Believers), *and assist her in whatever business she has need of you; for indeed she has been a helper of many and of myself also."* (Romans 16:1–2)

Now let's look at the hard questions about predestination and salvation:

The question of predestination is actually more a philosophical question than a theological or biblical question. The French theologian John Calvin (1509–1564) came up with the modern doctrine of predestination. He taught that those God has selected to be saved are irresistibly called into God's grace; all others have no chance of salvation, which has led to the philosophical question; that if God is truly all-powerful and all-knowing, He must have predestined the lives of all people from the beginning of time and have advance knowledge of all their actions. Therefore, God has predestined the fate, salvation or damnation, for all people. For there is no choice or free will for anyone to decide to follow Christ or not, it has already been predetermined by God.

There is of course support for this view recorded in scripture, and it is found in the epistles of the Apostle Paul:

"And we know that God causes all things to work together for good to those who love God, to those who are called according to His purpose. For those whom He foreknew, He also predestined to become conformed to the image of His Son, so that He would be the firstborn among many brethren; and these whom He predestined, He also called; and these whom He called, He also justified; and these whom He justified, He also glorified." (Romans 8:28–30)

"Also we have obtained an inheritance, having been predestined according to His purpose who works all things after the counsel of His will, to the end that we who were the first to hope in Christ would be to the praise of His glory." (Ephesians 1:11–12)

The Dutch theologian Jacobus Arminius (1560–1609) on the other hand, believed and taught that God's sovereignty and man's free will are compatible concepts. Thus the concept of free will is predominant throughout Scripture. We find that the New Testament portrays people as having the power and responsibility to choose or reject salvation, as found in many of the Gospels as well as in the epistles:

"For if you forgive others for their transgressions, your heavenly Father will also forgive you. But if you do not forgive others, then your Father will not forgive your transgressions." (Matthew 6:14–15)

"Not everyone who says to Me, 'Lord, Lord,' will enter the kingdom of heaven, but he who does the will of My Father who is in heaven will enter. Many will say to Me on that day, 'Lord, Lord, did we not prophesy in Your name, and in Your name cast out demons, and in Your name perform many miracles?' And then I will declare to them, 'I never knew you; DEPART FROM ME, YOU WHO PRACTICE LAWLESSNESS."
(Matthew 7:21–23)

"The good man brings out of his good treasure what is good; and the evil man brings out of his evil treasure what is evil. But I tell you that every careless word that people speak, they shall give an accounting for it in the Day of Judgment. For by your words you will be justified, and by your words you will be condemned." (Matthew 12:35–37)

"And a lawyer stood up and put Him to the test, saying, "Teacher, what shall I do to inherit eternal life?" And He said to him, "What is written in the Law? How does it read to you?" *And he answered,* "YOU SHALL LOVE THE LORD YOUR GOD WITH ALL YOUR HEART, AND WITH ALL YOUR SOUL, AND WITH ALL YOUR STRENGTH, AND WITH ALL YOUR MIND; AND YOUR NEIGHBOR AS YOURSELF." *And He said to him,* "You have answered correctly; DO THIS AND YOU WILL LIVE." (Luke 10:25–28)

"For those who are according to the flesh set their minds on the things of the flesh, but those who are according to the Spirit, the things of the Spirit. For the mind set on the flesh is death, but the mind set on the Spirit is life and peace, because the mind set on the flesh is hostile toward God; for it does not subject itself to the law of God, for it is not even able to do so, and those who are in the flesh cannot please God.

However, you are not in the flesh but in the Spirit, if indeed the Spirit of God dwells in you. But if anyone does not have the Spirit of Christ, he does not belong to Him. If Christ is in you, though the body is dead because of sin, yet the spirit is alive because of righteousness. But if the Spirit of Him who raised Jesus from the dead dwells in you, He who raised Christ Jesus from the dead will also give life to your mortal bodies through His Spirit who dwells in you.

So then, brethren, we are under obligation, not to the flesh, to live according to the flesh—for if you are living according to the flesh, you must die; but if by the Spirit you are putting to death the deeds of the body, you will live. For all who are being led by the Spirit of God, these are sons of God." (Romans 8:5–14)

"But what does it say? "THE WORD IS NEAR YOU, IN YOUR MOUTH AND IN YOUR HEART"—that is, the word of faith which we are preaching, that if you confess with your mouth Jesus as Lord, and believe in your heart that God raised Him from the dead, you will be saved; for with the heart a person believes, resulting in righteousness, and with the mouth he confesses, resulting in salvation. For the Scripture says, "WHOEVER BELIEVES IN HIM WILL NOT BE DISAPPOINTED." For there is no distinction between Jew and Greek; for the same Lord is Lord of all, abounding in riches for all who call on Him." (Romans 10:8–12)

A number of verses also suggest that salvation is potentially available to all people, not just a predestined group, i.e., only to the elect or only to the saints:

"Consequently, just as the result of one trespass was condemnation for all men, so also the result of one act of righteousness was justification that brings life for all men. For just as through the disobedience of the one man the many were made sinners, so also through the obedience of the one man the many will be made righteous." (1 Corinthians 15:21–23)

"So then as through one transgression there resulted condemnation to all men, even so through one act of righteousness there resulted justification of life to all men. For as through the one man's disobedience the many were made sinners, even so through the obedience of the One the many will be made righteous." (Romans 5:18–19)

"For God so loved the world that he gave his one and only Son, that whoever believes in him shall not perish but have eternal life." (John 3:16)

"This is good and acceptable in the sight of God our Savior, who desires all men to be saved and to come to the knowledge of the truth. For there is one God, and one mediator also between God and men, the man Christ Jesus, who gave Himself as a ransom for all, the testimony given at the proper time. For this I was appointed a preacher and an apostle (I am telling the truth, I am not lying) as a teacher of the Gentiles in faith and truth." (1 Timothy 2:3–7)

The majority of Christian churches today adhere to some form or variation of the Arminian view of Predestination and Free Will.

The German theologian Martin Luther (1483–1546), a professor of Scripture and Theology at the University of Wittenberg, taught that we can be justified (made acceptable to God) by faith alone. However, Luther did not deny the importance of doing good works. He wrote, *"For grace and faith are infused apart from our work, and when they are infused, then the works follow."*[6] In other words, when one is saved by the grace of God, he or she will practice good works as a result of that transformation. He also taught that a believer must consistently practice repentance throughout his or her whole life.

Now most Christians believe we are justified and saved by faith alone, and good works are the necessary result and evidence of that salvation. However, repentance of sins is required to maintain that salvation and keep us in fellowship with God.

In contrast, however, there is a modern doctrine, popularized by some evangelical evangelists and organizations which started at the start of the twentieth century in 1909 with the publishing of

---

[6.] *Augsburg Confessions* (Minneapolis: Augsburg Publishing House, 1959), 170.

the Scofield Reference Bible.[7] This doctrine states that believing in Jesus Christ as the Son of God and Savior is all that is required for salvation, and we can never lose that salvation. Now according to this doctrine of "Eternal Salvation," we are saved by belief in Christ alone; it is not necessary to repent, and do good works which do not necessarily result from being saved. This doctrine of Eternal Salvation is known as "Once Saved, Always Saved" and there are several scriptural passages that are cited to support this view:

> *"For God so loved the world that he gave his one and only Son, that whoever believes in him shall not perish but have eternal life."* (John 3:16)

> *"My sheep hear My voice, and I know them, and they follow Me; and I give eternal life to them, and they will never perish; and no one will snatch them out of My hand. My Father, who has given them to Me, is greater than all; and no one is able to snatch them out of the Father's hand."* (John 10:27–29)

> *"Who will separate us from the love of Christ? Will tribulation, or distress, or persecution, or famine, or nakedness, or peril, or sword? Just as it is written,* "FOR YOUR SAKE WE ARE BEING PUT TO DEATH ALL DAY LONG; WE WERE CONSIDERED AS SHEEP TO BE SLAUGHTERED." *But in all these things we overwhelmingly conquer through Him who loved us. For I am convinced that neither death, nor life, nor angels, nor principalities, nor things present, nor things to come, nor powers, nor height, nor depth, nor any*

---

7. C. I. Scofield; *Scofield Reference Bible* (Oxford: Oxford Publishing House, 1909), 1011. Scofield states "The new message of Jesus. The rejected King now turns from the rejecting nation and offers, not the kingdom, but rest and service to such in the nation as are conscious of need. It is a pivotal point in the ministry of Jesus. There is no longer legal obedience as the condition of salvation."

other created thing, will be able to separate us from the love of God, which is in Christ Jesus our Lord." (Romans 8:35–39)

"For as many as are the promises of God, in Him they are yes; therefore also through Him is our Amen to the glory of God through us. Now He who establishes us with you in Christ and anointed us is God, who also sealed us and gave us the Spirit in our hearts as a pledge." (2 Corinthians 1:20–22)

This doctrine has tremendous popular appeal because it teaches that we can be assured of our salvation without the obligation to change our sinful ways. In this view, God loves us and accepts us just as we are, and it is up to God to change us if He wants to.

This doctrine of "once saved, always saved" is identical to the doctrine of Cheap Grace, as detailed by Dietrich Bonheoffer; *"Cheap Grace is the grace we bestow on ourselves. Cheap grace is the preaching of forgiveness without requiring repentance, baptism without church discipline, Communion without confession... Cheap grace is grace without discipleship, grace without the cross, grace without Jesus Christ, living and incarnate*[8]*."* No contrition is required, still less any real desire to be delivered from sin. Cheap grace therefore according to Bonheoffer amounts to a denial of the living Word of God, in fact, *"a denial of the Incarnation of the Word of God."*

However, the overall weight of scriptural evidence against this false doctrine points to the conclusion that any person who goes on willfully sinning has either intentionally abandoned his or her faith or never sincerely made a faith commitment in the first place. True faith involves a commitment to trust God and to do our best to live according to His commandments, it's our obligation to Him.

[8.] Wayne Whitson Floyd Jr., editor; *Discipleship*, by Dietrich Bonhoeffer (Minneapolis: Fortress Press, 2003), p. 44.

"For if we go on sinning willfully after receiving the knowledge of the truth, there no longer remains a sacrifice for sins, but a terrifying expectation of judgment and THE FURY OF A FIRE WHICH WILL CONSUME THE ADVERSARIES. *Anyone who has set aside the Law of Moses dies without mercy on the testimony of two or three witnesses. How much severer punishment do you think he will deserve who has trampled underfoot the Son of God, and has regarded as unclean the blood of the covenant by which he was sanctified, and has insulted the Spirit of grace? For we know Him who said,* "VENGEANCE IS MINE, I WILL REPAY." *And again,* "THE LORD WILL JUDGE HIS PEOPLE." *It is a terrifying thing to fall into the hands of the living God."* (Hebrews 10:26–31)

"Keeping faith and a good conscience, which some have rejected and suffered shipwreck in regard to their faith." (1 Timothy 1:19)

"Now the deeds of the flesh are evident, which are: immorality, impurity, sensuality, idolatry, sorcery, enmities, strife, jealousy, outbursts of anger, disputes, dissensions, factions, envying, drunkenness, carousing, and things like these, of which I forewarn you, just as I have forewarned you, that those who practice such things will not inherit the kingdom of God. But the fruit of the Spirit is love, joy, peace, patience, kindness, goodness, faithfulness, gentleness, self-control; against such things there is no law. Now those who belong to Christ Jesus have crucified the flesh with its passions and desires. If we live by the Spirit, let us also walk by the Spirit. Let us not become boastful, challenging one another, envying one another." (Galatians 5:19–26)

Other relevant passages include Matthew 7:21–23, 10:22, 25:31–46, Luke 10:25–37, John 14:21–23, John 15:6, Romans 2:6–10, Galatians 6:8–9, 1 Timothy 1:18–20, 2 Timothy 2:12, Hebrews 6:4–6, James 2:14–24, and 2 Peter 2:20–21. Not to mention that all but one of the Seven Churches found in Revelation 2 and 3 are required to repent.

So Are All Believers Saved?

"Jesus answered and said to him, If anyone loves Me, he will keep My word; and My Father will love him, and We will come to him and make Our home with him. He who does not love me will not obey my teachings." (John 14:23–24)

"Let no one deceive you with empty words, for because of these things the wrath of God comes upon the sons of disobedience." (Ephesians 5:6)

"For the wrath of God is revealed from heaven against all ungodliness and unrighteousness of men, who suppress the truth in unrighteousness…" (Romans 1:18)

If we live a righteous life, repent of our sins on a regular bases, and do what is required of us, then we will be saved. Henceforth, they will know we are "Christians by our love." The love of God that compels us to live a life of obedience according to His word (teachings). However, on the other hand, if we live an unrighteous life (because of our bad choices through free will and we do not heed His discipline) even though we believe, then we are disobedient and we can expect God's displeasure and punishment, thus we can lose our salvation as the Apostle Paul tells us in Philippians 2:12, *"So then, my beloved, just as you have always obeyed, not as in my presence only, but now much more in my absence, work out your salvation with fear and trembling…"*

It is interesting that in Dr. Derek Prince's deliverance ministry over his many years of service, he has delivered many people from the demon of eternal salvation. This demonic entity and others like it (i.e., Jesus only, no pork, no bacon, Sabbath-only worship, once saved, always saved, etc....) are perverting the true Word of God and deceiving the church into following after many false doctrines which will only lead to Hell. This is why the Apostle Paul warns us that *"the Spirit explicitly says that in later times some will fall away from the faith, paying attention to deceitful spirits and doctrines of demons"* (1 Timothy 4:1) and he also goes on to tell us in 2 Timothy 4:3–4, *"For the time will come when they will not endure sound doctrine; but wanting to have their ears tickled, they will accumulate for themselves teachers in accordance to their own desires, and will turn away their ears from the truth and will turn aside to myths."*

So is the false doctrine "once saved, always saved" or "if you're going to sin, sin boldly" for it doesn't matter what we do considered the suppression of the truth? Could there be false doctrine (teachings) among the church today like there was with the churches at Ephesus, Pergamum, and Thyatira? Could these teaching lead us into a form of apathy like the church at Laodicea where we are no-longer seeking the truth because we are content with the status quo?

Revelation

CHAPTER 3

New American Standard Bible (NASB)

Message to Sardis

³ *"To the angel of the church in Sardis write:*

He who has the seven Spirits of God and the seven stars, says this: 'I know your deeds, that you have a name that you are alive, but you are dead. ² Wake up, and strengthen the things that remain, which were about to die; for I have not found your deeds completed in the sight of My God. ³ So remember what you have received and heard; and keep it, and repent. Therefore if you do not wake up, I will come like a thief, and you will not know at what hour I will come to you. ⁴ But you have a few people in Sardis who have not soiled their garments; and they will walk with Me in white, for they are worthy. ⁵ He who overcomes will thus be clothed in white garments; and I will not erase his name from the book of life, and I will confess his name before My Father and before His angels. ⁶ He who has an ear, let him hear what the Spirit says to the churches.'

Message to Philadelphia

[7] *"And to the angel of the church in Philadelphia write:*

He who is holy, who is true, who has the key of David, who opens and no one will shut, and who shuts and no one opens, says this:

[8] *'I know your deeds. Behold, I have put before you an open door which no one can shut, because you have a little power, and have kept My word, and have not denied My name.* [9] *Behold, I will cause those of the synagogue of Satan, who say that they are Jews and are not, but lie—I will make them come and bow down at your feet, and make them know that I have loved you.* [10] *Because you have kept the word of My perseverance, I also will keep you from the hour of testing, that hour which is about to come upon the whole world, to test those who dwell on the earth.* [11] *I am coming quickly; hold fast what you have, so that no one will take your crown.* [12] *He who overcomes, I will make him a pillar in the temple of My God, and he will not go out from it anymore; and I will write on him the name of My God, and the name of the city of My God, the new Jerusalem, which comes down out of heaven from My God, and My new name.* [13] *He who has an ear, let him hear what the Spirit says to the churches.'*

Message to Laodicea

[14] *"To the angel of the church in Laodicea write:*

The Amen, the faithful and true Witness, the Beginning of the creation of God, says this:

[15] *'I know your deeds, that you are neither cold nor hot; I wish that you were cold or hot.* [16] *So because you are lukewarm, and neither hot nor cold, I will spit you out of My mouth.* [17] *Because you say, "I am rich, and have become wealthy, and have need of nothing," and you do not know that you are wretched and miserable and poor and blind and naked,* [18] *I advise you to buy from Me gold refined by fire so that you may become*

rich, and white garments so that you may clothe yourself, and that the shame of your nakedness will not be revealed; and eye salve to anoint your eyes so that you may see. [19] Those whom I love, I reprove and discipline; therefore be zealous and repent. [20] Behold, I stand at the door and knock; if anyone hears My voice and opens the door, I will come in to him and will dine with him, and he with Me. [21] He who overcomes, I will grant to him to sit down with Me on My throne, as I also overcame and sat down with My Father on His throne. [22] He who has an ear, let him hear what the Spirit says to the churches.'"

Notes on Revelation 3

The Seven Churches

One of the things that I must point out is the fact that these seven letters to the Seven Churches were authored by Jesus Himself. They are not like the Gospels where the author recorded what Christ said after the fact, but these epistles were given to John and recorded directly from the Lord Himself. Henceforth, they must be of great importance and they are something we should pay close attention to for the Lord is addressing His Church.

As I have just mentioned in the preceding chapter there are three major themes we discover in the letters to the seven churches. The first theme that we discover is that three letters (Ephesus, Pergamum, and Thyatira) are dealing with heresy or false doctrine (teachings) among the church. These false doctrines have lead many in the church astray, both then and now. Some of these doctrines are Eternal Salvation, Jesus only, Sabbath-only worship, Dual Covenant Theology, and Replacement Theology (both of which leads to an Anti-Semitic attitude in the church), just to name a few. Keep in mind what the Prophet Hosea tells us about not knowing God's Word: *"My people are destroyed* (parish) *from lack of knowledge. Because you have rejected knowledge, I also reject you…"* (Hosea 4:6).

The second theme we discover about the seven churches is that two of the letters (Sardis and Laodicea) have no commendation and nothing good is said about these two churches. It is clear that God is not happy with these two churches: *"Therefore if you do not wake up, I will come like a thief, and you will not know at what hour I will come to you… He who overcomes…I will not erase his name from the book of life"* and *"because you are lukewarm, and neither hot nor cold, I will spit you out of My mouth."*

Both of these statements deal with believer's salvation. With the church of Sardis, if they do not wake up and overcome their temptations and trails than they may find it's too late to repent and their names will be erased from the Book of Life. That is a bold statement and should make each one of us take notice on where we stand with God. With the church of Laodicea, because they are apathetic, God will have nothing to do with them and spit them out of His mouth, thus their salvation is in jeopardy as well. Again both of these statements have raised concern about the believer's state of grace when it comes to their salvation. Will they or won't they be saved?

Our Prophecy Buffs won't even touch on this subject because they push the narrative that all who call on the Name of Jesus will be saved and raptured out of here. However, we need to understand what Christ taught concerning a believer's salvation as recorded in our scriptures? In Matthew 7:21–23 which is part of the Sermon on the Mount, Jesus says what has to be some of the most frightening words to religious people of anything He ever spoke, *"Not everyone who says to me, 'Lord, Lord', will enter the kingdom of heaven."*

What a statement: *Not everyone who says to me, 'Lord Lord', will enter the kingdom of heaven. Many will say to me on that day* (referring to the day of final judgment) *'Lord, Lord, did we not prophesy or preach in your name and in your name cast out demons and in your name perform many miracles?' And then I* (Christ) *will declare to them, 'I never knew you. Depart from me you who practice lawlessness.'*

Now it should be evident to us all, that Christ is talking about "believers" within the Church. That many who declare Him as their "Lord and Savior" who preach, prophecy, cast out demons and do miracles in His name, He is rejecting. Why? Because of unrepented sin in their lives. Christ will judge the nations as found in Matthew 25:31–46 and as revealed latter in the Book of Revelation, but that he will also judge us who are called by His name. These are Christians who know the Lord, they are casting out demons and doing miracles In the Lord's Name. Read Matthew 12:22–32, Can Beel'zebul cast out Be-el'zebul? Or are these things done by and through the Spirit of the Lord? If they are then why is Christ declaring, depart from me I knew you not?

This theme of judging His own people is also found in an Old Testament passage in the Book of Ezekiel:

> *For this is what the Sovereign Lord says: I myself (Jesus) will search and find my sheep. I will be like a shepherd looking for his scattered flock. I will find my sheep and rescue them from all the places to which they were scattered... And as for you, my flock, my people, this is what the Sovereign Lord says: I* (Christ) *will judge between one sheep and another, separating the sheep from the goats...* (Ezekiel 34:11–24)

Did you hear, *"As for you, my flock, my people, I will judge between one sheep and another."* We as Christians are His flock and His people (because we have been grafted into the vine of Judaism) and we will be judged. He will separate out the sheep from the goats and the goats will receive eternal punishment. Why? Because they are no longer spotless and pure, free from sin. They are tainted because of their sinful nature with filth and unrepentance, thus they retain their sins and cannot stand before a Holy God.

The Disciple Peter helps to clarify the fact that "Believers" within the Church will be judged first because of their sins:

> *Make sure that none of you suffers as a murderer, or thief, or evildoer, or a troublesome meddler* (because of your own sinful nature); *but if any-one suffers as a Christian, he is not to be ashamed, but is to glorify God in this name. For it is time for judgment to begin with the household of God; and if it begins with us first, what will be the outcome for those who do not obey the gospel of God? AND IF*

IT IS WITH DIFFICULTY THAT THE RIGHTEOUS IS SAVED, WHAT WILL BECOME OF THE GODLESS MAN AND THE SINNER? (1 Peter 4:12–19)

So why does judgment start with the household of God and why is it difficult for the righteous to be saved if all believers are saved when they confess that Jesus is Lord (the once saved always saved doctrine)? *"You believe that God is one. You do well; the demons also believe, and shudder"* (James 2:19).

It is interesting that even before the foundation of our great nation that Thomas Shepard, a pastor and the founder of Harvard University, wrote in 1636: *"Formal professors and carnal gospelers have a thing like faith, and like sorrow, and like true repentance, and like good desires, but yet they be but pictures; they deceive others and themselves too…most of them that live in the church shall perish."*[9] Can you now see the picture? Even in the Book of Proverbs King David wrote, *"There is a generation who is pure in their own eyes, yet is not washed from their filthiness"* (Proverbs 30:12).

Now the Apostle Paul confirms this when he tells us in 2 Timothy 3:1–4:

> *But mark this: There will be terrible times in the last days. People will be lovers of themselves, lovers of money, boastful, proud, abusive, disobedient, ungrateful, unholy, without love, unforgiving, slanderous, gossips, without self-control, brutal, not lovers of the good, treacherous, rash, conceited, lovers of pleasure rather than lovers of God—having a form of godliness but denying its power.*

[9.] Thomas Shepard: *The Works of Thomas Shepard, Volume 1* (Ligonier: Soli Deo Gloria Publications, 1992), 58.

Even the Prophet Isaiah joins in and tells us:

> *Woe to those who call evil good and good evil...*
> *what sorrow for those who are wise in their own*
> *eyes and think themselves so clever...for they have*
> *rejected the law of the Lord...they have despised*
> *the word of the Holy One of Israel. That is why the*
> *Lord's anger burns against his people and why He*
> *has raised His fist to crush them.* (Isaiah 5:20–25)

Jesus's own brother, James, warns us that our suffering is the result of our own sins and not because of God:

> *Let no one say when he is tempted, "I am being*
> *tempted by God"; for God cannot be tempted by*
> *evil, and He Himself does not tempt anyone. But*
> *each one is tempted when he is carried away and*
> *enticed by his own lust* (i.e., our own sinful nature).
> (James 1:13–14)

Looking back at the Gospel of Matthew again, Jesus tells a parable relating to the judgment. In chapter 13, verses 49–50, the Lord describes the fate of the wicked: *"So it will be at the end of the age; the angels shall come forth, and take out the wicked from among the righteous, and will cast them into the furnace of fire; there shall be weeping and gnashing of teeth"* (Matthew 13:49–50). If this is not referring to the Church than I don't know what is. There are "good people" sitting in the pews of our churches who think that are going to heaven, but will find they are not.

Now the third and most important theme we discover about these churches, is that all except one of the churches suffer some sort of reprove or discipline from the Lord if they do not repent. The one church that seems to miss out on any discipline is the church at Philadelphia, which is informed that they will be kept *"from the hour of testing, that hour which is about to come upon the whole world, to test those who dwell on the earth."*

Do not confuse this *"hour of testing"* as the *"tribulation,"* for it is not the same thing. The Greek word used here for testing is the word *peirasmos*, and means trail or temptation, which specifically is in reference to an individual's internal temptation to sin. It deals with the trial of one's fidelity, integrity, virtue and constancy toward God and His Word. The Greek word for tribulation is the word *philipses*, which means "pressure" (see notes on chapter 7 for a better understanding of the tribulation).

Going back to our passage we find that all the other six churches are disciplined by God in one form or another. As we read throughout the Old Testament, we discover that God has used the sword, famine, pestilence, and exile to discipline Israel in the past (Jeremiah 24:10 and Ezekiel 12:16), and which He also did to the early church (as recorded in our history books). So we must conclude that He will use the same discipline in the future. Jesus tells the Disciple John that five churches will be disciplined if they do not repent and wake up. The one church, which will suffer discipline, but is not required to repent, is the church of Smyrna which is the persecuted church and they are in right relationship with the Lord so there is no need to request them to repent. All the other five churches must repent.

The church at Ephesus: *"I am coming to you and will remove your lampstand out of its place, unless you repent."*

The church at Pergamum: *"Therefore repent; or else I am coming to you quickly, and I will make war against them."*

The church at Thyatira: *"Behold, I will throw her...into great tribulation, unless they repent of her deeds."*

The church at Sardis: *"Therefore if you do not wake up and repent...I will not erase his name from the book of life."*

And the church at Laodicea: *"Those whom I love, I reprove and discipline; therefore be zealous and repent."*

Each one of these churches must deal with the discipline God lays out and repent of their sins in order for them to be considered overcomers and receive their rewards in Heaven. If they do not repent, than they are destined to have their candle snuffed out and removed, which means they are destined for hell.

Now if we could only comprehend God's nature, that of holiness, and if we would understand what it means to be holy, pure, perfect, upright, and untainted by the least sin, then we would have a better idea of why God hates sin so much. Absolute holiness cannot tolerate even the smallest sin. The prophet Habakkuk writes, *"Thine eyes are too pure to approve evil, and Thou canst not look on wickedness with favor"* (Habakkuk 1:13).

So if we comprehend the holiness and purity of God and why he must punish the abominable nature of sin, then we would have no problem with understanding the absolute necessity of hell and why God must discipline His Church in order to assist us in the pursuit of Heaven. Like any good parent, we discipline our children out of love in order to correct their behavior so that they will grow up to be good, right, and just. That is just what God wants of His Church and what He has done throughout *"the Church Age."*

Revelation

CHAPTER 4

New American Standard Bible (NASB)

Scene in Heaven

⁴ *After these things I looked, and behold, a door standing open in heaven, and the first voice which I had heard, like the sound of a trumpet speaking with me, said, "Come up here, and I will show you what must take place after these things." ² Immediately I was in the Spirit; and behold, a throne was standing in heaven, and One sitting on the throne. ³ And He who was sitting was like a jasper stone and a sardius in appearance; and there was a rainbow around the throne, like an emerald in appearance. ⁴ Around the throne were twenty-four thrones; and upon the thrones I saw twenty-four elders sitting, clothed in white garments, and golden crowns on their heads.*

The Throne and Worship of the Creator

⁵ *Out from the throne come flashes of lightning and sounds and peals of thunder. And there were seven lamps of fire burning before the throne, which are the seven Spirits of God; ⁶ and before the throne there was something like a sea of glass, like crystal; and in the center and around the throne, four living creatures full of eyes in front and behind. ⁷ The first creature was like a lion, and the second creature like a calf, and the third creature had a face like that of a man, and the fourth crea-*

ture was like a flying eagle. [8] And the four living creatures, each one of them having six wings, are full of eyes around and within; and day and night they do not cease to say,

"HOLY, HOLY, HOLY IS THE LORD GOD, THE ALMIGHTY, WHO WAS AND WHO IS AND WHO IS TO COME."

[9] And when the living creatures give glory and honor and thanks to Him who sits on the throne, to Him who lives forever and ever, [10] the twenty-four elders will fall down before Him who sits on the throne, and will worship Him who lives forever and ever, and will cast their crowns before the throne, saying,

[11] "Worthy are You, our Lord and our God, to receive glory and honor and power; for You created all things, and because of Your will they existed, and were created."

Notes on Revelation 4

The Rapture

Chapter 4 opens up with the Disciple John being told to *"Come up here"* into the throne room of God from where Christ will show him what will take place in the *eschaton* after the "Church Age." Immediately, John was standing before the throne. This verse has baffled many Prophecy Buffs and has led to some false teachings about "the Rapture." They erroneous assume that this event is a chronical event and that John symbolically or spiritually represents the Church.

For them, the Church is "Raptured" to heaven here at the beginning of the Revelation and becomes an onlooker to the events which will take place throughout the Tribulation leading up to "the Day of the Lord." It never accrues to the Prophecy Buffs that this is just a metaphor to help the reader understand that John's vision comes directly from God and is used to enforce the authority of the revelation.

However, if this event is literal as they claim, than it applies only to John being taken up to heaven to be shown what will take place in the future and does not represent "the Church" being raptured. For in the vision John is both in heaven standing in the throne room of God chapter 4–7 and also on earth witnessing the rise of the Antichrist chapter 8–14, then he is back in heaven again chapters 15–16 and then back on earth chapters 16–18, then back in heaven chapter 19 and then on the earth once more chapter 19–20…see the picture, John is constantly moving between heaven and earth within the vision. So if he represents the church they are also moving from heaven to earth as well and we have a yoyo effect taking place.

So let's take a look at this event known as *the Rapture*. There are of course, many differing views, especially regarding *eschatology* (the study of "last things"). This diversity derives from several factors and disciplines associated with hermeneutics (the theory of interpretation) as well as the need to integrate an understanding of the entire plan of God's redemption.

This mysterious event known as *the Rapture* is clearly presented in Paul's first letter to the Thessalonians, in which he encourages the grieving Christians that, at the "great snatch," they will be reunited with those who have died in Christ before them.

> *But we do not want you to be uniformed, brethren, about those who are asleep (those who have died), that you may not grieve, as do the rest who have no hope. For if we believe that Jesus died and rose again, even so God will bring with Him those who have fallen asleep in Jesus. For this we say to you by the word of the Lord, that we who are alive, and remain until the coming of the Lord, shall not precede those who have fallen asleep. For the Lord Himself will descend from heaven with a shout, with the voice of the archangel, and with the trumpet of God; and the dead in Christ (Christian believers who have passed away) shall rise first. Then we who are alive and remain shall be caught up (raptured) together with them in the clouds, to meet the Lord in the air, and thus we shall always be with the Lord"* (1 Thessalonians 4:13–17)

There are many who claim that the word "rapture" is not in the Bible; well that's because they aren't reading from a Latin translation: "*Deinde nos qui vivimus qui relinquimur simul rapiemur cum illis in nubibus obviam Domino in aera et sic semper cum Domino erimu*" (1 Thessalonians 4:17). This verb is the first-person plural future passive indicative of the Latin word *rapio*, to snatch, grab or carry off.

However, the Greek word used in our New Testament scriptures for "caught up" is the word *harpazo*. The Latin equivalent of the Greek past participle is the verb *rapture*, "to take away by force" and as stated in the verse above it is found in the Latin Vulgate, one of the oldest Bibles in existence. At the Rapture, living believers will be "caught up," "snatched away," or taken by force" to be translated into the clouds, in a moment in time, to join the Lord in the air. I think the early Church Father's thought that to be "raptured" sound so much nicer then to be "harpazoed," henceforth, the doctrine became known as the Doctrine of the Rapture, not the Doctrine of the Harpazo.

Our scriptures teach us to expect Him at any moment and thus to be taken up with Him at any moment. At the Rapture, living believers, along with dead believers will be "caught up" in the air, translated into the clouds, in a twinkling of the eye, to join the Lord in the air. This is what the Apostle Paul clearly taught and what the Church holds to. So the Doctrine of the Rapture is true, however when will it take place is the ultimate question?

Now, there are many that hold to the view that emerged in the medieval church (both Catholic and Protestant) that the "Second Coming" of Christ and the "Rapture" are the same event. Yet today, many churches believe that there are a number of indications that these are distinct and separate events. This has led of course, too many differing views on the subject of the Rapture.

Before we move on we need to remember that the only certain barrier to understanding the truth in scripture is the presumption that you already have the truth and there can be no other. These presuppositions bar us from grasping the truth about the Word of God. So it is essential from time to time to step back and reestablish a fresh perspective and let God's Word speak to us through His Scriptures and not rely on what others have taught in the past.

Pre-Tribulation

The Pre-Tribulation Rapture is the view that the rapture will occur before the beginning of the Tribulation period. According to this view, the Christian Church that existed prior to that seven-year period has no vital role during the seven years of Tribulation, and will therefore be removed. Many people who accept Christ after the rapture (the Left Behind Theory) will be martyred for their faith during the Tribulation (Rev. 20:4).

The Disciple John is seen in Revelation 4:1 as representing the Church caught up to Heaven. John hears the Trumpet and a voice that says, *"Come up here,"* and he is translated in the Spirit to Heaven and then sees what will happen for those left on earth. The Pre-Tribulation rapture is the most widely held position among American Evangelical Christians today.

Some of those who believe in a Pre-Trib warn that the rapture is imminent, saying that all of the prophecies concerning the end-times have been fulfilled to the extent that the rapture could take place at any moment. Yet others suggest that certain requirements must first be met before the rapture can occur, such as the following:

- There will be peace in Israel (does Ezekiel 38 really refer to peace in Israel).
- The nations of the world must unify their currency onto a universal standard (think about what the EU has done for Europe, could this happen for the rest of the world).
- There will be a one-world government, to correspond to the seventh beast of Revelation, prior to the Antichrist's eighth beast government.
- The Jewish temple in Jerusalem must be rebuilt in its original place.
- There will be a great falling away and the Antichrist will be revealed (2 Thessalonians 2:3).
- Observance of Old Testament commandments concerning animal sacrifices must be reinstated.

Rapture as doctrine is sound biblical doctrine and it is clearly taught in Scriptures. The Pre-Tribulation Rapture Myth on the other hand is a distortion of that doctrine, which claims that: the Rapture will spare us from all time of trial, suffering, conflict and the need to do spiritual battle because we aren't going to endure God's wrath in the time of the Tribulation.[10] It also negates all the New Testament books for they all suggest that the whole Christian walk is made up of conflict and struggle. It never occurs to the Prophecy Buffs that we may well endure the world's wrath before Christ returns. Remember that it is the world's wrath and not God's wrath, which may be directed against believers.

Pre-Trib Rapture takes comfort in the erroneous assumption that there will be no time of trial in the run-up to the Rapture and Tribulation. It comforts itself with a "we're going to be outta here" mentality. Which has neutered the church and its followers to the point where they are indifferent to what is happening in the world around them. Don't worry about anything, i.e., the sad moral decline of our society or the corruption of the government and its hold over people, but just keep teaching the scripture as if the Bible were an end and goal unto itself. It fails to notice that the Scriptures are a manual for *action*, not just a study guide, and most definitely not an end in itself. As Jesus said, the Kingdom of Heaven consists in power, not words.[11]

The Pre-Tribulation Rapture Myth is identical to the doctrine of Cheap Grace, as detailed by Dietrich Bonheoffer in his book *Discipleship*: *"Cheap Grace is the grace we bestow on ourselves. Cheap grace is the preaching of forgiveness without requiring repentance, it is baptism without discipline of community; it is The Lord's Supper* (Communion) *without confession of sin; it is absolution without personal confession. Cheap grace is grace without discipleship, grace without the cross, grace without the living and incarnate Jesus Christ."*[12] No contrition is required, still less any real desire to be delivered from sin. Cheap grace therefore according to Bonheoffer amounts to a denial of the living Word of God, in fact, it's a denial of the Incarnation

10. C. I. Scofield; *Scofield Reference Bible* (Oxford: Oxford Publishing House, 1909), 1115.

11. John Loeffler, "Personal Update News Journal," *The Rapture Myth* (Coeur d'Alene: Koinonia House Inc, 2002), http://khouse.org/articles_cat/2002/.

12. Wayne Whitson Floyd Jr., editor; *Discipleship*, by Dietrich Bonhoeffer (Minneapolis: Fortress Press, 2003), p. 44.

of the Word of God. *"So the Christian need not follow Christ, since the Christian is comforted by grace!"*[13] Cheap Grace is the deadliest enemy of the Church in our time and is entwined throughout the Pre-Tribulation Rapture Myth.

The Pre-Trib debate all revolves around the Greek word *ek*, "out of" or "from" found in Revelations 3:10 and 7:14. Are those who are raptured removed from/out of before they have to endure the testing or tribulation, or are they removed after enduring the tribulation and come out of it or from it with their faith intact. Here the Prophecy Buffs get it wrong and have to do some theological gymnastics if you are to believe you do not have to endure the tribulation. If someone said to you *"did you come from that party or out of that house"* the assumption is automatic, that you were within the house or at the party. You would not automatically conclude that you did not go into the house or you did not attend the party, unless you add a clause behind the first statement to indicate that you did not go into the house or you did not go to the party.

Now let's look at the passage its self: *"These are the ones who come out of the great tribulation… They will hunger no longer, nor thirst anymore; nor will the sun beat down on them, nor any heat."* Sounds like the accompanying clause indicates that the believers have to endure something. They have to endure the tribulation, for they are not able to buy or sell because they did not receive the mark of the beast. They are NOT removed before it happens as our Prophecy Buffs would have you believe.

If history dictates that if the advancing liberal/socialism throughout the world continues its rapid approach, a time of trial will come and many will have their faith faltering, wondering where the Rapture is or whether the whole thing was just a giant fairy tale in the first place (this will be the great falling away). Many Christians from persecuted countries of the twentieth century (i.e., Brother Yun in China) have warned of this. Standing firm in a time of trial requires aggressive action and preparation ahead of time just in case

---

[13.] Ibid., p. 44.

this isn't the immediate end of times and the time of testing or trial comes first.

Christ states in all His seven letters to the seven Churches that they are to stand firm and become victorious in the face of heresy, persecution, false doctrine, immortality, and apathy. Are these not trials which we undergo to prove we are conquerors? Christ also makes it very clear when asked by His disciples about the sign of the end times found in Matthew 24:9 that *"Then we will be handed over to tribulation and they will killed you."* Sounds to me like we will have to endure some sort of tribulation even to the point of death.

Most of the adjectives and verbs found in our Scriptures (specifically in Paul's Epistles) imply a conflict: contend, run to win, race, stand, fight, resist, and defend. So as he clearly states, *"In defenso fidei"* (in defense of the faith) must once again become the battle cry for us and the church.[14] The Christian spiritual life is a life of rewarding but often painful sacrifice and struggle; its all-out war and it's not a picnic. Yes, we do win in the end, but many expect to win without participating in the fight. Remember the Apostle Paul calls us to suffer with Christ. To quote Dietrich Bonheoffer again, *"When Christ calls a person, he bids him come and die."*[15]

Mid-Tribulation

Mid-Tribulation theology, a minority view with few proponents today, is that the rapture happens and takes place halfway through the seven-year Tribulation period. This view is supported by the seventh chapter of Daniel (verse 25), where it says the saints will be given over to tribulation for *"time, times, and half a time"* which is interpreted to mean 3.5 years. This seven year period is divided into half—the first 3.5 years are the "beginning of sorrows" and the last half is the "great tribulation" proper or the "time of Jacob's troubles."

[14.] John Loeffler, "Personal Update News Journal," *The Rapture Myth* (Coeur d'Alene: Koinonia House Inc, 2002), http://khouse.org/articles_cat/2002/.

[15.] Wayne Whitson Floyd Jr., editor; *Discipleship*, by Dietrich Bonhoeffer (Minneapolis: Fortress Press, 2003), p. 287.

At this midpoint juncture, the Antichrist commits the "abomination of desolation" by desecrating the Jerusalem temple (to be built on what is now called The Temple Mount) as recorded by the Apostle Paul in 2 Thessalonians 2:1–13. It is at this point the Mid-Triber's believe they will be raptured. They will experience some sort of tribulation but not the real tribulation or "time of Jacob's troubles," which the Antichrist brings, that's for the unbelievers left behind. However, if they are unbelievers why would it matter to the Antichrist? He would persuade them to follow after him; thus, there is no need to continue the tribulation period into the last 3.5 years, is there?

Post-Tribulation

The Post-Tribulation Rapture (or "Post-Trib") view places the rapture at the end of the Tribulation period. From this perspective, Christian believers will be on the earth as witnesses for Christ during the entire seven years, until the last day of the tribulation period when Christ returns to pour out God's Wrath on mankind. The Post-Tribulation view brings Christ's "appearing" and his "coming" together in one all-encompassing, grand event as found in Matthew 24:29–31:

> *"But immediately after the tribulation of those days the sun shall be darkened, and the moon shall not give its light, and the stars shall fall from heaven, and the powers of the heavens shall be shaken: and then shall appear the sign of the Son of man in heaven: and then shall all the tribes of the earth mourn, and they shall see the Son of man coming on the clouds of heaven with power and great glory. And He shall send forth His angels with a great sound of a trumpet, and they shall* (rapture) *gather together His elect from the four winds, from one end of heaven to the other."*

Another supporting scripture for Post-Trib is John 17:15–16, where Jesus prays that the Father *"not take His* (Jesus's) *disciples from the earth, but to keep them from the evil one."* Thus the Christian goes through the tribulation but is spared the horrors that the Antichrist brings.

Pre-Wrath

The Pre-Wrath Rapture view is that the tribulation of the church begins 3.5 years into the seven-year period, being Daniel's seventieth week, when the Antichrist is revealed and desecrates the temple found in 2 Thessalonians 2. The great Tribulation, according to this view, is of the Antichrist against the church at this time, otherwise known as the time of Jacob's Troubles. The duration of this tribulation is unknown, except that it begins and ends during the second half of Daniel's seventieth week, presumable it will be the last 3.5 years of the seven-year period.

References supporting this view come from Matthew 24, Mark 13, and Luke 21 and are all used as evidence that this tribulation will be cut short by the coming of Christ to deliver the righteous by means of rapture, which will occur after the sixth seal is opened and the Sun is darkened and the moon is turned to blood. However, by this point many Christians will have been slaughtered as martyrs by the Antichrist. After the rapture comes God's seventh-seal wrath of trumpets and bowls (a.k.a. "the Day of the Lord"). The Day of the Lord's wrath against the ungodly will follow for the remainder of the seven years, which will then usher in the millennial reign of Christ when he returns from Edom having defeated and trampled His enemies with His robes dripping in blood, Isaiah 63:1–6 (see my notes on chapter 20, part B, The Armageddon Campaign).

Yet when our Lord comes to gather His church, there will be a generation alive at that time. In his discussion of the Resurrection in his first letter to the Corinthians, the Apostle Paul again deals with this astonishing event:

> *Behold, I tell you a mystery; we shall not all sleep,*
> *but we shall all be changed, in a moment, in the*
> *twinkling of an eye, at the last trumpet; for the*

trumpet shall sound, and the dead shall be raised imperishable, and we shall be changed (raptured). *For this perishable must put on the imperishable, and this mortal must put on immortality. But when this perishable shall have put on the imperishable, and this mortal shall have put on immortality, then shall come about the saying that is written, Death is swallowed up in victory. O death, where is thy sting? O grave, where is thy victory?* (1 Corinthians 15:51–55)

Clearly, our scriptures teach us to expect Him at any moment. This is called the Doctrine of Imminency. (The word "imminent" should not be confused with "immanent," which, in theological contexts, means that God is not only transcendent, or far above us, but that He is always with us and active on our behalf. Nor should it be confused with "eminent," which is a title of honor reserved for persons of outstanding distinction.)

Imminency expresses the hope and a comforting spirit of expectancy, 1 Thessalonians 1:10, which should also result in a victorious and purified life, 1 John 3:2, 3. Believers are taught to expect the Savior from heaven at any moment, Philippians 3:20; Titus 2:13; Hebrews 9:28; 1 Thessalonians 1:10, 4:18, 5:6; Revelation 22:20.

Keep in mind 2 Thessalonians 2:1–8, where the Apostle Paul reveals what will take place leading up to Christ's Second Coming:

"Now, brethren, concerning the coming of our Lord Jesus Christ and our gathering together (rapture) *to Him, we ask you, not to be quickly shaken in mind or disturbed either by a spirit or a message or a letter as if from us, as to the effect that the day of Christ had come. Let no one deceive you, for it* (the day of the Lord, God's wrath) *will not come unless the apostasy comes first and the man of lawlessness is revealed* (the Antichrist), *the son of destruction, who opposes and exalts himself above every so-called*

god or object of worship, so that he takes his seat in the temple of God, displaying himself as being God…

Continuing with 2 Thessalonians verse 7:

Do you not remember that when I was still with you, I told you these things? And now you know what restrains him now, so that in his time he may be revealed. For the mystery of lawlessness is already at work; only He (Christ) *who now restrains will do so until he* (Satan) *is taken out of the way. And then that lawless one* (the Antichrist) *will be revealed whom the Lord will slay with the breath of His mouth* (the Sword of the Spirit) *and bring to an end* (the tribulation) *by the appearance of His coming."*

In contrast to the imminent gathering of His church, there are numerous passages that deal with precedent events that must transpire prior to the "Second Coming" to establish His kingdom on the earth.

Revelation

CHAPTER 5

New American Standard Bible (NASB)

The Book with Seven Seals

⁵ I saw in the right hand of Him who sat on the throne a book written inside and on the back, sealed up with seven seals. ² And I saw a strong angel proclaiming with a loud voice, "Who is worthy to open the book and to break its seals?" ³ And no one in heaven or on the earth or under the earth was able to open the book or to look into it. ⁴ Then I began to weep greatly because no one was found worthy to open the book or to look into it; ⁵ and one of the elders *said to me, "Stop weeping; behold, the Lion that is from the tribe of Judah, the Root of David, has overcome so as to open the book and its seven seals."*

⁶ And I saw between the throne (with the four living creatures) and the elders a Lamb standing, as if slain, having seven horns and seven eyes, which are the seven Spirits of God, sent out into all the earth. ⁷ And He came and took the book out of the right hand of Him who sat on the throne. ⁸ When He had taken the book, the four living creatures and the twenty-four elders fell down before the Lamb, each one holding a harp and golden bowls full of incense, which are the prayers of the saints. ⁹ And they *sang a new song, saying,*

"Worthy are You to take the book and to break its seals; for You were slain, and purchased for God with Your blood men from every tribe and tongue and people and nation.

[10] "You have made them to be a kingdom and priests to our God; and they will reign upon the earth."

Angels Exalt the Lamb

[11] Then I looked, and I heard the voice of many angels around the throne and the living creatures and the elders; and the number of them was myriads of myriads, and thousands of thousands, [12] saying with a loud voice,

"Worthy is the Lamb that was slain to receive power and riches and wisdom and might and honor and glory and blessing."

[13] And every created thing which is in heaven and on the earth and under the earth and on the sea, and all things in them, I heard saying,

"To Him who sits on the throne, and to the Lamb, be blessing and honor and glory and dominion forever and ever."
[14] And the four living creatures kept saying, "Amen." And the elders fell down and worshiped.

Notes on Revelation 5

The Literary Style

There are of course, many differing views, especially regarding *eschatology* (the study of "last things"). This diversity derives from several factors and disciplines associated with *hermeneutics* (the theory of interpretation) as well as the need to integrate an understanding of the entire plan of God's redemption. So it is important to remember how scripture is used here in the Book of Revelation, thus understanding the literary style of allegory, metaphor, and symbolism is vital to interpreting each verse and each chapter as a whole, especially starting here in chapter 5 and throughout the rest of the book.

Allegory is the method of indirect representation of ideas or truths. It is a literary form where abstract ideas and principles are described in terms of characters, figures, and events to tell a story with a purpose of teaching or explaining an idea or a principle:

> *"And I saw between the throne (with the four living creatures) and the elders a Lamb standing, as if slain, having seven horns and seven eyes, which are the seven Spirits of God, sent out into all the earth"* (Rev. 5:6) or like in Revelation 13:1, *"Then I saw a beast coming up out of the sea, having ten horns and seven heads."*

Metaphor is the literary form of expressing an analogy or simile. It is a way to compare two different things to make an interesting connection in the reader's mind like a word-picture:

"The dragon, the serpent of old, who is the devil and Satan" (Rev. 20:2) or in Revelation 8:3, *"For all the nations have drunk of the wine of the passion of her immorality, and the kings of the earth have committed acts of immorality with her, and the merchants of the earth have become rich by the power of her luxury."*

Symbolism is the method of comparison whereby something stand for something else by reason of relationship or association:

The lion is used as the symbol of courage or kingship; *"Behold, the Lion that is from the tribe of Judah"* (Rev. 5:5) also in Revelation 17:5, we understand that Babylon symbolizes all that which is evil; *"Babylon the Great, the Mother of Harlots and of the Abominations of the Earth."*

So as we read chapters 5–21 we find all the literary forms of allegory, metaphor and symbolism are all displayed in their various form and sometime all entwined to paint a picture for the reader that will be memorable. One that is not easily forgotten and one that is sure to bring hope to the believer or fear and despair to the nonbeliever in hopes that they might believe, repent and be saved.

Notes on Revelation 5

Angels

Here in chapter 5, we start to encounter the multitude of references to angels and specifically specialized angels found throughout the book:[16]

(1) Four Angels holding back the four winds (Rev. 7:1)
(2) Angel with seal of the living God (Rev. 7:2)
(3) Seven angels with Seven Trumpets (Rev. 8–9, 11)
(4) Angel with a golden censer (Rev. 8:3)
(5) Angel with little book and measurer (Rev. 10:1, 2, 11:1)
(6) Angel with Everlasting Gospel (Rev. 14:6–7)
(7) Angel warning against Mark of the Beast (Rev. 14:9–10)
(8) Angel with Harvest Sickle (Rev. 14:18–19)
(9) Seven Angels with Seven Vials of Wrath (Rev. 16)
(10) Angel with message of doom (Rev. 14:8, 18:1–2, 21)
(11) Angel with strange fowl invitation (Rev. 19:17)
(12) Angel with key and great chain (Rev. 20:1)

Thus, it becomes imperative to take a moment in order to gain an understanding of who and what angels are as we begin our study of the revelation. Angels have always been a popular topic of discussion; however, most people do not understand the biblical identity or use of angels found throughout Scripture. They believe a number of myths about them—i.e., some people pray to angels, thinking they are on the same level as God himself, and others believe that people

---

16. Bob Chadwick, *Revelation Seminar* (Wisdom Press, 2013).

become angels when they die, going around helping those still here on earth.

Here is what some of our Scriptures teach about angels. Note this is not an all-inclusive list; there are many, many more references found in our scriptures:[17]

God created angels (Ps. 148:2, 5; Col. 1:15–17)

They are immortal (Lk. 20:36) and spiritual beings (Heb. 1:14)

Angels worship God (Neh. 9:6) and are holy (Mt. 25:31)

They are wise (2 Sam. 14:17, 20) and powerful (Ps. 103:20)

They are celibate (Mt. 22:30) and not perfect (Job 4:18)

They minister to God's people (Heb. 1:13–14) and comfort them (Acts 27:23)

They guard and protect God's people (Ps. 34:7, 91:9–12; Dan. 6:22; Acts 12:7–10)

They are given special assignments by God (Mt. 1:20, 4:6; Lk. 1:26)

God's angels rejoice when we repent of sin (Lk. 15:7, 10)

Angels can take on human form (Gen. 19:1)

They bring destruction to unbelievers (Gen. 19:13) and persecution (Ps. 35:5–6)

There are Fallen Angels (Is. 14:12–15, Jude 6) who make war against the saints (Rev. 12:7–17)

They can be imprisoned (2 Pet. 2:4) and they can suffer eternal fire and torment (Mt. 25:41)

Angels are known by several terms and are organized in ranks:

(1) Chief of Princes (Dan. 10:13)
(2) Archangels (Jude 1:9, 1 Thess. 4:16)
(3) Cherubim (2 Kings 19:15)
(4) Seraphim (Isa. 6:1–3)
(5) Warrior Angels (Dan. 10:5–6, 12–13, 20–21)
(6) Heavenly Hosts (Lk. 2:13)
(7) Angels of Light (2 Cor. 11:14)

[17.] Chuck Missler, *Revelation: An Expositional Commentary* (Coeur d'Alene: Koinonia House Inc, 1996).

Where angels are concerned, only God deserves our worship, but absolutely no angels do, for that would be an abomination. They are not to be worshiped or adored (Heb. 1:6) for man is created a little lower than the angels (Heb. 2:7). And Jesus is at God's right hand—with angels, authorities, and powers all in submission to him (1 Pet. 3:22). Thus all angels are the messengers of God and do His bidding.

According to the Book of Enoch, there are seven archangels *'iyrin we-ḳaddishim*, "holy ones who watch":

(1) Uriel ["*God is Light*"], set over the world's luminaries and over Sheol

(2) Raphael, ["*God Heals*"], set over the spirits of men

(3) Raguel ["*the Terrifier*"], who chastises the world of the luminaries

(4) Michael, ["*God Protects*"], set over the best part of mankind, over the nation of Israel

(5) Sariel ["*God Turned*"], set over the spirits who seduce the spirits to sin

(6) Gabriel ["*God is Great*"], set over paradise, the seraphim, and the cherubim

(7) Jerahmeel ["*God is Merciful*"], whom God set over the resurrection

The reason Michael is listed as the fourth, is probably because he stands in the middle as chief of the angels, for Enoch tell us that he is the leader of the seven. Jerahmeel the seventh angel was a replacement for Hallel (i.e., Lucifer or Satan) when he was cast out of heaven.

The Book of Enoch also mentions the seven classes of angels:

(1) The Cherubim

(2) The Seraphim

(3) The Ofanim

(4) All the angels of power

(5) Principalities

(6)   The Elect One (The Messiah when he appears as an angel of light)

(7)   The Elementary powers (They are endowed with seven angelic virtues—of faith, wisdom, patience, mercy, judgment, peace, and goodness)

Now that we have a quick understanding of what the Judeo-Christian's teachings are about angels, we need to remember that what God has created, Satan will counterfeit. So be aware that not all that appear holy is holy.

Revelation

CHAPTER 6

New American Standard Bible (NASB)

The First Seal—Rider on White Horse

⁶ *Then I saw when the Lamb broke one of the seven seals, and I heard one of the four living creatures saying as with a voice of thunder, "Come." ² I looked, and behold, a white horse, and he who sat on it had a bow; and a crown was given to him, and he went out conquering and to conquer.*

The Second Seal—War

³ *When He broke the second seal, I heard the second living creature saying, "Come." ⁴ And another, a red horse, went out; and to him who sat on it, it was granted to take peace from the earth, and that men would slay one another; and a great sword was given to him.*

The Third Seal—Famine

⁵ *When He broke the third seal, I heard the third living creature saying, "Come." I looked, and behold, a black horse; and he who sat on it had a pair of scales in his hand. ⁶ And I heard something like a voice in the center of the four living creatures saying, "A quart of wheat for a denarius, and three quarts of barley for a denarius; and do not damage the oil and the wine."*

The Fourth Seal—Death

⁷ When the Lamb broke the fourth seal, I heard the voice of the fourth living creature saying, "Come." ⁸ I looked, and behold, an ashen horse; and he who sat on it had the name Death; and Hades was following with him. Authority was given to them over a fourth of the earth, to kill with sword and with famine and with pestilence and by the wild beasts of the earth.

The Fifth Seal—Martyrs

⁹ When the Lamb broke the fifth seal, I saw underneath the altar the souls of those who had been slain because of the word of God, and because of the testimony which they had maintained; ¹⁰ and they cried out with a loud voice, saying, "How long, O Lord, holy and true, will You refrain from judging and avenging our blood on those who dwell on the earth?" ¹¹ And there was given to each of them a white robe; and they were told that they should rest for a little while longer, until the number of their fellow servants and their brethren who were to be killed even as they had been, would be completed also.

The Sixth Seal—Terror

¹² I looked when He broke the sixth seal, and there was a great earthquake; and the sun became black as sackcloth made of hair, and the whole moon became like blood; ¹³ and the stars of the sky fell to the earth, as a fig tree casts its unripe figs when shaken by a great wind. ¹⁴ The sky was split apart like a scroll when it is rolled up, and every mountain and island were moved out of their places. ¹⁵ Then the kings of the earth and the great men and the commanders and the rich and the strong and every slave and free man hid themselves in the caves and among the rocks of the mountains; ¹⁶ and they *said to the mountains and to the rocks, "Fall on us and hide us from the presence of Him who sits on the throne, and from the wrath of the Lamb; ¹⁷ for the great day of their wrath has come, and who is able to stand?"

Notes on Revelation 6

The Seven Seals

Throughout Jesus's ministry, many of His followers questioned Jesus about the signs of His coming, and of the end of the age. In the Book of Matthew, chapter 24 we are given Christ's response to those questions. His replay lays out for us in chronological order the framework for how we are to view the revelation John is given with the Seven Seals. This becomes the overall big picture of what will happen. In John's revelation the Lord goes on to refine the picture through the seven trumpets and then focuses the picture into specifics in the wrath of God found in the seven bowls. So before we start looking at the overall picture of John's revelation in chapter 6, we need to look back at the Gospel of Matthew to understand just what Jesus was conveying to His followers.

Christ lets us know right from the start that many will try to mislead you regarding the end of the age, wither intentionally or unintentionally. *Jesus answered and said to them, "See to it that no one misleads you."* This is important for us to grasp for there are many different teachings regarding eschatology and most of them will lead you to a false sense of hope and security, whereby you might lose not only your faith (part of the great falling away), but also your salvation. I know this is hard to hear, but someone must speak the truth and awaken believers to the harsh reality of scriptures. For even Jesus warns us that, *"Not everyone who says to Me, 'Lord, Lord,' will enter the kingdom of heaven."*

Now going back to verse 5 in Matthew 24, Jesus lays out to us what John records in his vision of the seven seals, *"for many will come in My name, saying, 'I am the Christ,' and will mislead many."* Jesus is giving us an outline to exactly what will take place in the future by letting us know that there will be many Antichrists claiming to be *"the way"* throughout history, but only one will emerge at the end of the age who will lead many astray. Now if we compare this to John's revelation he states when he saw the first seal broken: *"behold, a white horse, and he who sat on it...went out conquering and to conquer."* This white rider is the Antichrist and wears the color white to mock that which is holy and to appear Christ like. This Antichrist will make a future covenant or peace treaty with Israel and the surrounding nations for seven years according to Daniel 9:27. (See my notes on the Four Horsemen.)

Verse 6 continues by letting the reader know that *"you will be hearing of wars and rumors of wars. See that you are not frightened, for those things must take place, but that is not yet the end."* Here now we have the second seal in John's vision, *"and another, a red horse, went out; and to him who sat on it, it was granted to take peace from the earth, and that men would slay one another; and a great sword was given to him."* This passage is in reference to verse 6 where there will be wars which will take peace from the earth.

"For nation will rise against nation, and kingdom against kingdom, and in various places there will be famines and earthquakes. But all these things are merely the beginning of birth pangs." Verse 7 continues with wars and rumors of war but changes tune and mentions famines and earthquakes which will kill many. This is reflected again in the breaking of the third and fourth seal. The black horse represents famine as well as social and economic injustice in John's vision, while the pale horse represents death brought on by sword, famine, and natural disasters, i.e., earthquakes, and storms, etc., all of which will slay and take many lives. Can you now start to see the parallel between these two scriptural passages?

The fifth seal now parallels verses 9–11 and follows the chronological sequence, *"Then they will deliver you to tribulation, and will kill you, and you will be hated by all nations because of My name. At that time many will fall away and will betray one another and hate one another. Many false prophets will arise and will mislead many."* Jesus is making it clear in this verse to His followers (us believers) that we will go through tribulation and be killed on account of their hatred for us Christians who bear His name. While those who are not prepared to suffer will fall away and betray us, so that we will also suffer to the point of death for our faith.

Than John *"saw underneath the altar the souls of those who had been slain because of the word of God, and because of the testimony which they had maintained...until the number of their fellow servants and their brethren who were to be killed even as they had been, would be completed also."* Christ informs us that we will be killed on account of our testimony and faith, while John see the future where it has already taken place for many, where the saint have been martyred and are waiting for God's justice and wrath to be poured out. However, the key point here is that John not only see those who have died for their faith throughout history, but he also understands that in the future more saints will be martyred and killed through the tribulation once the Antichrist appears on the scene. *"Until the number of their fellow servants and their brethren who were to be killed even as they had been, would be completed also."*

Suffering has always been part of the believers' walk of faith. The false hope that we will not have to endure the tribulation and subsequent suffering brought on by the Antichrist is a hearsay taught by many of our Prophecy Buffs. These false teachings are still misleading many in the church today. No matter how you look at it the followers of Christ will suffer and be killed according to these two passages. The first passage states they will be killed and hated because of "Christ's name." The second passage clearly reveals that these were slain because of the testimony (there belief in Christ) which they held and clung too and that there would be more martyred saints to follow.

"Because lawlessness is increased, most people's love will grow cold. But the one who endures to the end, he will be saved." The overall question which I will put forth is; why will we have to endure to the end if we are going to be raptured before the tribulation begins? Or do our Prophecy Buffs have it wrong. If we are raptured out of here, what then do we have to endure? I submit to you that we will have to go

through and endure the Antichrist's tribulation to the end if we are to be refine as pure gold and made righteous.

Now if this passage in Matthew is the overall big picture as I believe it is, then following the four horsemen will come the great tribulation for the believers and many will give up there life for their faith. Now verses 15–24 change the tone by letting the reader (us believers) know just when the "Great Tribulation" will begin.

> *Therefore when you see the* ABOMINATION OF DESOLATION *which was spoken of through Daniel the prophet, standing in the holy place (let the reader understand), then those who are in Judea must flee to the mountains... For then there will be a great tribulation, such as has not occurred since the beginning of the world until now, nor ever will.*

The idea that this passage is referring only to the Jews who are "left behind" after the Christians have been raptured is preposterous, for the context of the passage is in reference to believers, both Christians and Jews, who if they want to save their lives they must flee the persecution which will now start taking place. The Antichrist is the cause of this persecution and tribulation, not God. This persecution will make Hitler's Holocaust look like a picnic, *"such as has not occurred since the beginning of the world until now."*

Now we know that the tribulation will last seven years according to Daniel and in the middle of it the Antichrist will cause the temple to be desecrated as stated above, ushering in what is known as "the Great Tribulation." This is where Satan will use men's wrath to persecute the believers and followers of Christ Jesus, and many will fall away because they are not prepared to go through such severe suffering. We also know that this persecution/tribulation will be cut short, for verse 22 make it very clear. *"Unless those days had been cut short, no life would have been saved; but for the sake of the elect those days will be cut short."*

Verses 29–31 finish off the remainder of the overall big picture and parallels the sixth seal in John's revelation.

> But immediately after the tribulation of those days
> THE SUN WILL BE DARKENED, AND THE MOON WILL NOT
> GIVE ITS LIGHT, AND THE STARS WILL FALL from the sky,
> and the powers of the heavens will be shaken. And
> then the sign of the Son of Man will appear in the
> sky, and then all the tribes of the earth will mourn,
> and they will see the SON OF MAN COMING ON THE
> CLOUDS OF THE SKY with power and great glory. And
> He will send forth His angels with A GREAT TRUMPET
> and THEY WILL GATHER TOGETHER His elect from the
> four winds, from one end of the sky to the other.

Immediately after the tribulation, let me repeat that, *"But immediately after the tribulation of those days,"* Christ now returns (this is the Second Coming otherwise known as the *Parousia*) to pour out His/God's Wrath on mankind (all those who have received the mark of the beast). While He is still in the clouds of the sky, He will gather together His followers (this is the *harpazo* or *Rapture* where the remaining believers will be "caught up," "snatched away," or taken by force" to be translated into the clouds, in a moment in time, to join the Lord in the air, 1 Thessalonians 4:16–17). He will then send them to be with the Father while He defeats His enemies on earth and sets up His earthly Kingdom. All this must take place before the return of Bride, *"and I saw the holy city, new Jerusalem, coming down out of heaven from God, made ready as a bride adorned for her husband."* (See my notes on Revelation 21.)

Thus, we are given signs in the heavens to look for which will signal the end of the tribulation and the Rapture of the believers. *"THE SUN WILL BE DARKENED, AND THE MOON WILL NOT GIVE ITS LIGHT, AND THE STARS WILL FALL from the sky."* Now compare this to John's vision of the sixth seal, *"the sun became black as sackcloth made of hair, and the whole moon became like blood; and the stars of the sky fell to the earth."* Both events are the same, and both the darkening of the sun and moon as the stars fall from the sky follow after the tribulation and precede the Wrath of God's justice, *"for the great day of their* (the Trinity's) *wrath has come, and who is able to stand?"*

Now once the seventh seal is opened there is silence in heaven because no one can believe that God; this slow to anger, compassionate, all-loving God of grace and mercy is now pouring out His Wrath on mankind. It's an OMG moment! John does not go into great detail here because he will focus the picture more with what will transpire in the vision of the Seven Trumpets and then he will refine the picture into specifics with the Seven Bowls. Jesus on the other hand, lets the reader know exactly what will transpire on that *"Great and Awesome Day of the Lord."* For verses 50–51 make it very clear to the reader that *"The master…will come on a day when he* (the servant/unbeliever) *does not expect him and at an hour which he does not know, and will cut him in pieces and assign him a place with the hypocrites; in that place there will be weeping and gnashing of teeth."*

Both Jesus's account as recorded in Matthew 24 and John's account recorded in Revelation 6 are describing the same event in the same chronological order. Of this I am certain and there can be no doubt. Hence, in both passages we are given the complete overall big picture of the signs of His coming, and of the end of the age.

Notes on Revelation 6

The Four Horsemen of the Apocalypse

The Book of Revelation, like many other books within the Bible was written in the apocalyptic literary genre; however, the Disciple John wrote his "Apocalypse" to get his audience to pay attention to the important message that he had received and wanted to impart. Like other Jewish apocalyptic writings, John reshaped the well-known literary tradition of his day to portray heroes and villains of the first century world. It is among this literary style, that we must look at in order to understand John's use of the imagery of war and violence throughout the book. Unfortunately, we have a tendency to look at images of violence and military language through the eyes of someone living in the twenty-first century and not through the eyes of a first century reader.

When we read the harsh tone of the book with all its violence, war and judgment language we are taken aback and feel that the author was describing something completely out of the normal. However, in the first century AD, war and violence were rather commonplace. There is nothing extraordinary about the imagery of war, for John's readers were well acquainted with oppression and harsh cruelty at the hands of the Roman Empire.

In the epistles (letters) to the Seven Churches John warns and admonishes the believer of the church to hold on to their faith, to persevere and endure, to overcome the trials that come with the wickedness of this world. His main point through the imagery and language of the book is for the reader to get ready, to repent now, for when judgment comes it will be too late. The urgency of his message is rather apparent, for John's consistency in the use of military language and the violence, which comes along with such force, is seen throughout the whole apocalypse. If the reader is ready, then there is no fear for the approaching Day of Judgment.

The Four Horsemen

After "these things" have taken place (in reference to the *"Church Age"* as viewed through the prophetic lens of the seven letters to the Seven Churches), then comes the breaking of the first four seals which release John's four horsemen of the apocalypse. The literary genre of Zechariah's prophecy may have inspired John to use the same type imagery of four horses as an appropriate commentary on the Roman Empire and the element of social injustice associated with the *Pax Romana* (Peace of Rome). As Nelson Kraybill, *Imperial Cult and Commerce in John's Apocalypse,* puts it: "In Zechariah's vision, horses patrol the earth in service to God (Zech. 1:8–11, 6:1–8); in Revelation they are evil agents of Roman oppression." I agree with Kraybill that they are evil agents, but not of Roman oppression for Rome does not fit the paradigm of eschatological prophecy as we shall see.

The First Rider

As the first seal is broken, the first rider comes out upon a white horse and is told to go and to conquer. The Greek word *nikao* means "to conquer" or "to be victorious" by military force or might (Rev. 6:2, 15:2). This rider also carries with him a bow, which will be used as he conquers; it was the characteristic weapon of the mounted Parthian soldier, to whom also white was deemed a sacred color. First-century readers would have made the connection to the Parthians and this first rider immediately, because in 103 AD the Emperor Trajan would launch a campaign against the Parthians who had been moving steadily into Roman territories west of the Euphrates River. However, the Roman Legions were defeated one hundred miles from Babylon and never went any further, nor did they even attempt to cross the Tigris River to push eastward.

The Parthians were fierce warriors who were also expert horsemen and equally efficient with the war bow. It is a said that they could shoot an arrow behind them with supreme accuracy at an enemy as they rode way. Hence, the Parthian shot has become known as "the parting shot." However, the connection to the Parthians should not be lost to us at this point, for I believe we will see them again as we continue our study.

Now the word for "bow" is the Greek word *toxon*, which is normally used as a weapon of warfare, though it usage here is in reference to an instrument of peace which corresponds with Daniel 8:25 and 9:27. The Septuagint, otherwise known as LXX, translates *toxon* as a covenant or contract as we find in Genesis 9:13, Daniel 8:25, 9:27, and Zachariah 11:17. Thus this first rider carries a peace treaty with him which allows him to conquer by it.

This white rider wears the color white to mock that which is holy and can only be the Antichrist (for Christ is the one breaking the seals and is not the one sent out). This Antichrist will make a future covenant or peace treaty with Israel and the surrounding nations for seven years according to Daniel 9:27 and halfway into the seven-year treat he will break it in which he will be revealed as the Antichrist himself.

The Second Rider

When the second seal was broken, the second horse and rider is sent forth, this time the rider rode a red horse and he was given a sword to slay and kill men in order to take peace from the earth. Bruce M. Metzger. *Breaking the Code, Understanding the Book of Revelation* claims that this obviously symbolized war and bloodshed. He is absolutely correct, but there is more to it than just dismissing it off as war and bloodshed.

This rider is given the *machaira*, or short sword, which is the distinctive short sword of the Roman Infantry; no other army in history has used the short (fifteen- to eighteen-inch blade) *gladius* or *pompeii* style sword. Josephus in *The Wars of the Jews* describes how the Roman Legionaries used the *machaira/gladius* in their tactics of combat. Thus the reference to military conquest is unavoidable throughout the Book of Revelation.

In the first century when John's prophecy was being read, his audience would have known that the Roman army was one of the finest fighting machines the world had ever seen. Thirty legions, comprising 4,800 to 6,000 men in each (today we would consider this a Brigade), were spread across the empire, including five legions in Pannonia and Moseia, four in Germania, and three in Britain and Syria. Each legion was divided into smaller units called cohorts, numbering about six hundred men (battalion), but the basic battlefield unit was called the century and was composed of a hundred men (company), hence the eventual usage of the word to denote a hundred years.

Not only were Roman soldiers well disciplined, they were also superbly trained. Every waking moment was spent in training; the only thing that distinguished a training field from a field of battle was the absence of blood. R. Manning Ancell, *Rome's Warrior Supreme*, described the training that a Roman soldier received as anything that "could add strength to the body, activity to the limbs, or grace to the motions. The soldiers were diligently instructed to march, to run, to leap, to swim, to carry heavy burdens, to handle every species of arms..."

The Roman military showed their genius for adaptability by abandoning the Greek Phalanx formation in the first century BC and created the *linier penta* formation or the five-line formation. This formation consisted of the *hastati* in the front, the *principes* forming the second row; the third through fifth rows were the *triarii, rorarii,* and *accensi* in the rear.

At the front stood the *hastati*, who were most likely the spearmen in the former phalanx. The *hastati* contained the young fighters; they wore body armor and carried a rectangular shield, the *scutum*, which was the distinctive equipment of the legionary throughout Roman history. They also carried as their main weapons the *gladius* or the *pompii* as described earlier, and a *pilum*, a well-crafted seven-foot wooden spear with a three-foot iron tip. Attached to the *hastati* were far more lightly armed skirmishers (*leves*), carrying the *pilum* and several *javelins*. The *javelins* that were carried were short compared to the *pilum*, only about four feet long, but with a tip nine inches long, well hammered, and so fashioned that it bent on impact so that it could not be returned by the enemy.

The older experienced soldiers, consisting of the *principes* in the second line and the *triarii* in the third line formed the heavy infantry. The *principes* were the picked men of experience and maturity. They were similar, though better equipped than the *hastati*. In fact the *principes* were the best-equipped men in the legion. The *triarii* were veterans of former battles and functioned like the heavily armed hoplites of the old Greek phalanx. The last two lines consisted of the *rorari* and the *accensi*. The *rorarii* were younger, inexperienced men, and the *accensi* were the least dependable fighters.

During a battle their tactics were thus; the *hastati* would engage the enemy. If things got too hot, they could fall back through the lines of the heavy infantry *principes* and reemerge for counter attacks. Behind the *principes,* kneeling a few yards back were the *triarii* who, if the heavy infantry was pushed back, would charge forward with their spears, shocking the enemy with suddenly emerging new troops and enabling the *principes* to regroup. The *triarii* were generally understood as the last line of defense, behind which the *hastati* and *principes* could retire, if the battle was lost. If this should happen then behind the closed ranks of the *triarii* the army would then try to withdraw. The old Roman saying, "*It has come to the triarii*" described a desperate situation.

General Marius in the second century BC is given credit for changing the construction of the *pilum* by replacing one of the iron nails with a wooden pin, so that the connection would break under impact and be impossible to return. Once the *pilum* is thrown at the enemies' shields the shaft would break off leaving the three-foot tip stuck into the shield, rendering the shield useless. The enemy would then have to discard their shields and charge into the Roman line of attack. This is where the short sword became famous, after the Roman soldiers threw their *pilum;* they drew their short sword and closed with the enemy face to face. The formation would then stab between their wall of shields at the enemy's vulnerable areas, the face, the stomach or under the arm, which ever was exposed and not protected by body armor. The Roman formation probably look a lot like a buzz-saw, with all the blood, carnage and wounded enemy lying about the field of battle.

The color of this second rider's horse is red and is also unmistakable, for red and white were the color of the Roman legions throughout Syria and Judaea. Titus's six legions were all raised and made up from recruits from Asia Minor, Syria and Egypt, not to mention the soldiers form Arabia who came as well. Hence, John's audience would have known this and would make the connection to the ancient enemies of Israel who sacked Jerusalem in 70 AD and not to the Roman Empire itself. They would have also have understood the Apostle Paul's reference to the *"Armor of God"* described in his letter to the Ephesians (Eph. 6:14–17) as coming into play here, for what Paul was describing was the armor and tactic of the Roman Legionaries.

However, with this second red rider the *machaira* represents and symbolizes not only war and bloodshed, but also coming judgment, which Paul also denotes as the sword of the Spirit, probing the conscience and subduing the impulse to sin (Hebrews 4:12). Judgment is also what God will do to the world, he will judge all nations for their treatment of Israel.

The Third Rider

When the third seal was broken a black horse came forth and the rider had a pair of scales in his hands in which to weigh the wheat and barley in order to bring economic strife, inflation and famine. The black horse symbolizes famine, which typically follows any war. Thus economic strife, inflation and famine follow right behind the warfare that is brought about because of the second rider. However, God Himself has set limits as to what this third rider can accomplish and do (i.e., the rider is not allowed to harm the oil and the wine, which are the by-products [fruit] of the vine). Do not attempt to allegorize or symbolize the reference to the oil and wine, it is just what is says it is—oil from the olive tree and grapes to make wine.

In the year 91 AD, due to a shortage of grain that was being experience throughout the empire, Emperor Domitian issued an edict forbidding any one from planting more vineyards in Italy and in the controlled provinces, while they were also to destroy at least half of their vineyards. There was obviously an abundance of wine, but no grain. If the edict had been carried out, the wealthy commercial vineyard owners would have lost income, but grain would have been cheaper. Kraybill explains that "Domitian never enforced the edict, apparently fearing the wrath of people invested in the wine business," and I might add the wrath of the drunken mob or maybe as the case would be, the sober mob. People do like their wine, don't they?

Black also represents the color of social and economic injustice, which was evident throughout the empire. The Romans got wealthy and so did anyone who supported them, however for those who did not capitulate to Rome felt the oppression of Rome upon them. The scales in the rider's hand would also indicate not only the weight and price of grain but it would also symbolize justice or in this case injustice. Justice is blind as she weighs out justice equally with her scales, but our rider is not and he knows what he is doing as he weighs out injustice to all through this judgment.

The Fourth Rider

When the fourth seal was broken out went a pale green horse whose rider was named Death and Hades follow with him. This rider was given authority to kill by sword, famine, pestilence and by the beast. The word for sword that Death carries is *rhomphaia*, or the "great sword" which is referred to as a great, long, heavy sword, almost as tall as a man (about forty-one inches long with a curved blade with only the inside curve sharpened) that is wielded with both hands. This is where the image found in the middle ages of Death robed in black carrying a scythe comes from.

However, this sword was a weapon used by the "Thracians" in Alexander's great Macedonian Army, which symbolizes the cavalry saber, the *spatha*, of the Roman Cavalry which brought sudden death.

For when the cavalry appears out of nowhere, it suddenly strikes terror by slashing and cutting at all in its path. This mayhem and killing spree can only be achieved by the use of a long cavalry type sword which can reach to the ground to slash at those lying on the ground.

But Death does not only use the sword, he also uses famine, pestilence and the beast of the earth to accomplish his mission, all of which come upon society quickly and without warning. Death slays those on the earth and Hades snatches them away all in the same moment. It is sudden, quick and without warning. This judgment comes upon the unbeliever swiftly and is a sure warning for the Christians of John's day to be prepared. They should repent now for they will not know the hour or the day in which judgment comes.

The pale green color of the horse, *chloros*, is fitting because it is the color of death and rotting flesh. It is not, as depicted in art, a horse that is all skin and bones weak from hunger. This horse is strong and robust, a charger, which can run the length of the earth in, a moments time and appear suddenly out of nowhere. Unlike the other three horses this horse carries on his back both Death and Hades together for they are one in this judgment.

Ekolouthei meta autou would be better translated as "accompanying him," not "followed him," otherwise there would be another horse following somewhere behind Death, which in turn would mean there is time between the killing and the entrance into Hell. However, this is not the case, for in one swift motion death suddenly comes to an individual and they find themselves in Hell being tormented. There is no time for repentance. No time to cry out for forgiveness, only the tormenting fire of judgment, which they find themselves in.

John cannot make his case any stronger to his Judeo-Christian audience then with these four apocalyptic judgments, which will befall man. For now is the time to repent in order to be ready for the coming day, which John claims is upon them now. You cannot be faithful to God and serve the world, or become complacent about the world and neglect Christ. For John, they would have to make a stand, either to be on God's side or to stand with the world; you cannot do both.

It is interesting to note that the colors of the four horsemen; white, red, black, and green which encompass the Middle East and the one fourth of the world, are also the four holy colors of Islam which encompass that exact area. Just food for thought.

Notes on Revelation 6

The Key to Understanding Revelation 6:1–8

When we come to our Scriptures we need to view it, not in our western American-centric worldview, but on an eastern Jerusalem-centric Hebraic worldview of the first century AD. This mind-set helps us to visualize the audience to whom the Revelation was given and how it would be interpreted.

Though John was writing to the Seven Churches in Asia Minor, his vision like the other prophets of the Old Testament and Christ as well, is specifically Jerusalem-centric dealing with the nations surrounding Israel. In other words, the ten nations who were historically the enemies of Israel found in Jeremiah 25:19–26 and throughout the Old Testament (whose judgments against them were not completed through historical events) will in the future be involved in God's Wrath and will be brought to judgment when Christ returns.

So when we read Revelation 6:8, *"They were given power over a fourth of the earth to kill by the sword, famine and plague, and by the beast of the earth,"* we realize that John is not talking about the last horseman, but all four. The key to unlocking the whole revelation is understanding the *"fourth* (part) *of the earth,"* which is quantitative and symbolizes the extent of the influence that these four horsemen have over the whole world.

If you take a globe and divide it at the North Pole into four equal parts, placing Jerusalem in the center of one of the parts (one fourth), the surrounding area will be the Middle East and the historical enemies of Israel. This fourth part of the earth will come under the influences of a *"one world leader"* (a.k.a. the Antichrist) who will unite the nations to war against Israel, not the *"whole world."*

This fourth of the earth will experience war, famine, injustice, pestilence, and attacks by the beast (a.k.a. the Antichrist) of the earth, all of which lead up to God's Wrath and Christ's Second Coming. This does not mean that the rest of the world will not experience the ripple effect of what takes place in this fourth part of the world (i.e., Revelation 8:6–12 which mentions a third of the earth will experience cataclysmic event, thus our fourth part is now enlarged), but the whole world is not the center of John's Revelation, Israel is!

Notes on Revelation 6

The Wild Beasts of the Earth

If we look at Revelation 6:8 and the four horsemen of the apocalypse, we see our scriptures translate this passage as *"authority was given to them over a fourth of the earth, to kill with sword and with famine and with pestilence and by the wild beasts of the earth."* However, I submit to you that this passage is mistranslated and should be changed regarding the last portion of the passage and should read *"by the beast of the earth."*

This passage is commonly translated *"and by the wild beasts of the earth"* as mention above to make it fit in with the preceding part of the passage associated with famine and pestilence which occurs because of the result of war. Prophecy Buffs are quick to find an Old Testament parallel for this phrase in scripture. While it is true that God has used the sword, famine, and pestilence to discipline Israel in the past as we find in the books of Jeremiah 24:10 and Ezekiel 12:16. There is no prophecy of a future judgment of this kind against Israel. There is only one occurrence where "wild beasts" are added to the list and that is found in the book of Ezekiel 14:21 and the context of the passage limits that judgment only to the city of Jerusalem and not the fourth of the world.

The fact that the term "wild beasts" is used in some translations has led to a misinterpretation of the passage. It should be first admitted that "wild beast" is not the correct translation for this passage in Revelation 6:8, for nowhere in history has wild animals come out after war and famine to ravage and kill mankind who have suffered the scourges of war. Thus, the passage should be translated as *"and by the beast of the earth"* in reference to Revelation 13:11.

The Greek rendering for Rev. 6:8b is written as:

kai upo twn therion tes ges
and by the beast the earth
(brute)

The Greek word translated as "beasts" is the word *tharion* and at its basic meaning is beast. It is translated as beast in the book of Titus 1:12 or wild beast in the book of Acts 11:6. Context of the passage always determines which translation is best used. Here in the book of Revelation it is used thirty-nine times. In thirty-eight of the occurrences, the term refers either to the first beast, Revelation 13:1 or the second beast (the Antichrist), Revelation 13:11. It is also correctly translated beast in the description for the image of the beast. However, the translators attempting to clarify the meaning in Revelation 6:8 incorrectly translated the text as wild beasts.

When translating scripture we also need to look to extra biblical sources to understand how words were used by writers of their day. The Jewish General Flavius Josephus who fought the Romans in 68–70 AD, wrote in his book, *The Wars of the Jews or The History of the Destruction of Jerusalem,* describes Titus Vespasian as a brute, using the same Greek word *therion*, this is why I placed it in parentheses under the word beast.

Now if we do a word study on the Greek word *therion*, we find in *Strong's Exhaustive Concordance;* #2342, that they translate it as the generic term for wild animal ("beast"); (figuratively) a brutal ("bestial") nature. Even when the word is used elsewhere in scriptures Strong's translates it as an animal of some sort. However, Strong's is not the definitive word on the subject. So let's look at the Greek word and how it is used in language and by other Lexicon's, Concordance's or References:

Therion: Beast: An animal other than human: metaphorically, a brutal, bestial man, savage, ferocious, Jer 24:10; Ez 12:16; and Titus 1:12; Ez 14:21; Act 11:6; Rev. 6:8; 13:1; and 13:11.[18]

Therion: Brute: a brutal person, Rev. 13:1; 13:11: physical; brute strength savage and cruel, Rev. 13:1; 13:11.[19]

Therion: A Beast: Under the figurative of a 'beast' is depicted Antichrist, both his person and his kingdom and power, Rev. 6:8; 13:1; and 13:11; A brute: usually with a violent display of a harsh and cruel nature, Rev. 6:8; 13:1; 13:11 and 13:15[20]

There is therefore no grounds for the translation of wild beast in Revelation 6:8. So now when we compare the actual written Greek of Revelation 6:8 to Revelation 13:11 we get a different conception then a wild animal.

The Greek rendering for Revelation 13:11 is written as:

kai	*eidon*	*therion*	*anabainon*	*ek*	*tes*	*ges*
and	I saw	beast	from beneath	out	the	earth
		(brute)	(come up)			

When translating this passage, it will mean *"and I saw a beast come up out of the earth."* So I will submit to you that the two passages are the same and refer to this second beast who comes up out of the earth. Thus, as we look back to Revelation 6:8 we have a new understanding of the passage, *"authority was given to them* (all four horse-

[18]. Joseph Thayer, *Greek-English Lexicon of the New Testament* (Milford: Baker Book House Co., 1977), 4578–4579 reference numbers numerically coded to Strong's Exhaustive Concordance.

[19]. William Arndt and Wilbur Gingrich, *A Greek-English Lexicon of the New Testament* (Chicago: Chicago Press, 1979), 746.

[20]. W. E. Vine, *A Comprehensive Dictionary of the Original Greek Words with their Precise Meaning for English Readers* (McLean: MacDonald Publishing Co.,), 771, 921, 1038.

men) *over a fourth of the earth, to kill with sword and with famine and with pestilence and by the beast* (who is the Antichrist) *of the earth."* Even if you make the word plural, *twn therwn*, it refers to both the first and second beast and not to wild animals.

The Greek rendering for Revelation 13:1 is written as:

kai	eidon	ek	tes	thalasses	therion	anabainon
and	I saw	out	the	sea	beast	from beneath
					(brute)	(come up)

Thus now when translating Revelation 13:1 we have *"and I saw out of the sea a beast coming up,"* which correlates with the rest of the chapter regarding this first beast that comes up out of the "sea of humanity," which is understood to be *"every tribe, tongue, people, and nation,"* and which is indicated clearly in the text. So in reality both passages Revelation 13:1 and 11 refer to the beast (the Antichrist) of the earth that in chapter 6 all have power to put to death and kill one fourth of mankind.

Just some more things to consider.

Revelation

―――――― ❦ ――――――

CHAPTER 7

New American Standard Bible (NASB)

An Interlude

⁷ After this I saw four angels standing at the four corners of the earth, holding back the four winds of the earth, so that no wind would blow on the earth or on the sea or on any tree. ² And I saw another angel ascending from the rising of the sun, having the seal of the living God; and he cried out with a loud voice to the four angels to whom it was granted to harm the earth and the sea, ³ saying, "Do not harm the earth or the sea or the trees until we have sealed the bond-servants of our God on their foreheads."

The 144,000

⁴ And I heard the number of those who were sealed, one hundred and forty-four thousand sealed from every tribe of the sons of Israel:

⁵ from the tribe of Judah, twelve thousand were sealed, from the tribe of Reuben twelve thousand, from the tribe of Gad twelve thousand, ⁶ from the tribe of Asher twelve thousand, from the tribe of Naphtali twelve thousand, from the tribe of Manasseh twelve thousand, ⁷ from the tribe of Simeon twelve thousand, from the tribe of Levi twelve thousand, from the tribe of Issachar twelve thousand, ⁸ from the tribe of Zebulun twelve thousand, from the tribe of Joseph twelve thousand, from the tribe of Benjamin, twelve thousand were sealed.

A Multitude from the Tribulation

[9] *After these things I looked, and behold, a great multitude which no one could count, from every nation and all tribes and peoples and tongues, standing before the throne and before the Lamb, clothed in white robes, and palm branches were in their hands;* [10] *and they cry out with a loud voice, saying,*

"Salvation to our God who sits on the throne, and to the Lamb." [11] *And all the angels were standing around the throne and around the elders and the four living creatures; and they fell on their faces before the throne and worshiped God,* [12] *saying,*

"Amen, blessing and glory and wisdom and thanksgiving and honor and power and might, be to our God forever and ever. Amen."

[13] *Then one of the elders answered, saying to me, "These who are clothed in the white robes, who are they, and where have they come from?"* [14] *I said to him, "My lord, you know." And he said to me, "These are the ones who come out of the great tribulation, and they have washed their robes and made them white in the blood of the Lamb.* [15] *For this reason, they are before the throne of God; and they serve Him day and night in His temple; and He who sits on the throne will spread His tabernacle over them.* [16] *They will hunger no longer, nor thirst anymore; nor will the sun beat down on them, nor any heat;* [17] *for the Lamb in the center of the throne will be their shepherd, and will guide them to springs of the water of life; and God will wipe every tear from their eyes."*

Notes on Revelation 7

The Interlude between the Sixth and Seventh Seal

The Interlude of the 144,000 and the multitudes in chapter 7 tie in with the fifth seal and the martyrs under the altar of chapter 6, which completes the thought of those who have been martyred, those who are sealed, and those who will be raptured and will be in heaven before the wrath of God is poured out. This interlude between the sixth and seventh seal, sixth and seventh trumpet, and the sixth and seventh bowl are considered redactive story telling. It is where the story teller needs to inform the reader about something in the story to help explain something that the reader will need to know for later on before the story can continue, and are thus inserted to shed light on the overall theme of the book. In other words, it is information that helps the reader understand specific details of the revelation.

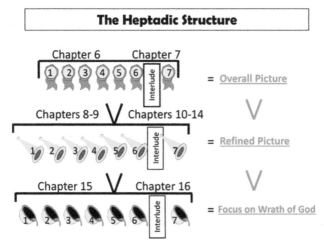

The above chart is modified from Chuck Missler's *Revelation Video Series*.

The interlude is placed here in chapter 7 in this order because it shows the chronological progression of what will take place in the future. For example, with the seals we have first; the Four Horsemen of war, famine and death, brought on by the Antichrist, followed by those who are martyred during this time, then comes the interlude and the sealing of the 144,000 in which the four winds of destruction are held back. The four winds of the earth are in reference to the directions north, south, east, and west (Ezekiel 37:9; Jeremiah 49:36; and Daniel 7:2, 8:8, and 11:4). After the sealing, now comes the cataclysmic events of God getting mankind's attention here on earth. Culminating with the rapture where the multitudes are then taken up to heaven whereby they will see Christ in the air as He returns for the Second Advent otherwise known as the *parousia*, which then leads to the Wrath of God being poured out.

The sealing of the 144,000 clearly identify each one sealed as God's agent. The context also demonstrates what the purpose of the seal or mark is. Many Prophesy Buffs argue that the seal is salvation, but there is no evidence for this claim. Those who take this position are reading into this text ideas taken from Ephesians 1:13 and the writings of the Apostle Paul.

There are also those who claim that the sealing is to prevent harm. That this is sealing for protection, which is found in Revelation 9:4, where those who have the seal of God are protected from the fallout of the fifth trumpet. However, I believe this to be a miss-rendering of both text by erroneously asserting that Revelation 9:4 applies here. This marking is the devil's counterpart or duplication of the sealing of God's 144,000, in Revelation 7:2–17. However, in Revelation 9:4 and the fifth trumpet judgment, I would submit to you that the seal/mark also applies to the followers of the beast who also receive a seal or mark, *chragma* in Revelation 13:16, who are the tormentors of mankind, for they will not harm each other as they inflict their torment on those who do not follow after or belong to their god.

The Greek word used here in this passage is *sphragida* and means "sealed," it is the perfect, passive, participle, genitive, plural, masculine of the word *chragma*, which can mean either "a seal or a mark, in order to mark a person or a thing."[21] Thus the action of sealing has already taken place at the time of John's revelation.

What most Prophesy Buffs find strange is that the term bond-servant is used to designate 144,000 Jews. Strange because this term in the New Testament is usually used to refer to believers. However, clearly the ones who are sealed are not believers, or are they! What does Romans 11:2, 5–7 tells us, that *"God did not reject his people* (the Jews), *whom he foreknew...So too, at the present time there is a remnant chosen by grace... What then? Israel has not obtained what it seeks; but the elect* (the remnant) *have obtained it..."*

The primary argument against the notion that the sealed are believers is the fact that only a limited number are sealed. Only by spiritualizing the number 144,000 can one make the argument that this number refers to the whole Church. Slave or bond-servant is used here in the true sense of ownership. God owns, claims, and seals His agents. Such a view is not inconsistent with the long held biblical notion that Israel is God's unique chosen people.

Now the 144,000 number has received much speculation. It is disappointing that Prophesy Buffs do not take this number literally. However, the book of Revelation cannot be interpreted literally, allegorically, metaphorically, or symbolically, for interspersed throughout the narrative are all four types of metaphorical hermeneutics which are typical of any apocalyptic literary genres. However, there are times where we need to interpret a passage literally, and this is such a passage. Thus, we are not told why 144,000 are chosen, but that twelve thousand from each tribe are chosen is made evidently clear.

So who are these 144,000? There is absolutely no textual basis to support those who claim that the 144,000 are any entity other than physical descendants of Abraham, Isaac, and Jacob. To spiritualize the 144,000 into a Christian group violates the text. The Disciple John gives the reader every detail necessary to correctly identify this group, and to the first century believer it would be unmistakably

---

[21.] Joseph H. Thayer, *A Greek-English Lexicon of the New Testament* (Milford: Baker Book House Co., 1977), 609.

clear. The critical phrase *"from every tribe of the sons of Israel"* should settle any debate about who they are. This phrase always refers to physical descendants of Abraham, Isaac and Jacob and is found six hundred and thirty-five times throughout the Scriptures.

The interlude changes its focus and now give us more information on who the multitudes are. The multitudes have to suffer the Great Tribulation and wash their robes through what they endure in maintaining their faith before they are made white in heaven. The martyrs under the altar in Revelation 6:9–11 are given white robes because of what they have already been through, i.e., they were beheaded in Revelation 20:4 for their testimony in Jesus Christ for which they gave the ultimate sacrifice, their lives. The robes given to the martyrs are called *stoles* and are considered Symbols/Robes of State. They are different from the robes *himatia*, which the multitudes and the seven churches receive, for these are everyday type robes, which are made white because of what the churches overcame throughout the prophetic Church Age.

The multitudes are the ones coming out of the tribulation, *ek tas phlipeoos*, who are being refined by fire. They are not spared the trials but have to endure them and come out the far side with their faith intact. What most Prophecy Buffs miss is the statement following the fact that the multitudes are serving the Lord in his sanctuary. *"They shall not hunger any more, nor shall they thirst any more, nor shall the sun beat down upon them, nor any heat."*

The imagery here is used to recall hardship and suffering, trials and afflictions, pain and weariness, etc....something they have to go through in-order to receive their white robes. It sounds to me like they can't buy or sell anything, nor do they have any shelter to keep the sun off their backs, thus they are at the mercy of their oppressors because they have not received the mark of the beast (Rev. 13:16).

However, as they experience and suffer through the tribulation, the Lord will *"shepherd them and lead them to springs of living water,"* where God will ultimately *"wipe away every tear from their eyes,"* as he embraces them and welcomes them into heaven at the rapture. This is now our promises *"But the one who endures to the end, he will be saved.*" So enduring to the end of the tribulation period becomes the key to our salvation and receiving the crown of life.

The seventh seal and verse 8:1 should stand alone or be connected with chapter 7 and become verse 7:18. Once this seal is opened there is silence in heaven because no one can believe that God; this slow to anger, compassionate, all-loving God of grace and mercy is now pouring out His Wrath on mankind. It's an OMG moment!

The scene changes with 8:2 and should become a new chapter where John now shows us a refined picture of what is taking place during this period of the Seven Seals. More on this to follow.

Notes on Revelation 7

The Tribe of Dan

Our passage here in Revelation 7:4–8, is concerned with the Remnant of Israel who are sealed by God. They number 144,000 individuals and there is absolutely no textual basis to support those who claim that the 144,000 are any entity other than physical descendants of Abraham, Isaac and Jacob. To spiritualize the 144,000 as the Christian Church violates the text. The Disciple John gives the reader every detail necessary to correctly identify this group, and to the first century believer it would be unmistakably clear. The critical phrase *"from every tribe of the sons of Israel"* should settle any debate about who they are. John then goes on to give us a list of the Tribes, however, the tribe of Dan is excluded from this list!

Now there is much speculation as to why Dan is missing and many Prophesy Buffs have been perplexed by the apparent omission of the tribe of Dan from the list of *"every"* tribe of Israel. This has led to much speculation in an attempt to explain this strange occurrence. So let's look closely at our passage to gain a better understanding of what is taking place.

The Disciple John states those who were sealed were *"from every tribe of the sons of Israel"* (NASB). The Greek word used here in this passage is *pas* and is translated as "every" or "all"—i.e., *"all the tribes of the children of Israel"* (KJV). Now the Greek word *huios* translated as "children" in the KJV literally means "a son" according to *Strong's Exhaustive Concordance.* Thus, the 144,000 are literally "the sons" of Israel.

Notice the language, it specifically indicates that it pertains to "all" the tribes of Israel. Thus by that definition itself, the tribe of

Dan cannot be excluded. The verse does not say "all the tribes of Israel except Dan," what it states is "all the tribes of Israel." However, the listing of the tribes in verses 5–8 does not mention and excludes the tribe of Dan. So what is going on here?

Before we move on we need to remember that the only certain barrier to understanding the truth in scripture is the presumption that you already have the truth and there can be no other. These presuppositions bar us from grasping the truth about the Word of God. So, it is essential from time to time to step back and reestablish a fresh perspective and let God's Word speak to us through His Scriptures and not rely on what others have taught in the past.

One possible explanation according to the *Pulpit Commentary* is that Dan was omitted due to a scribal error.

> Ewald believes that St. John wrote *Δαν*, and that *Μαν.*, the abbreviated form of "Manassas," was substituted by error; and he appeals to manuscripts 9, 13, which, however, have "Dan" in place of "Gad." Moreover, Irenaeus, Origen, Arethas, have "Manasseh," and state plainly that Dan was omitted. It is certainly curious in connection with this conjecture that, if it were true, that is to say, if "Dan" should be read in place of "Manasseh," we should have a more intelligible order of arrangement...

A second possible explanation is that there are many translational errors which are found in our Scriptures and I submit were placed there intentionally. For example: the King James Version (KJV) translators deliberately mistranslated the Greek word for "Passover" as "Easter" in the book of Acts 12:4. They likely did so because King James was head of the Church of England and he did not want his "King James Version" to "Judaize" in the text. They also substituted the word "unicorn" for the word "wild oxen" in Numbers 23:22 and in Psalms 22:21. Unicorns were vogue and in fashion at the time so they thought that a unicorn fit the passage better than a wild oxen. However, the New American Standard Bible (NASB) and many other more modern versions of the Bible saw this obvious error and they restored the word "Passover" and "wild oxen" to their translations of Scripture.

Now if there was an ancient scribal error as described above in copying from the original manuscripts (Ewald appeals to at least two manuscripts 9 and 13, which have Dan recorded as part of the list, there many have been more) than this error has persisted up until now. But by the time the New Testament scripture was canonized around the fourth century Dan was missing from the list, wither intentional or by error we cannot know.

However, I still draw your attention back to verse 4 which specifically states the intent was to include "all" the tribes of Israel. So, the omission of Dan must be an error by some scribe or translator who became confused when he recorded the tribal listings. This is the only way that the listing makes sense with the language of verse 4, which makes no mention that one tribe was to be mentioned twice and one tribe not at all. In all the genealogical listing throughout scripture the tribe of Dan is listed and it is only here in Revelation 7:5 that it is not.

The double inclusion of Joseph in the passage presents for us another problem that must be questioned. This is apparent by the appearance of Joseph, who was the leader of the tribe and whose name usually represented both Ephraim and Manasseh, for they were the sons of Joseph and would be included under the tribe of Joseph. Whenever Joseph is not listed then both Ephraim and Manasseh are listed in that order, Numbers 2:3–29, Joshua 15–22; thus when Joseph was mentioned, the direct mention of Joseph's sons were unnecessary when the name of the father appears.

Remember that the mention of Joseph in verse 8 is to be understood that it includes both Ephraim and Manasseh. And if we include Manasseh as the son of Joseph, than what we have is the same tribe mentioned twice (once directly and once indirectly) and Dan not at all. This is totally inconsistent with the wording in verse 4, that "all" the tribe of Israel were to be included in the "sealing" of the 144,000. The tribe of Ephraim is also not named, but Ephraim is understood to be included within the definition of the tribe of Joseph. So the naming of Manasseh in place of Dan must be a scribal error.

Genesis 36:23-26	Numbers 1:5-15	Numbers 2:3-29	Deuteronomy 33:1-29	Joshua 15-22	1 Chronicles 2:1	Ezekiel 48:1	Revelation 7:5-8
Reuben	Reuben	Judah	Reuben	Judah	Reuben	Dan	Judah
Simeon	Simeon	Issachar	Judah	Ephraim	Simeon	Asher	Reuben
Levi	Judah	Zebulun	Levi	Manasseh	Levi	Naphtali	Gad
Judah	Issachar	Reuben	Benjamin	Benjamin	Judah	Manasseh	Asher
Issachar	Zebulun	Simeon	Joseph	Simeon	Issachar	Ephraim	Naphtali
Zebulun	Joseph	Gad	Zebulun	Zebulun	Zebulun	Reuben	Manasseh
Joseph	Benjamin	Levi	Issachar	Issachar	Dan	Judah	Simeon
Benjamin	Dan	Ephraim	Gad	Asher	Joseph	Levi	Levi
Dan	Naphtali	Manasseh	Dan	Naphtali	Benjamin	Benjamin	Issachar
Naphtali	Gad	Benjamin	Naphtali	Dan	Naphtali	Simeon	Zebulun
Gad	Naphtali	Dan	Asher	Levi	Gad	Issachar	Joseph
Asher		Asher		Reuben	Asher	Zebulun	Benjamin
		Naphtali		Gad		Gad	
	Levi left off		Simeon left off				Dan Left off

Now there are many Prophecy Buffs who claim that because both Dan and Ephraim fell into idolatry that they were blotted out and would not receive an inheritance. However, Jeremiah 31:20 clearly states, *"Is Ephraim my dear son? Is he my darling child? For as often as I speak against him, I do remember him still. Therefore my heart yearns for him; I will surely have mercy on him, declares the LORD."*

As I have stated before, Joseph is interchangeable with Ephraim and Manasseh as we can see in the chart above, and many passages verify this. When Joseph is mentioned, Ephraim and Manasseh are not, and when Ephraim and Manasseh are mentioned, Joseph is excluded. Now remember what Jeremiah stated earlier in verse 9 that God is not done with Ephraim: *"With weeping they will come, And by supplication I will lead them; I will make them walk by streams of waters, On a straight path in which they will not stumble; For I am a father to Israel, And Ephraim is My firstborn."*

So our Prophecy Buffs solution for Dan needs to be made separate from Ephraim if you still think they will be blotted out.

However, connecting Dan's idolatry to Ephraim's works against their arguments, because what about the Levities who also went astray after idols, are they blotted out as well? *"But the Levites who went far from Me when Israel went astray, who went astray from Me after their idols, shall bear the punishment for their iniquity…"* (Ezekiel 44:10–16).

To continue to deflate their argument, during the Millennium, Dan will be allotted the first territory or portion of land *"Now these are the names of the tribes: from the northern extremity, beside the way of Hethlon to Lebohamath, as far as Hazarenan at the border of Damascus, toward the north beside Hamath, running from east to west, Dan, one portion…"* (Ezekiel 48:1). The passage goes on to state that Joseph will receive a double-portion because both Manasseh and Ephraim will receive their own territories *"Beside the border of Naphtali, from the east side to the west side, Manasseh, one portion. Beside the border of Manasseh, from the east side to the west side, Ephraim, one portion"* (Ezekiel 48:4, 5). It is also interesting that Joseph is not mentioned, which confirms the fact that they are interchangeable. When Joseph is mentioned, Ephraim and Manasseh, in that order are not.

Furthermore, God is merciful and will not break His everlasting promises; ultimately, the land will be given to "all" the tribes of Israel even the Levites. For Ezekiel states that *"the holy allotment shall be for these, namely for the priests, toward the north. It shall be for the priests who are sanctified of the sons of Zadok, who have kept My charge, who did not go astray when the sons of Israel went astray as the Levites went astray"* (Ezekiel 48:10–11). Hence Levi is also included in the promise.

Now the Apostle Paul assures us, *"All Israel will be saved; just as it is written, "THE DELIVERER WILL COME FROM ZION, HE WILL REMOVE UNGODLINESS FROM JACOB. THIS IS MY COVENANT WITH THEM, WHEN I TAKE AWAY THEIR SINS." But from the standpoint of God's choice they are beloved for the sake of the fathers; for the gifts and the calling of God are irrevocable,"* (Romans 11:26–29). Thus, it is reassuring to know that Dan and all the other tribes of ancient Israel to include the others who fell away to idolatry, Levi and Ephraim, will be saved!

The other argument against Dan that our Prophecy Buffs like to manipulate, is what they believe are several obscure prophecies in scripture which they claim point to the fact that the tribe of Dan will produce the Antichrist. Now this heresy is not new and I will submit to you that it is in reference to one of the things the seven churches are dealing with throughout the church age which has led to the church distancing itself from its Jewish roots and becoming "anti-Semitic" throughout history.

This heresy deals with the tribe of Dan, who they call the Synagogue of Satan, attempting to steal the messianic birthright from the tribe of Judah and establish a false messianic kingdom in Israel. The church father, Irenaeus writing in the first century around 180 AD, *Against Heresies*, is one of the first to claim that the Antichrist will be a Jew, and apparently of the tribe of Dan, which he based on Jer. 8:16 and because of the absence of Dan in Revelation 7:5–8. Hippolytus writing around 203 AD in the second century *Treatise on Christ and Antichrist*, picks up on this heresy and runs with it, basing it upon Deuteronomy 33:22, Genesis 49:16–17; and he considered that as the opposite of Christ the Antichrist must also descend from Israel.

So let's consider these prophecies about the Antichrist that leads to this heresy:

1. That the Antichrist is of Jewish decent they claim is found in the Book of Daniel 11:37: *"He will show no regard for the gods of his fathers or for the desire of women, nor will he show regard for any other god; for he will magnify himself above them all."*

2. That the Antichrist is from the tribe/region of Dan, found in the Book of Jeremiah 8:16–17: *"From Dan is heard the snorting of his horses; At the sound of the neighing of his stallions The whole land quakes; For they come and devour the land and its fullness, The city and its inhabitants. "For behold, I am sending serpents against you, Adders, for which there is no charm, and they will bite you," declares the LORD."*

3. That the Antichrist is from the serpent's root, found in the Book of Isaiah 14:29–31: *"Do not rejoice, O Philistia, all of you, Because the rod that struck you is broken; For from*

the serpent's root a viper will come out, And its fruit will be a flying serpent. "Those who are most helpless will eat, and the needy will lie down in security; I will destroy your root with famine, and it will kill off your survivors. "Wail, O gate; cry, O city; Melt away, O Philistia, all of you; for smoke comes from the north, and there is no straggler in his ranks."

As you can see, these are three obscure texts which are taken out of context and misapplied to support the lie that the Antichrist derives from the tribe of Dan. I have always said that context, context, context is everything. So let's put this in proper prospective and context by looking at each one of these three heresies.

1. The passage in Daniel 11:37 tie in with verses 36–39, overlapping between Antiochus IV Epiphanes and the Antichrist, for both act the same toward the Jewish people and do what they please as if they were god. Both speak arrogant words and blasphemies against God, Revelation 13:5 and Daniel 11:36, and both will exalt themselves above every so-called god or object of worship, 2 Thessalonians 2:4 and Daniel 11:36. Both distribute plunder and booty, Isaiah 10:5–7 and Daniel 11:24, and both have a hatred and disregard of women, Revelation 12:17 and Daniel 11:37.

    However, where Antiochus worshiped the Greek gods of his father, the Antichrist will worship a different god who is a god of fortresses or forces; in other words, a god of war who exults warfare and death as a major component of the religion (Allah and Islam fit this description nicely). What is interesting is the fact that Assyria, the kingdom of the north, Asia Minor and modern-day Turkey where the Antichrist will come from (Antiochus is from Assyria and is the model/archetype for the Antichrist) have worshiped three sets of religions throughout their history. The Greek gods under Alexander the Great were exulted from 332 BC until 52 AD when the Disciple Thomas evangelized the area from Syria to Taxila in present-day Pakistan establishing Christianity as the religion of the north. It wasn't until the eleventh century, a thousand years later, when the Seljuk Empire brought Islam to Assyria.

Thus, where our Prophecy Buffs teach that the passage in verse 37, *"And he will show no regard for the gods of his fathers"* is in reference to the Jewish God, *Elohim*, found in the previous verse 36, making the Antichrist Jewish, is complete bunk. Yes, the word *Elohim* elsewhere in scriptures does mean the God of the Old Testament, i.e., *"In the beginning God (Elohim) created the heavens and the earth"* (Genesis 1:1), is in reference to the Trinity (Father, Son, and Holy Spirit) the three in one Triune God which is found in both Deuteronomy 6:4 and Isaiah 48:16.

However, verse 36 reads; he, in reference to the Antichrist *"will speak monstrous things against the God of gods,"* which in the Hebrew it reads *El elohim*. El is the singular word which represents the God of the Old Testament. The word elohim in this verse is the plural word which means many gods and is used in contrast to the God (*El*) of the Old Testament. So what this means is that the Antichrist will speak blasphemies against the God of the Christians and Jews who worship the same Lord God.

The Hebrew word for gods in verses 37 and 38 are *elohah* and *elohe* both of which mean "any god or idol" other than the God of the Old Testament. Thus, the antichrist will show no regard for any god or idol that came before the god of war (Allah) that he worships and forces everyone to submit too, Revelation 13:14 and 15. This is the same "foreign god" that will allow him rule over the many nations that surround Israel today (Daniel 11:39).

So as you can see, this first heresy about the Antichrist being of Jewish decent is totally taken out of context and either by ignorance or by guile is misapplied to support their false agenda. For it is dealing with Antiochus who is the model for the Antichrist, thus the Antichrist comes from the northern land of Assyria and not Israel and was not raised a Jew.

Now let us look at the second part of the heresy:

2. The passage in Jeremiah 8:16–17 belongs with the whole section of chapter 7 and 8 dealing with the idolatry that Judah committed in the House of the Lord there in Jerusalem. *"The word that came to Jeremiah from the LORD, saying, "Stand in the gate of the LORD's house and proclaim there this word and say, 'Hear the word of the LORD, all you of Judah, who enter by these gates to worship the LORD!'" Thus says the LORD of hosts, the God of Israel, "Amend your ways and your deeds, and I will let you dwell in this place"* (Jeremiah 7:1–3).

    To put this in perspective the children of Israel, specifically the tribe of Judah was committing idolatry in the land, so God punished them by sending a foreign army against them. In 607 BC, Nebuchadnezzar, the Crown Prince Regent of Babylon besieges Jerusalem and takes Jehoiachin the King of Judah, Daniel, and the sons of Israel into exile. This starts what has become known as the seventy years of servitude for the nation of Israel.

    Ten years later in 597 BC, the Second Siege of Jerusalem take place because of rebellion and unrest, so Nebuchadnezzar puts down this revolt, tears down the gates of Jerusalem and takes more of the sons of Israel into exile. The prophet Ezekiel is also taken to Babylon at this time.

    Yet again, having not learned their lesson, ten years later in 587 BC, the prophet Jeremiah appears on the scene warning the people of Jerusalem to amend their ways and not rebel a second time against the authority of the Babylonian Empire otherwise God will judge them a third time for their iniquity. However no one listens and the Jewish rebellion now leads to the Third Siege of Jerusalem, only this time King Nebuchadnezzar destroys the Temple in Jerusalem along with the remaining walls of the city. The followers of Jeremiah escape the city taking Jeremiah with them to Egypt so that he is not deported to Babylon in this third exile.

So again as we look at the text, we find Jeremiah prophesying a warning to the tribe of Judah. *"For the sons of Judah have done that which is evil in My sight,"* declares the LORD, *"they have set their detestable things in the house* (the Temple) *which is called by My name, to defile it. They have built the high places of Topheth, which is in the valley of the son of Hinnom, to burn their sons and their daughters in the fire* (child sacrifice to the Canaanite god Molech), *which I did not command, and it did not come into My mind"* (Jeremiah 7:30–31)

Chapter 8:1–3 continues to state what will happen to them if they do not repent and turn from their wicked ways. *"At that time,"* declares the LORD, *"they will bring out the bones of the kings of Judah and the bones of its princes, and the bones of the priests and the bones of the prophets, and the bones of the inhabitants of Jerusalem from their graves. They will spread them out to the sun, the moon and to all the host of heaven, which they have loved and which they have served, and which they have gone after and which they have sought, and which they have worshiped. They will not be gathered or buried; they will be as dung on the face of the ground. And death will be chosen rather than life by all the remnant that remains of this evil family, that remains in all the places to which I have driven them,"* declares the LORD of hosts."

So now we come to the misapplied text in Jeremiah 8:16–17: *"From Dan is heard the snorting of his horses; At the sound of the neighing of his stallions The whole land quakes; For they come and devour the land and its fullness, The city and its inhabitants. "For behold, I am sending serpents against you, Adders, for which there is no charm, and they will bite you,"* declares the LORD." The tribe of Dan was the most northern tribe and would have been the first one invaded when the Babylonian Army came back into Israel to punish them a third time.

Now let's read this passage in context as it is meant to be understood: *"From Dan* (the northeastern part of the country) *is heard the snorting of his* (Nebuchadnezzar's) *horses; At the sound of the neighing of his stallions The whole land quakes; For they* (the Babylonian Army) *come and devour the land and its fullness, The city and its inhabitants. "For behold, I am sending serpents* (the Babylonians) *against you, Adders* (the Babylonians), *for which there is no charm, and they will bite you," declares the* LORD." And this is exactly what the Babylonians did to the tribe of Judah. They came in from the northeast and completed devoured the land taking everything left after the first two conquests captive and into this final exile.

Here again, we have a misapplied text to support a false heresy. The snorting of "his" horses does not apply to Dan, it is in reference to the enemy of Israel and the one carrying out the punishment from God, i.e., the Babylonians. The "serpent" also does not apply to the tribe of Dan even though the serpent is the symbol for the tribe. This again is in reference to the ones carrying out God's punishment.

Now we need to lay to rest the rest of this false lie and heresy:

3. The passage from Isaiah 14:29–31 that claims that the Antichrist comes from the serpent's root stems from the Jacob's/Israel's prophecies concerning his twelve sons found in Genesis 49:1–27. Which says, *"Dan shall judge his people, as one of the tribes of Israel. "Dan shall be a serpent in the way, a horned snake in the path, that bites the horse's heels, so that his rider falls backward. "For Your salvation I wait, O* LORD."

    Jacob's prophecy for his son Dan makes it clear that Dan will provide justice for Israel and be a serpent along the roadside, a viper that will bite at the enemies' horses' heel. But what does this mean? That Dan will protect Israel from her enemies who will attempt to do harm to Israel (prophesy about the Babylonian invasion). It is interesting, that when people see the word "serpent" they immediately refer to it as being something evil.

So how does God use the "serpent" to administer justice? Let's looks at a few passages to help in our understanding: In Exodus 4:2–5, God took the staff of Moses and turned it into a serpent to show Israel that the God of their fathers Abraham, Isaac, and Jacob had appeared to Moses and had come to set them free from bondage. Again in Exodus 7:8–12, God took the staff of Aaron and turned it into a serpent that swallowed up the two serpents that Pharaoh's wizard's, Jannes and Jambres, had produced through witchcraft.

In Numbers 21:6, when Israel became impatient and spoke against the Lord Most High, God sent venomous serpents to attack those who spoke out against Him. Also in verse 9, the only way that Israel could be healed from the snake bites was that they had to look at a bronze serpent on a pole that God had instructed Moses to erect in the wilderness order to heal Israel.

Even Jesus's Himself tells us *"Behold, I send you out as sheep in the midst of wolves; so be shrewd as serpents and innocent as doves"* (Matthew 10:16). So the serpent is not always the sign of evil and treachery, and in the case of Dan, it is used not only to fight against Israel's enemies, but also to bring about Justice to the people, that is why it became a standard for the tribe to follow in the wilderness.

Now we need to look at chapters 13–23 of Isaiah in order to understand what the prophet Isaiah was referring to when he wrote 14:29–32. *"Do not rejoice, O Philistia, all of you, Because the rod that struck you is broken; For from the serpent's root a viper will come out, And its fruit will be a flying serpent. "Those who are most helpless will eat, and the needy will lie down in security; I will destroy your root with famine, and it will kill off your survivors. "Wail, O gate; cry,*

O city; Melt away, O Philistia, all of you; for smoke comes from the north, and there is no straggler in his ranks." Was this in reference to the Antichrist who would come from the tribe of Dan? Is Dan the serpent's root? I don't think so.

Isaiah chapters 13–23 all deal with the ten nation Judgment of God against the enemies of Israel which are both historical and prophetic: Babylon, Assyria, Philistia, Moab, Damascus, Ethiopia, Egypt, Edom, Arabia, and Tyre. This passage has nothing to do with the tribe of Dan. It is judgment against the enemies of Israel.

I submit to you that these ten nations are the ten toes of the Book of Daniel which are also found in the Book of Ezekiel: Assyria/Ionia, Babylon, Persia/Elam, Egypt, Edom, Moab/Ammon, Philistia, Damascus, Tyre/Sidon, and Cush/Put. They also correspond to the ten horns/ kings and the modern nations of Turkey, Iraq, Iran, Egypt, Arabia, Jordan, Gaza, Syria, Lebanon, and Sudan/Somalia/ Libya.

If we look at Daniel 2:43 we discover that the ten toes represent the people groups of these nations. *"So to the people will be a mixture and will not remain united,"* the Hebrew word for mixture or as some translations state comingled, is the word *"arab,"* which is pronounced as ar-ab. I believe this is a word play on the word Arab meaning those Semites (a member of any of a number of peoples of ancient southwestern Asia including the Akkadians, Phoenicians, Hebrews, and Arabs who spoke a common language—i.e., Aramaic) who live in the Arabian Desert who were also known as the Midianites whom Gideon defeated in Judges 6:1–8:35. So if I were to translate this passage I would translate it as *"So the people will be Arabs and will not remain united."*

These ten Arab kings are the leaders of the above nations which will join together with the Antichrist (the eleventh horn), for they receive their power and authority from the Beast with the seven heads and lead their nations to unite with the Antichrist in rebellion against God. Both the kings and the empires belong to the seven headed Beast and are part of the Beast, though they function differently. However, they will ultimately be destroyed together when *"the Day of the Lord's Wrath"* is poured out (Rev. 19:20–21). More on this to follow when we study Revelation chapters 13–21.

So now you see that the reference made, that the tribe of Dan were serpents and that the Antichrist will come out of the tribe of Dan is a lie from the enemy and will only cause more heresies with in the church if not corrected. Thus, it is important to understand that the tribe of Dan is referred to as the one who will administer "justice." Samson, a descendent of Dan was one of the judges who administered justice to Israel for twenty years. They are the ones who were the Judges of Old that Jacob prophesied about in Genesis 49:16, and who Isaiah claims God promises to *"restore your judges as at the first, And your counselors as at the beginning,"* found in Isaiah 1:26.

I hope this solves the question once and for all about why Dan was left off the list in Revelation 7 and ends the false heresy that from the tribe of Dan will come the Antichrist.

Notes on Revelation 7

The Great Tribulation

Chapter 7:9–16 now deals with the multitudes who came from the Great Tribulation, and here again our Prophecy Buffs get it wrong. They would have you believe that the church will not suffer any persecution and be *"raptured outa here"*; thus, there would be no believers left on the earth to face the Antichrist. Now, is this really the case?

The Tribulation is often used as a generic term for the entire seven years of the seventieth week of Daniel. However, the Great Tribulation is actually defined as the last half of the week: the last three and a half years, once the Antichrist has revealed himself by desecrating the temple as found in 2 Thessalonians 2.

Now the Preterist view the Nazi Holocaust in Germany as its fulfillment where an estimated one in three Jews were exterminated. However devastating as that was, many of our Prophecy Buffs today (myself included) hardly believe that it fits the text of scripture, because it is to be followed by dramatic cosmic signs and the Second Coming of Christ:

> *Immediately after the tribulation of those days, the sun will be darkened, and the moon shall not give her light, and the stars shall fall from heaven, and the powers of the heavens shall be shaken: And then shall appear the sign of the Son of man in heaven: and then shall all the tribes of the earth mourn, and they shall see the Son of man coming in the clouds of heaven with power and great glory.* (Matthew 24:28, 29)

In the same vein of thinking one would assume that the seventieth week follows immediately after the sixty-ninth week of Daniel, but as we have seen there seems to be a time gap of about two thousand years. So the tribulation may not immediately precede cosmic events; however, I believe it will according to the verse above, for *"Immediately after the tribulation..."* the text states this clearly.

> *Now at that time shall Michael, the great prince which stands guard over the sons of your people, will arise. And there will be a time of distress such as never occurred since there was a nation until that time; and at that time your people, everyone who is found written in the book, will be rescued.* (Daniel 12:1)

Note, too, that although it is worldwide, the focus is on God's people, Israel: *"Alas! for that day is great, there is none like it; And it is the time of Jacob's distress; but he will be saved from it"* (Jeremiah 30:7). Even the Prophet Zechariah confirms that one-third of Israel will be refined by experiencing the fire of the tribulation.

> *Awake, O sword, against My Shepherd, and against the man, My Associate, declares the LORD of hosts. Strike the Shepherd that the sheep maybe scattered; and I will turn My hand against the little ones. And it will come about in all the land, declares the LORD, that two parts in it will be cut off and perish; but the third will be left in it. And I will bring the third part through the fire, refine them as silver is refined, and test them as gold is tested. They will call on My name, and I will answer them; I will say, 'They are My people,' and they will say, 'The LORD is my God,'* (Zechariah 13:7–9)

The purpose of this ordeal (the Time of Jacob's Trouble) is to drive Israel *en extremis*, to return to God: *"I will go and return to my place, until they acknowledge their offense, and seek my face: in their affliction they will seek me earnestly"* (Hosea 5:15).

This is an interesting Old Testament passage: God says, *"I will go and return to my place,"* so He must have left it! When did he leave and when did he return? God left heaven to become one of us to fulfill the requirement of a sacrifice. After the crucifixion Christ returned to heaven to be with the Father.

Watch those until(s) in the text: they often denote significant milestones and context is everything. The term *offense* is both singular and very specific. Apparently, a prerequisite condition for the Second Coming of Christ is for Israel to acknowledge her Messiah and to petition His return. (This would help explain why Satan continues to be so intensely committed to the destruction of the Jews.)

There are many who believe that the Church will not go through the Great Tribulation. In exploring this issue, it is essential to distinguish between persecution, which clearly has been the case of the Church for the past nineteen centuries, and "the Great Tribulation" of eschatology. The persecution—and tribulation—of the Church was clearly promised to us: *"These things I have spoken to you, that in me you might have peace. In the world you shall have tribulation: but be of good cheer; I have overcome the world"* (John 16:33).

The Greek word for tribulation is the word *philipses*, which means "pressure." It is a word that was used in torture, where heavy rocks were places upon the chest of the victim which would ultimately suffocate them by crushing them to death. Now that's what I call pressure, tribulation. It is outward pressure that is placed upon the believer that may ultimately result in their death. Are you ready and willing to die for your faith?

> *Then you will be handed over to be persecuted and put to death, and you will be hated by all nations because of me. At that time many will turn away from their faith and will betray and hate each other, and many false prophets will appear and deceive many people.* (Matthew 24:9–11)

Revelation 20:4 clearly lets us know that we Christians will suffer this tribulation for we will be *"beheaded because of the testimony of Jesus and because of the word of God, and those who had not received the mark upon their foreheads and upon their hand."* These are the martyrs under the altar in Revelation 6:9–11. They are given white robes because of what they have already been through, i.e., they were beheaded in Revelation 20:4 for their testimony in Jesus Christ for which they gave the ultimate sacrifice, their lives. The robes given to these martyrs are called *stoles* and are considered Symbols/Robes of State. They are different from the robes *himatia*, which the multitudes and the seven churches receive, for these are everyday type robes which are washed and made white because of what the churches overcame throughout the Prophetic Church Age.

The source of this tribulation is the world and, of course, Satan. However, "the Great Tribulation" of major significance is quite another matter. *"For then shall be great tribulation, such as was not since the beginning of the world to this time, no, nor ever shall be"* (Matthew 24:2, 1). The Great Tribulation leads up to the wrath of God being poured out upon the world and Satan. It involves the indignation and wrath of God, Revelation 6:16, 17; 11:18; 14:10, 19; 15:1, 17; 16:1, 19; 19:15. In contrast, the Church has been promised: *"For God has not appointed us to wrath, but to obtain salvation by our Lord Jesus Christ"* (1 Thessalonians 5:9), and *Much more then, being now justified by his blood, we shall be saved from wrath through him* (Romans 5:9).

There appears to be a difference between the Great Tribulation and the Wrath of God poured out on a rebellious world. Chapter 8 of Revelation, the breaking of the seventh seal announces the Day of the Lord, which is the start of God's out pouring of his Wrath. The Great Tribulation precedes this at the three-and-a-half mark with the Antichrist desecrating the Temple. The Antichrist will than persecute the believers *"such as was not since the beginning of the world."* The Wrath of God however is poured out against the ungodly and the enemies of Israel.

So who is this *"Great Multitude"* found in Revelation 7:9–16 and why are they giving praise to the one who sits on the throne?

Well, these are the Tribulation Saints who have been raptured to Heaven and who are now singing praises to the Lord. They are the ones who suffered and endured for their faith as they went through the Great Tribulation. This multitudes are those coming out of the tribulation *"ek tas phlipeoos"* who have been refined by fire. They were not spared the trials of Satan but had to endure them and come out with their faith intact, that is why they are given the *himatia*, the white robes. These multitudes have to go through and suffer the Great Tribulation before they can wash their robes white through what they endured in maintaining their faith.

As I have stated in chapter 4, the whole debate all revolves around the Greek word *ek* "out of" or "from" found in Revelation 3:10 and here in 7:14. Are these the ones who were removed "out of" or "from" the tribulation before it started; or are these the ones who came "out of" or "from" the tribulation as if they went through a tunnel and came out of the other end with their faith intact having endured what the world threw at them?

Remember that even Christ Jesus himself asked the Father to *"not take His* (Jesus') *disciples from the earth, but to keep them from the evil one"* (John 17:15–16). In other words, Jesus asked our Heavenly Father to assist and help the saints (believing Christians) through the tribulation so they could endure all that the beast and the Antichrist brought upon them.

Here the Prophecy Buffs get it wrong and have to do some theological gymnastics if you are to believe you do not have to endure the tribulation. If someone said to you *"did you come from that party or out of that house"* the assumption is automatic, that you were within the house or at the party. You would not automatically conclude that you did not go into the house or you did not attend the party, unless you add a clause behind the first statement to indicate that you did not go into the house or you did not go to the party.

Now let's look at the passage its self: *"These are the ones who come out of the great tribulation... They will hunger no longer, nor thirst anymore; nor will the sun beat down on them, nor any heat."* Sounds like the accompanying clause indicates that the believers have to endure something. They have to endure the tribulation, for they are not able to buy or sell because they did not receive the mark of the beast. They are NOT removed before it happens as our Prophecy Buffs would have you believe.

Context is everything and the imagery is quite clear in this passage, for it recalls the hardship and suffering, trials and afflictions, pain and weariness, etc. something they have gone through. Thus the multitudes can't buy or sell anything (i.e., food and drink, nor do they have any shelter to keep the sun off their backs because they can't buy homes or rent living places), and so they are at the mercy of their oppressors because they have not received the mark of the beast:

> And he (the Antichrist) *causes all, the small and the great...to receive a mark on their right hand or on their foreheads, so that no one could be able to buy or to sell unless he had the mark, which is the name of the beast...* (Rev. 13:16)

Who is the above passage referring to? Well, everyone except the Tribulation Saints (i.e., *"Great Multitude"*), for they are the ones who refuse to receive the mark of the beast and will have to suffer at his hands by enduring and going through "The Tribulation." They are the ones who endure to the end, whom Christ will save. For Matthew 24:13 clearly states, *"But the one who endures to the end, he will be saved."*

Revelation

CHAPTER 8

New American Standard Bible (NASB)

The Seventh Seal

⁸ *When the Lamb broke the seventh seal, there was silence in heaven for about half an hour.*

The Trumpets

² *And I saw the seven angels who stand before God, and seven trumpets were given to them.*

³ *Another angel came and stood at the altar, holding a golden censer; and much incense was given to him, so that he might add it to the prayers of all the saints on the golden altar which was before the throne.* ⁴ *And the smoke of the incense, with the prayers of the saints, went up before God out of the angel's hand.* ⁵ *Then the angel took the censer and filled it with the fire of the altar, and threw it to the earth; and there followed peals of thunder and sounds and flashes of lightning and an earthquake.*
⁶ *And the seven angels who had the seven trumpets prepared themselves to sound them.*

The First Trumpet

7 The first sounded, and there came hail and fire, mixed with blood, and they were thrown to the earth; and a third of the earth was burned up, and a third of the trees were burned up, and all the green grass was burned up.

The Second Trumpet

8 The second angel sounded, and something like a great mountain burning with fire was thrown into the sea; and a third of the sea became blood, 9 and a third of the creatures which were in the sea and had life, died; and a third of the ships were destroyed.

The Third Trumpet

10 The third angel sounded, and a great star fell from heaven, burning like a torch, and it fell on a third of the rivers and on the springs of waters. 11 The name of the star is called Wormwood; and a third of the waters became wormwood, and many men died from the waters, because they were made bitter.

The Fourth Trumpet

12 The fourth angel sounded, and a third of the sun and a third of the moon and a third of the stars were struck, so that a third of them would be darkened and the day would not shine for a third of it, and the night in the same way.

13 Then I looked, and I heard an eagle flying in midheaven, saying with a loud voice, "Woe, woe, woe to those who dwell on the earth, because of the remaining blasts of the trumpet of the three angels who are about to sound!"

Notes on Revelation 8

A Whole Lot of Shaking Going On

In John's Revelation, he is taken up into heaven and is standing in the throne-room of God where he is given insight into what will happen in the last days leading up to and including what will take place on the Day of The Lord.

> Most commentaries agree that Revelation 6:12 is allegorical: "The earthquake, the eclipse of the sun and moon, the falling of the stars, etc., are to him (John) figurative of "grievous and disturbed times," which impend by God's judgment over his enemies…the shaking down is only from the standpoint of the appearance to human vision; while the human eye sees the stars sinking as stars to earth, yet must they in reality sink, and pass far from the earth in the void expanse. The context itself should have been sufficient protection from all these aberrations; for here, just as in the proceeding seal-visions, the simple admonition is entirely valid, that everything portrayed in vv. 12–17 is subject of a vision, and not something objectively real."[22]

[22.] Friedrich Dusterdieck, and edited by Henry Jacobs, *Critical and Exegetical Handbook to the Revelation of John* (Winona Lake: Alpha Publications, 1980), 232–233.

There are no real stars striking the earth and no earthquake felt because of the impact of the stars being cast down. They are removed out of their natural place to a distant place where their light does not shine upon the earth leaving it in complete darkness with only an eerie red glow of the blood moon appearing. Thus the shaking and quaking relates to what John experiences in heaven and not what is happening on earth.

To add more emphases to what is happening in the throne-room of heaven, chapter 8:2–5 describes the angel taking coal from the altar and hurling it to earth. Yet earth is not the object of the scene, heaven is. Thus when the trumpets blow, then the vision shift to earth.

> According to Lenski, one of the leading Greek experts: *"There occurred thunders and sounds and lighting and quaking,"* and the seven angels reached for their trumpets and are ready to trumpet in their turn. We must consider these thunders, etc., together. Review 4:5 (cf., 11:19; 16:18): *"lightning and sounds* (not voices) *and thunders"* which are there said to proceed *"out of the throne."* The Omnipotent on his throne is proceeding to act. John witnesses these tremendous manifestations; they are a part of this vision. Neither here nor in 4:5 does *seismos* mean "earthquake"; it does not mean "earthquake" even in 6:12. It means "shaking or quaking" and accompanies "thunder," etc. Only when the earth shakes may we render this Greek word "earthquake.""[23]

So John standing in heaven does not see the earth shake (an earthquake taking place) but he feels the heavens quake or vibrate where he is standing (in the throne room of God) where the thunder,

---

[23.] R. C. H. Lenski, *The Interpretation of St. John's Revelation* (Minneapolis: Augsburg Publishing House, 1963), 272.

lighting and sounds emanate from the throne. Chapter 11:19 confirm the fact that these *"flashes of lightning, peals of thunder, rumblings and shaking along with a great hailstorm"* are emanating from God's temple and throne-room, which is in heaven, specifically, from the Ark of his Covenant.

However, chapter 16:18 is obviously an actual earthquake because the object or scene of the vision is the earth where *"the great city is split in three parts and the cities of the nations all collapsed."* Here thought the judgment proceeds from the temple or throne-room of God and are brought to earth via the wrath, so we can render the word *seismos* here as an actual "earthquake" that is felt in the world.

Now if we do a word study on the Greek word *seismos*, we find in *Strong's Exhaustive Concordance* that they translate it as earthquake even when the word is used elsewhere in scriptures to refer to a storm at sea. However, Strong's is not the definitive word on the subject. So let's look at the Greek word and how it is used in language and by other references:

> *Seismos.* Rev. 6:12—present, passive, participle, nominative, singular, feminine of the word *seio:* to shake or to quake.[24]

> *Seismos.* Shaking; is accompanied by peals of thunder, Rev. 8:5; 11:19—Earthquake; a severe earthquake, Rev. 6:12, 11:13, 16:18[25]

> *Seio-.* To shake to and fro, is rendered to shake in Rev. 6:12; usually a violent concussion, Rev. 6:12; shake or tremble, Rev. 4:5; 8:5[26]

---

24. Nathan Nan, *A Parsing Guide to the Greek New Testament* (Wheaten: Herald Press), 443.

25. William Arndt and Wilbur Gingrich, *A Greek-English Lexicon of the New Testament* (Chicago: Chicago Press, 1979), 746.

26. W. E. Vine, *A Comprehensive Dictionary of the Original Greek Words with their Precise Meaning for English Readers* (McLean: MacDonald Publishing Co.), 771, 921, 1038.

Seismos. To shake, agitate, cause to tremble, Rev. 6:12; a shaking, a commotion, Rev. 6:12; 8:5; 11:13 and 19; 16:18.[27]

Seio-. To shake or agitate, as an earthquake or storm at sea, Rev. 6:12; 8:5; 11:19; 16:18.[28]

So as we can see, most Lexicons and/or Greek-English dictionaries translate our word as shake, agitate, or tremble and then the context determines whether it applies to the earth as an earthquake or storm at sea.

As we look back at Revelation 8:5, we discover that the scene is in heaven (the throne-room of God) where *"there occurred thunders and sounds and lighting and shaking/trembling."* The fact that fire was thrown down to earth does not change the location of where the event occurs. We will see what happens on earth when the first trumpet blows, and thus any shaking going on then will mean that it is an earthquake, because the context of the vision determines that the earth is now the major scene of the vision.

---

27. Joseph Thayer, *Greek-English Lexicon of the New Testament* (Milford: Baker Book House Co., 1977), 4578–4579 reference numbers numerically coded to Strong's Exhaustive Concordance.

28. George Berry, *Interlinear Greek-English New Testament* (Milford: Baker Book House, Co., 1982), 4578–4579 reference numbers numerically coded to Strong's Exhaustive Concordance.

Notes on Revelation 8 and 9

The Seven Trumpets

In John's Revelation, he is taken up into heaven and is standing in the throne-room of God where he is given insight into what will happen in the last days leading up to and including what will take place on the *"Day of The Lord."* This insight is revealed to us in two parallel, but separate set of interwoven visions which take place both in heaven and on Earth. Both sets of visions start with a broad overall big picture of what will take place, then the picture is refined with more detail, and finally the picture is brought into focus.

The first set of visions are depicted in the Seven Seals, Seven Trumpets, and the Seven Bowls, which culminates with the focus on the Wrath of God. The second set of visions which I call the First, Second, and Third Previews depict the struggle between the forces of God and Satan and finally focuses with the Third Preview on the Victorious Christ, but more on the previews when we start looking at chapter 12.

The Heptadic Structure

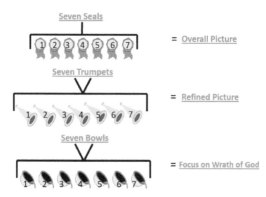

With the opening of the Seven Seals, we have been shown the overall big picture of what will take place at the end of the age. Now with the sounding of the Seven Trumpets the picture is refined to show us more detail on just what will take place within the scheme of the overall picture. The Seven Seals are a literal, chronological series of events leading up to the return of the Lord. The Seven Trumpets on the other hand, which I submit to you, should be viewed as allegory. Why, because allegory forces the reader to look for the hidden meaning behind what is being stated, for it is the method of indirect representation of ideas or truths. The Rabbi's and Sages of old would tell their student's to look for the deeper meaning, *sod*, throughout scripture each time you read and not rely on first impressions to reveal the truth.

So if we look at all of chapters 8 and 9 allegorically, we see the six trumpet blasts are a progression of supernatural destructive religious delusions which have been sent to those who have rejected the truth as the Apostle Paul teaches in 2 Thessalonians 2:9–13:

> *"The coming of the lawless one* (the Antichrist) *will be in accordance with the work of Satan displayed in all kinds of counterfeit miracles, signs and wonders, and in every sort of evil that deceives those who are perishing. They perish because they refused to love the truth and so be saved, For this reason God sends them a powerful delusion* (a false religion) *so that they will believe the lie and so that all will be condemned who have not believed the truth but have delighted in wickedness."*

We gather a deeper understanding of why these destructive delusions were sent to earth as we look at the Old Testament prophecies of Isaiah. In Isaiah's vision he was standing in the throne-room of God when an angel flew to him with a burning coal from the altar of incense and touched Isaiah's lips which we are told took away his guilt and atoned for his sin. He is then told by God to go tell the people that God has hardened their hearts against his word:

> *"He* (God) *said, "Go and tell this people: 'Be ever hearing, but never understanding; be ever seeing, but never perceiving.' Make the heart of this people calloused; make their ears dull and close their eyes. Otherwise they might see with their eyes, hear with their ears, understand with their hearts, and turn and be healed...so that only the Holy seed will be the stump in the land."*

Thus God is telling us that he is stopping up ears from hearing the truth, blinding those from seeing the truth and to making hearts callous to understanding the Word of God's Truth. For, what better way of doing this then by sending religious delusions to deceive those who do not want to listen to the truth. His purpose is to leave only the Holy stumps of the vine left in the land whereby believers might be grafted into the vine of Judaism to spring forth a stronger vine Holy unto himself.

This progression of supernatural destructive religious delusions which have been sent to those who have rejected the truth, is carried out through the vision of John's Revelation as the angel throw's down fire/burning coals from altar of incense to the earth. Once the fire has reached the earth (Psalm 11:1–7), then the angels sound the trumpets which then starts the progression of deception and falsehood for those who will not believe the Truth.

The Seven Trumpets

First Trumpet: Scripture tells us that Life is in the blood, so having it mixed with Hail and Fire in this judgment indicates that one-third of mankind will run hot and cold in their faith or the lack of and not believe the Word of God. Thus, the burning of nature does not afford them the opportunity to find comfort in their environment apart from what God brings. For those who buy into the Global Warming/Climate Change Theory and who worship the creation rather than the Creator may find that this is a huge delusion which God has allowed to take hold and spread in our time.

Second Trumpet: Throughout the Old Testament the allegorical use of mountains representing kingdoms or nations and seas representing multitudes of people throughout the world is abundant. Thus a mountain burning with fire represents a nation consumed with a false religion, which has deluded its population with its destructive lie. It is hurled into the sea of the world's populace whereby one-third of the creatures (mankind) and one-third of the ships (institutions of religion/higher learning) are destroyed because of the lie or fall prey to the lie and spread the false religious lie to others. It is this sea of humanity in which the beast in Revelation 13:2 rises out of, it is this same sea/waters that the prostitute sits upon in Revelation 17:1.

Third Trumpet: Scriptures tell us that rivers of Life flow from the Word of God, thus when they are made bitter by Wormwood even some of the elect will be deceived and have their faith deluded. The one-third of mankind who believe the lie will not be refreshed by the rivers of Life and so they will die in their sins because they have not repented.

Fourth Trumpet: This is the climax of the first four trumpets where the destructive religious delusions, i.e., the lie, removes one-third of the Light of Truth from the world. Mankind is then doomed to spend time in the darkness of their wickedness where evil permeates every area of life. Woe to those who call good evil and evil good.

Fifth Trumpet: This trumpet marks the first of the three Woes where we are no-longer looking at the whole world per say, but are now looking at a geographical area where the hellish delusion is allowed to torment mankind. With the opening of the bottomless pit, *"smoke went up out of the pit, like the smoke of a great furnace... Then out of the smoke came locusts upon the earth..."* Satan carries out his designs through blinding the eyes of men and extinguishing the light of truth and knowledge. He also carries out his schemes by promoting ignorance and error, for he deceives mankind first and then he destroys them.

This swarming delusion is an inescapable curse of judgment on mankind. Hell's smoke thus completely blots out the Light of the Truth from men's souls. This has been evident in the Mid-East where the fastest growing religion has taken root and has been spread to the rest of the world by terror. Now this hellish army is restricted from harming the earth or any green thing, nor are they allowed to harm those who have the seal/mark of their god on their foreheads. The Greek word used here to mean "seal" is *sphragida* and is the perfect, passive, participle, genitive, plural, masculine of the word *chragma*, which can mean either "a seal or a mark, in order to mark a person or a thing."[29] This marking is the devil's counterpart or duplication of the sealing of God's 144,000, in Revelation 7:2–17. However, here in this fifth trumpet judgment, I would submit to you that the seal/mark also applies to the followers of the beast who also receive a mark, *chragma* in Revelation 13:16, who are the tormentors of mankind, for they will not harm each other as they inflict their torment on those who do not belong to their god.

This army is led by the angel from the abyss called *Abeddon*, which means the "Destroyer." It is interesting that several of the titles or ninety-nine beautiful names of Allah are "Destroyer of Nations" and the "Destroyer of Men's Souls." It is also interesting that the Qur'an forbids the Muslim from cutting down trees, for the Qur'an states that when the Mahdi (the Muslim Messiah) and Isa (the Muslim Jesus) return "the rocks and the trees will cry out that there is a Jew hiding behind me come and kill him." That's why they are restricted from doing harm to the earth or anything green.

Sixth Trumpet: Here we have the companion to the fifth trumpet which marks the second Woe in which the Hellish delusion completes God's judgment by adding to the torment from the previous trumpet, only now adding the killing blow in order to slay one-third of mankind. For those who do not worship their god are put to the sword. The four angels are not evil angels, but are angels of restraint, which are restraining the armies from beyond the great river Euphrates. They act like the four angels of Revelation 7:1 holding back the destructive winds from the four corners of the earth from blowing until the appointed time. These angels in 7:1 are waiting to release God's judgment on those who do not repent.

---

29. Joseph H. Thayer, *A Greek-English Lexicon of the New Testament* (Milford: Baker Book House Co., 1977), 609.

The killing blow of this trumpet is also accomplished through the use of war. As described, *"the heads of the horses are like the heads of lions; and out of their mouths proceed fire and smoke and brimstone."* This slaughter is a prediction of great artillery pieces, which had been used as instruments of cruelty and destruction by the Turks at the siege of Constantinople. This strange Turkish weapon of warfare could hurl a 1 ton projectile a half mile which ultimately destroyed the walls of Constantinople allowing the city to fall, thus paved the way for the Islamic invasion up to the door steps of Central Europe.

Now, the fifth and sixth trumpets are the worst of the religious delusions and describe the rise of Islam as smoke and locusts spreading across the land. According to the *Commentary Critical and Explanatory on the Whole Bible*, several of the titles or ninety-nine beautiful names of Allah are "Lord of the Locusts" and the "Destroyer of Nations,"[30] There are many modern scholars today who are beginning now to realize the theological implications of this religious delusion. Dr. Dan Green for one and co-author of the book *Sword of Islam* calls it "a Religion of Smoke and Mirrors,"[31] reinforcing the idea that this fifth and sixth trumpet are in-fact a false theology and religion which will delude mankind's knowledge of the true Word of God through deception disguised as "the only true faith," which is intolerant of any faith other than Islam itself.

Seventh Trumpet: This trumpet marks the Second Coming of Christ and the beginning of God's Wrath being poured out on mankind. Up until now the Six Trumpets have been judgments by God bestowed and issued on mankind in order to get them to repent of their sins and turn from their wickedness, but now with the blowing of this seventh Trumpet, God releases his Wrath on the world and any repentance that now may take place is in vain, for it's too late. Christ has returned and judgment has come to the earth.

[30.] Robert Jamieson, A. R. Fausset, and David Brown. *Commentary Critical and Explanatory on the Whole Bible* (New York: 1871).

[31.] John F. Murphy and R. Dan Green. *Sword of Islam, Muslim Extremism from the Arab Conquest to the Attack on America.* (New York: Prometheus Books, 2002), 73.

Revelation

CHAPTER 9

New American Standard Bible (NASB)

The Fifth Trumpet—the Bottomless Pit

⁹ Then the fifth angel sounded, and I saw a star from heaven which had fallen to the earth; and the key of the bottomless pit was given to him. ² He opened the bottomless pit, and smoke went up out of the pit, like the smoke of a great furnace; and the sun and the air were darkened by the smoke of the pit. ³ Then out of the smoke came locusts upon the earth, and power was given them, as the scorpions of the earth have power. ⁴ They were told not to hurt the grass of the earth, nor any green thing, nor any tree, but only the men who do not have the seal of God on their foreheads. ⁵ And they were not permitted to kill anyone, but to torment for five months; and their torment was like the torment of a scorpion when it stings a man. ⁶ And in those days men will seek death and will not find it; they will long to die, and death flees from them.

⁷ The appearance of the locusts was like horses prepared for battle; and on their heads appeared to be crowns like gold, and their faces were like the faces of men. ⁸ They had hair like the hair of women, and their teeth were like the teeth of lions. ⁹ They had breastplates like breastplates of iron; and the sound of their wings was like the sound of chariots, of many horses rushing to battle. ¹⁰ They have tails like scorpions, and stings; and in their tails is their power to hurt men for five months. ¹¹ They have as king over them, the angel of the abyss; his name in Hebrew is Abaddon, and in the Greek he has the name Apollyon.

[12] The first woe is past; behold, two woes are still coming after these things.

The Sixth Trumpet—Army from the East

[13] Then the sixth angel sounded, and I heard a voice from the four horns of the golden altar which is before God, [14] one saying to the sixth angel who had the trumpet, "Release the four angels who are bound at the great river Euphrates." [15] And the four angels, who had been prepared for the hour and day and month and year, were released, so that they would kill a third of mankind. [16] The number of the armies of the horsemen was two hundred million; I heard the number of them. [17] And this is how I saw in the vision the horses and those who sat on them: the riders had breastplates the color of fire and of hyacinth and of brimstone; and the heads of the horses are like the heads of lions; and out of their mouths proceed fire and smoke and brimstone. [18] A third of mankind was killed by these three plagues, by the fire and the smoke and the brimstone which proceeded out of their mouths. [19] For the power of the horses is in their mouths and in their tails; for their tails are like serpents and have heads, and with them they do harm.

[20] The rest of mankind, who were not killed by these plagues, did not repent of the works of their hands, so as not to worship demons, and the idols of gold and of silver and of brass and of stone and of wood, which can neither see nor hear nor walk; [21] and they did not repent of their murders nor of their sorceries nor of their immorality nor of their thefts.

Notes on Revelation 9

The Church Fathers

The focus of chapter 9 is on the swarming hellish delusion coming out of the earth, which is allowed to torment mankind through the fifth and sixth trumpets. This delusion is an inescapable judgment of God allowed to deceive mankind for not seeking the Light of the Truth as many of our Church Fathers believed. Thus it is apropos to stop here and look at what many of our Church Father taught.

Many of the Post-Nicene Church Fathers and some of our best Western scholars on biblical prophecy believed that Islam would be a major player and would revive in the end of days as the end-time beast of Revelation 13. Below are just a few who thought and taught that Islam would be a major player in eschatology:

Cyril of Jerusalem (315–368 AD) in his *Divine Institutes* believed that Antichrist proceeds forth from the region of ancient Assyria, which today extends from Syria well into portions of Asia Minor (Turkey).

Sophronius, Patriarch of Jerusalem (560–638) and Maximus the Confessor (580–662) identified Islam with Antichrist and lived through Islam's invasion of Jerusalem. Maximus, who was also an important theologian and scholar of the early Church who helped defeat the Monothelite heresy, referred to the Muslim invasions as "announcing the advent of the Antichrist."

John of Damascus (676–749) was another very important figure in the early church. In his famous book, *Concerning Heresies*, he identified Muhammad as a "pseudo-prophet" (false prophet) and also identified Islam (which he calls the heresy of the Ishmaelites), as the "forerunner of the Antichrist," *prodromos tou Antichristou.* In his famous treatise on the faith, *De fide orthodoxa*, he acknowledged that many antichrists were "bound to come" in addition to the final Antichrist, and that any one of many expected antichrists can be identified by the fact that he "confesses not that the Son of God came in the flesh and is perfect God and became perfect man, after being God."

Eulogius, Paul Alvarus, and the Martyrs of Cordova (all living in the ninth century) believed Muhammad to be a false prophet and the precursor to the Antichrist.

Peter the Venerable (1092–1156) who, in the prologue of his translation of the Qur'an into Latin, referred to Muhammad as the maximal precursor of the Antichrist and the elect disciple of the devil: *maximus precursor Antichristi et electus discipulus diaboli Mahumet.*

Gregory Palamus of Thessalonica (1296–1359) interpreted that the martyrdom of Christians during the Great Tribulation would come from Islam.

Many are not aware that while Martin Luther (1483–1546), father of the Protestant Reformation, believed that the Papacy played the role of the Spiritual Harlot, he also believed that the Muslims were the Kingdom of Antichrist. Luther felt that Islam was inhumanly violent, treacherous, and demonically lascivious and that the Turks whole existence was to extirpate all of Christianity.

Luther spent considerable effort attacking the beliefs of the Turks in his treatises especially in *On War against the Turk* and demonstrated that it is "a religion of lies, murder and the disregard of marriage, of these he was most certain." He saw the Turk as the devil and the pope as the antichrist, both of which were raging furiously against Christ. "When the Turk comes, judgment and hell will follow." Luther saw the four horseman of the apocalypse in the wake of the Turkish armies march through the Balkans to the gates of Vienna; he understood that Islam was the little horn in the book of Daniel, and that Gog and Magog were interpreted to be the Turks who would rule and have dominion for a time before they would be destroyed by Christ in the book of Revelation. Luther wrote: *"Ego usque ad mor-*

tem luctor adversus Turcas et Turcarum Deum," "I will always struggle to the death against the Turks and the god of the Turks."

John Calvin (1509–1564) interpreted Daniel 2 and 7 as the Roman Empire prior to the rule of Trojan, stating that the prophecies were fulfilled at "the time when Christ's reign began… From the time when the Gospel began to be promulgated, we know the Roman monarchy to have been dissipated and at length to vanish away." He also interpreted the little horn to be Caesar. "I have no doubt the *the little horn* relates to Julius Caesar and the other Caesars who succeeded him, namely, Augustus, Tiberius, Caligula, Claudius, Nero, and others."

However, Calvin interpreted Islam's fall at the sound of the great trumpet in Revelation. "The Turkish Empire, indeed, at this day, excels in wealth and power, and the multitude of nations under its sway; but it was not God's purpose to explain future events after the appearance of Christ." So according to Calvin, the sound of the great trumpet carries Islam into the Great Tribulation where he believed Islam would be removed prior to Christ's second coming.

John Wesley (1703–1791) along with his brother Charles Wesley founded the Methodist movement. In John's writings, *Works*, published in 1841, he interpreted both the two Iron legs in Daniel 2 as Islam and not Rome.

Jonathan Edwards (1703–1758) the great American preacher and orator, who helped bring about the Great Awakening and who fueled the American Revolution, saw Islam as the beast and the premier elements of the Antichrist's Kingdom. He wrote in his book *History of Redemption* in 1753; that "America's last war will be fought against the rising tide of the Islam at the dawn of the twenty-first century."

Josiah Litch (1809–1886) interpreted Revelation as the ushering in of Islam; claiming that all Christians understand the role of Islam in end times. He even described the magnitude of Islam's role as being Antichrist to the extent of calling it the "general agreement among Christians, especially protestant commentators."

Even Sir Robert Anderson (1841–1918) perhaps one of the best prophecy experts who unlocked the seventy weeks of Daniel, in his remarkable book, *The Coming Prince*, insists on focusing on the Levant (Eastern) part rather than the Adriatic (West) in Daniel 2, because the Islamic nations surrounding Israel in his day would not change to something else in the future.

Hilaire Belloc (1870–1953) an Anglo-French writer and historian foresaw Islam's rise as the Beast of Revelation.

Dr. Francis Nigel Lee (1934–2011) who sums up the traditional view in his excellent work, *Islam in the Bible* wrote: "from the seventh century onward—the two legs would degenerate respectively into the Papacy (which progressively took over the West) and Islam (which progressively took over the East)."

However, here I disagree with Dr. Lee and Sir Robert and submit or suggest that our Scriptures profile this period of history in terms of seven major empires: These would appear to be Egypt, Assyria, Babylon, Persian, Greece, and Islam, this last one in two phases: Islam under the Caliphate ("Phase I") and the final re-emergent revival of the Caliphate ("Phase II"). Islam and the Caliphate makes more sense as we look closer; it was put to death with the ending of the Ottoman Empire in 1918 and will be brought back and reestablished in the "last days," remember that the head that had the fatal wound, was healed. Rome does not fit this image because Rome will not come back and rule over this area. Also the only kingdom to conquer all the territories that made up the Babylonian-Persian Empire was the kingdom of Islam, not Rome. The head wound does not equate to a person, but to a government; thus the Caliphate which ceased being after 1923 will rise again and reestablish itself once more over the entire geographical area (from Turkey to Egypt, from Libya to Iran).

There are many other countless Bible commentators who have warned about Islam being the Kingdom of Antichrist—Selnecker, Nigrinus, Chytraeus, Bullinger, Foxe, Napier, Pareus, John Cotton, Thomas Parker, Increase Mather, Cotton Mather, and William Henry.

However, we do not hear of these warnings after the Second Great Awakening, because in 1830, John Nelson Darby created Dispensation and Replacement Theology which by 1909 Cyrus

Ingersoll Scofield promoted in his Scofield Reference Bible and usurped center stage by bringing in the idea which became so very popular; that the Church replaces the Elect and then we are Raptured out of here before the tribulation. Hence, there is no need to focus on understand eschatology or worrying about what happens in this present life other than what we can get for ourselves, because we will not be here and we will not suffer in the hellish world that the Antichrist brings about.

Hal Lindsey increased the confusion when he wrote the book, *The Great Late Planet Earth* in 1970. All the Prophecy Buffs were then focused on Russia and China (the two communist countries) which are anti-God as being the nations (Gog and Magog, and the kingdoms of the East) which will attack Israel in the Battle of Armageddon. They used a mistranslated scripture passage from Ezekiel 39:2, that included the word ROSH, which they then claimed was the ancient term for Russia. However, the Hebrew *ro'sh* translates as *"chief or head"* and not Russia (see my notes on chapter 20).

The Prophecy Buffs also focused in on the erroneous teachings of Luther claiming the Pope is the Antichrist to enforce their anti-Catholic agenda. However, Luther understood that the Beast of Revelation was Islam, but he was fighting the battle of Faith with the Catholic Church and saw the spirit of antichrist in the dictates of the Pope, thus he started to call the Pope "the antichrist" to get the church to focus in on *Sola Scriptura*, "Scripture Alone," and not on the Office of the Pope as the sole authority of the Word of God. Remember that there were several Bad Popes (Rodrigo Borgia a.k.a. Pope Alexander VI, being the worst) leading up to and during Luther's time, so his criticism was accurate.

The last century also brought to the forefront the lie which has been propagated since Mohammad's day; that we worship the same god. Here it is not just our Prophecy Buffs who get it wrong, but it is also many pastors in our churches who have been blinded and have repeated the lie that "Allah" is the Islamic word for god. IT IS NOT!

The word Allah is a proper noun; it is a name, not a title. You cannot say the first pillar or creedo of Islam, the *Shahadah*, by saying there is no god but god and Mohammad is his prophet, nor can you say that there is no Allah but, Allah and Mohammad is his prophet. It must be stated as such, that there is no god (*ilah*) but Allah and Mohammad is his prophet. Thus, Allah is the proper name for their god,[32] but it is not the same God we (Christians and Jews) worship as *Adoni, Elohim, Yahwah, or Messiah.*

[32.] Yoel Natan. *Moon-o-Theism.* (New York: Edition 1.0. 2006). 364.

Notes on Revelation 9

Islam and the End of Times

Martin Luther, the great Church Reformer wrote: *"Ego usque ad mortem luctor adversus Turcas et Turcarum Deum,"* "I will always struggle to the death against the Turks and the god of the Turks."[33] This sets the stage for the conflict between Christianity and Islam which was already well over nine hundred years old before the Turkish invasion of Europe which threatened Germany and helped shape the Reformation.

The question which arises for us today is, so what? How does all this play out through our Scriptures and our study of Revelation? In comparing the Reformation world to scripture, Luther believed that they were living in the last days as we do today. The Turks and Islam played an important role in this interpretation. Because the end of the world is near, Luther argued, the devil rages with his two weapons: the antichrist (the papacy) and the Turks. Luther wrote: "The Turks are certainly the last and most furious raging of the devil against Christ...after the Turk comes the judgment."[34]

Luther interpreted both Daniel and Revelation as prophecies that the Turks would be allowed dominion for a time, but then would be destroyed on the "Day of the Lord" when God pours out His Wrath. The Turks entered the interpretation of Daniel in chapter 7. Muhammad and his faith rose as the little horn amid the ten horns on the fourth beast. The eyes of the horn are Muhammad's Qur'an, "In whose law there is no divine eye, but mere human reason without

---

33. *Luther's Works, Volume 46* (Minneapolis: Augsburg Publishing House, 1959), 170.
34. Ibid., 205.

God's word and spirit."[35] The mouth that speaks blasphemous things is Muhammad, exalting himself over Christ.[36]

The Book of Revelation also offered insights on the contemporary situation of that day. For Luther, he saw the four horsemen of the apocalypse in the wake of the Turkish army's march toward Central Europe, which brought with it both judgment and hell.[37] He recognized that the trumpet blast of the fifth angel in Revelation 9 recording the opening of the abyss and the smoke rising from it was the false religion of Islam itself.

Luther saw the locusts as the soldiers of Muhammad, who were given permission to harm all mankind who did not have the mark of their god (Allah) on their foreheads. He clearly recognized the description of them in verse 7–11 as the hordes who conquered the Holy Lands, moved across North Africa and up into Spain. The sixth trumpet and the second Woe, he saw as the two million manned army of Suleiman "the Magnificent's" campaign as they marched up the Balkans to the door step of Vienna and Central Europe.

Luther also understood that Gog and Magog in Revelation 20:8, is the biblical designation for the Turks. This was such an important point for him that he published his translation of Ezekiel 38 and 39 as separate treaties with an introduction underscoring the whole connection.[38] Though he was waging war with the Pope and the Catholic Church, he understood from scriptures that the Worthless Sheppard (a.k.a. the Antichrist) would arise out of Assyria and be a Turk (a Muslim).[39]

For Luther, the Islamic invasion through the Holy Lands to the doorstep of Central Europe was the fulfillment of the first two Woes of Revelation 9. The last Woe which is still to follow will be the finial contest in Revelation (the battle of Armageddon) which will ulti-

---

35. *LW 45,* 103.
36. Ibid., 103.
37. Timothy J. Wengert, ed. "Luther on the Turks and Islam," *Harvesting Martin Luther's Reflections on Theology, Ethics, and the Church* (Grand Rapids: Eerdmans Publishing, 2004), 200–201.
38. *LW 16,* 263.
39. Timothy J. Wengert, 248.

mately be fought out between the Kingdom of God (the Christians) and the kingdom of Satan (Islam) at a future date.

Keeping this in mind, could chapter 9, the fifth and sixth trumpets also be over with as Luther taught? The fact that the Woe is past according to our scriptures does not mean that it took place prior to John's writing. The phrase regards the vision of the first Woe, which is now over, and the vision of the second Woe, which will now commence or take place. Both Woes will take place in the future sometime after the Revelation was recorded by John. Thus, the future for John would be the Middle Ages and Luther's time, which is now the past for us. Isn't it interesting how scripture can be past, present, and future all at the same time?

I would submit to you that the first Woe is the rise of Islam which ends with the first Muslim civil war (the first Fitna) in 657 which split Islam into two sects (Sunni and Shia) thus making Jerusalem the center of worship for the Shia followers of Islam. Jerusalem is thus no longer the center of Judeo-Christian worship but now has been usurped by the kingdom of Satan.

The second Woe starts when Suleiman's father, Selim "the Grim," the founder of the Ottoman Empire, marched through the Balkans. He was known for making it illegal to be a Christian within the empire and was far more ruthless in his dealings with Christians, especially the Orthodox Church which controlled this area of Europe. Selim was the first Islamic Emperor to use the title "Caliph of Islam."

The Second Woe ends not as Luther inferred with the ending of chapter 9 but in the middle of chapter 11, for I believe this was fulfilled in 1917 when Jerusalem was liberated from Ottoman control by General Allenby on December 11, thus *the Holy City will be trampled underfoot by the Gentiles for 42 months"* (Revelation 11:14).

Dates and times in scripture are always difficult to understand, but it is interesting that forty-two months equal 1,260 days or 3.5 years, however if you convert the 1,260 days into years and add the date when Jerusalem became the center of Islamic worship for the Shia Muslims 657, you end up with the date that Jerusalem was liberated from Islamic control in 1917. A coincidence, I think not.

However, when the title of the "Caliph of Islam" is resurrected we need to watch out for the third Woe will be near.

Now if you look back at Revelation 9:20–21 we see that they did not stop worshiping the works of their hands, i.e., *"idols of gold, silver, bronze, stone and wood—idols that cannot see or hear or walk."* Again, I submit to you that this is in reference to the practice of both the Catholic and Orthodox Churches in the way they "so call" venerate their saints. It also besmirches the church leadership and hierarchy (for there was a string of evil popes and bad patriarchs during this time which lead to the Great Schism between the two churches whereby they excommunicate each other) for the evil practices they committed all in the name of the Lord. *"Nor did they repent of their murders, their magic arts, their sexual immorality or their thefts."* Which indicates that the heretical theology and pagan practices that found their way into the Church was practiced in both the east and the west. They were not very Christ like where they.

However, if we are to date this period to correlate with the *"very hour and day and month and year,"* according to Ellicott, Barnes, Mauro and others, it equals out to be 396 years, from the Great Schism in 1057 culminating with the fall of Constantinople on May 29, 1453, which paved the way for the Islamic invasion through the Balkans, thus starting the second Woe in which the "Caliph of Islam" was established.

If the second Woe has not yet happened, then it will come at a future date. It will come from the east of the Euphrates River and the area of Iraq and Iran which are still Islamiclly controlled, bringing with it two myriads of myriads of cavalry to defeat Israel (a myriad is regarded as the Turkish way of counting an army like the way the Romans used the legion). No matter how we look at it we find ourselves dealing with the religion of Islam, past, present, or future.

If we look at all of chapter 9 allegorically as many teach today, we see the six trumpet blasts are a progression of destructive religious delusions which have been sent to those who have rejected the truth as the Apostle Paul teaches in 2 Thessalonians 2:9–13:

> *"The coming of the lawless one* (the Antichrist) *will be in accordance with the work of Satan displayed*

*in all kinds of counterfeit miracles, signs and won-
ders, and in every sort of evil that deceives those who
are perishing. They perish because they refused to
love the truth* (the Word of God) *and so be saved,
For this reason God sends them a powerful delusion*
(the religion of Islam) *so that they will believe the
lie and so that all will be condemned who have not
believed the truth but have delighted in wickedness."*

Isaiah 9:15 clearly lets us know that *"the prophets who teach lies
are the tail,"* which God will cut off. Hence the tails of this religious
delusion found in Revelation 9:10 and 19 become the lie which will
deceive and torment mankind. So I ask does this fit in with what
Luther taught or are we missing something altogether.

Now the third Woe which is still to come is then the final cam-
paign/battle of Armageddon which will bring about God's Wrath.
More on this to follow (see my notes on chapter 20).

Revelation

CHAPTER 10

New American Standard Bible (NASB)

The Angel and the Little Book

[10] *I saw another strong angel coming down out of heaven, clothed with a cloud; and the rainbow was upon his head, and his face was like the sun, and his feet like pillars of fire;* [2] *and he had in his hand a little book which was open. He placed his right foot on the sea and his left on the land;* [3] *and he cried out with a loud voice, as when a lion roars; and when he had cried out, the seven peals of thunder uttered their voices.* [4] *When the seven peals of thunder had spoken, I was about to write; and I heard a voice from heaven saying, "Seal up the things which the seven peals of thunder have spoken and do not write them."* [5] *Then the angel whom I saw standing on the sea and on the land lifted up his right hand to heaven,* [6] *and swore by Him who lives forever and ever,* WHO CREATED HEAVEN AND THE THINGS IN IT, AND THE EARTH AND THE THINGS IN IT, AND THE SEA AND THE THINGS IN IT, *that there will be delay no longer,* [7] *but in the days of the voice of the seventh angel, when he is about to sound, then the mystery of God is finished, as He preached to His servants the prophets.*

[8] *Then the voice which I heard from heaven, I heard again speaking with me, and saying, "Go, take the book which is open in the hand of the angel who stands on the sea and on the land."* [9] *So I went to the*

angel, telling him to give me the little book. And he *said to me, "Take it and eat it; it will make your stomach bitter, but in your mouth it will be sweet as honey." ¹⁰ I took the little book out of the angel's hand and ate it, and in my mouth it was sweet as honey; and when I had eaten it, my stomach was made bitter. ¹¹ And they *said to me, "You must prophesy again concerning many peoples and nations and tongues and kings."

Notes on Revelation 10

Interlude—Sealing up These Things

The scene in heaven changes with the opening of chapter 10. In this first part of the interlude, between the sixth and seventh trumpet of our second heptadic (sevenfold) preview. John is no longer in the throne room of God where the *"flashes of lightning, peals of thunder, rumblings and shaking"* emanate and where he views the progression of supernatural destructive religious delusions (2 Thessalonians 2:11–12), which have been sent to earth upon those who have rejected the truth through the sounding of the six trumpets. The seventh trumpet which ushers in *"the Day of the Lord's Wrath,* has not yet occurred. Here now in chapter 10, John is told to *"Seal up the things which the seven peals of thunder have spoken and do not write them."*

The focus of the vision is twofold; first, it gives us the locale of the *mighty angel* coming down from heaven to earth where *"he placed his right foot on the sea and his left on the land."* This is in direct contrast to what we will read in chapter 13, that Satan stood on the sands of the shore, where the earth and sea meet in which he has one beast coming up out of the sea and the second coming out of the earth. Hence, the significance of our scene here in chapter 10, is to remind us that God is sovereign over the earth and the sea and all that takes place therein.

Second, the focus of the vision is the message that the angel brings. It has its origin in heaven emanating from God and is of great importance. John, however, is not allowed to record the words issued forth from the *"seven peals of thunder"* or what was written in the little scroll, like Daniel, *"for these words are concealed and sealed up until the end time"* (Dan. 12:9).

Now, we can only assume as Richard Bauckham claims that these seven thunders are a "process of increasingly severe warning judgments which are not to be extended any further because such judgments do not produce repentance."[40] Bauckham continues to imply that these judgments are canceled simply because John did not write them down.

However, here I must disagree, for John has heard and knows far more than he is communicating to us. If anything, the seven thunders are more mysterious and frightening, simply because they are not described in detail. Which means that there is a fourth heptadic (sevenfold) preview, which we know nothing about and which I will submit is a complete detail of God's Wrath and Judgment being poured out on those who have rejected the truth.

Now verses 6 and 7 state, *"That there will be delay no longer, but in the days of the voice of the seventh angel, when he is about to sound, then the mystery of God is finished, as He preached to His servants the prophets."* So what's going on here?

Well, let's look at the phrase *"that there will be delay no longer,"* in Greek it is *chronos ouketi estai*, and it translates as *"Time no longer."* So if we look at it literally, it means the time we live in today which will end and then usher in eternity; or is it referring to metaphorical time, which will come when salvation's door is finally closed; or is it symbolic time, where a day represents a year?

Dates and times in scripture are always difficult to understand as I have said before and this cryptic declaration is such. However, in order to understand the issue of "time no longer" here, we need to go to Daniel, where again we find an angel imparting a message. Daniel 12:6–7 says,

> *"How long will it be until the end of these wonders?" I heard the man dressed in linen, who was above the waters of the river, as he raised his right hand and his left toward heaven, and swore by Him*

---

[40]. Richard Bauckham. *The Theology of the Book of Revelation.* (Cambridge: Cambridge University Press, 1993), 82.

who lives forever that it would be for a time, times,
and half a time; and as soon as they finish shattering
the power of the holy people, all these events will be
completed."

"Time no longer" and "events being completed" then seem to take on the same meaning. It is interesting that a "week" in scripture is equivalent to "seven years" and we know that the Antichrist appears in the middle of the "week." The middle of the week or this seven year period has been understood in the above passage of Daniel 12:7 to be *"time, times, and a half of time"* or 3.5 years.

However, if we look at these dates/times differently than our presuppositions, we discover something completely new. Three and a half years (3.5 years) equals forty-two months, which equal 1,260 days, however if you convert the 1,260 days into 1,260 years and add the date when Jerusalem became the center of Islamic worship for Shia Muslims in 657 AD, you end up with the date that Jerusalem was liberated from Islam and Ottoman control by British Forces under General Allenby on December 11, 1917. Thus fulfilling the scripture which states that *"the Holy City will be trampled underfoot by the Gentiles for forty-two months"* (Rev. 11:14). Something to think about!

In Daniel 12 verse 11, we are told that *"From the time that the daily sacrifice is abolished and the abomination that causes desolation is set up, there will be 1,290 days."* That's thirty days more than the 1,260 days allocated for the climactic 3.5-year period known as the "Great Tribulation," or the "Time of Jacobs Troubles." So does that mean that we have to wait thirty days after the tribulation is over until the *Rapture* takes place and we are taken to heaven, or does the dating mean something else?

If we change the 1,290 days into 1,290 years and subtract the date of the Restoration of Israel 1948, we once again come up with 658 AD when the Nation of Israel fell to complete Islamic control following the desecration of the Temple Mount by Islamic worship of Allah the year before. Is it a coincidence that Israel was controlled by Islamic forces for 1,290 years to the day, I think not.

Now in verse 12 we are told *"Blessed is the one who waits for and reaches the end of the 1,335 days."* So now we are told that we are blessed if we reach the 1,335th day, which is seventy-five days after the 3.5 years of the tribulation have ended and forty-five days after the *Rapture* should have taken place and all believers have been taken to heaven. So is this the *parousia*, the Second Coming where God's wrath is poured out? Doesn't that mean we missed the *Rapture* and are *"Left Behind"* and have to experiencing God's punishment? So why are we blessed, or does the dating again here mean something else as well?

Again if we change the 1,335 days into 1,335 years and subtract the date of the Restoration of Jerusalem, 1967, when Israel won the Six Day War and took control of the Old City and restored Jewish worship to the Temple Mount, albeit, the Western Wall otherwise known as the "Wailing Wall," we come up with the date 632 AD the year Mohammad died.

It is a blessing for those who have witnessed not only the rebirth of the Nation of Israel in 1948, but also of the Restoration of Jerusalem where the Old City was put back in the hands of God's chosen people once more in 1967. The dating works out exactly, again a coincidence, I think not. I might also remind you that *the* Book of Daniel starts off with Israel being carried away into exile and ends with the future prophecy of the Restoration of Israel and Jerusalem which will be a Blessing to all who live during these end days.

Hence, we are instructed to be aware of the *"times and the seasons"* and to be aware of the Devil's devices, *"in order that Satan might not outwit us. For we are not unaware of his schemes"* (2 Corinthians 2:11). Thus it is very timely to study the Scriptures and to be able to recognize the *"signs of the times,"* and know that the end is near.

Now the second major aspect of this part of the first interlude for John is consuming the scroll.

> *"Then the voice which I heard from heaven, I heard again speaking with me, and saying, "Go, take the book which is open in the hand of the angel who*

stands on the sea and on the land...and he said to me, "Take it and eat it; it will make your stomach bitter, but in your mouth it will be sweet as honey" (Rev. 10:8–9).

Again I ask, what's going on here? Well, we must know Ezekiel's story in order to understand actually what is happening. Ezekiel had a vision much like John's where he witness a scroll being unrolled in front of him and *"it was written on the front and back, and written on it were lamentations, mourning and woe"* (Ezek. 2:9). Ezekiel too was told to eat a scroll in which he was then told *"Son of man, go to the house of Israel and speak with My words to them"* (Ezek. 3:4). The Lord continues telling Ezekiel *"yet the house of Israel will not be willing to listen to you, since they are not willing to listen to Me. Surely the whole house of Israel is stubborn and obstinate"* (Ezek. 3:7). Like John, when he ate it, *"it tasted as sweet as honey,"* suggesting that Ezekiel's message like John's, would be sweet to him, though bitter to his hearers.

However, John's experience is more complex and nothing is said of what is written on the scroll, but the message is sweet as "honey" in John's mouth and "bitter" in his stomach. Just as in Ezekiel's experience, God's messages to His servants have often been a mixture of sweetness and bitterness, for they reveal both God's love and God's judgments. It should be noted that many of the Prophets of God have experienced both the ecstasy of divine visions as well as the bitterness of delivering messages of rebuke and judgment to the people.

John, like Ezekiel is told *"You must prophesy again concerning many peoples and nations and tongues and kings."* Now this message for John to impart, which I believe is God's Judgment on mankind, is not meant for believers, but for the unbelievers who will fallow after the Beast. As we shall see in chapter 13, Satan (the Dragon) who desires to *"make himself like the Most High,"* creates a destructive religious delusion which will deceive and torment mankind. This lie *"rises out of the sea"* of humanity and *"rising out of the earth"* in reference to *"those dwelling in it"* which envelopes all the unbelievers of *"every tribe, tongue, people, and nation,"* who are apart or separated from God through their own unbelief.

For John's message can only be one of Woe, Morning and Lamenting for those who do not following after the Truth because of their abstinence and stubbornness for it is concealed least they repent and turn from their wicked ways:

> *"He* (God) *said, "Go* (referring to Isaiah) *and tell this people: 'Be ever hearing, but never understanding; be ever seeing, but never perceiving.' Make the heart of this people calloused; make their ears dull and close their eyes. Otherwise they might see with their eyes, hear with their ears, understand with their hearts, and turn and be healed..."* (Isaiah 6:9–10)

Hence, God does not want this message (the fourth heptadic sevenfold preview of complete judgment) that John hears revealed, least those who deserve Hell (the wicked, evil and corrupt) be saved. Remember, God is just and will bring about Justice for all mankind, therefore he must punish the wicked as his Word states; otherwise He is a liar.

Revelation

CHAPTER 11

New American Standard Bible (NASB)

The Two Witnesses

11 Then there was given me a measuring rod like a staff; and someone said, "Get up and measure the temple of God and the altar, and those who worship in it. ² Leave out the court which is outside the temple and do not measure it, for it has been given to the nations; and they will tread underfoot the holy city for forty-two months. ³ And I will grant authority to my two witnesses, and they will prophesy for twelve hundred and sixty days, clothed in sackcloth." ⁴ These are the two olive trees and the two lampstands that stand before the Lord of the earth. ⁵ And if anyone wants to harm them, fire flows out of their mouth and devours their enemies; so if anyone wants to harm them, he must be killed in this way. ⁶ These have the power to shut up the sky, so that rain will not fall during the days of their prophesying; and they have power over the waters to turn them into blood, and to strike the earth with every plague, as often as they desire.

⁷ When they have finished their testimony, the beast that comes up out of the abyss will make war with them, and overcome them and kill them. ⁸ And their dead bodies will lie in the street of the great city which mystically is called Sodom and Egypt, where also their Lord was crucified. ⁹ Those from the peoples and tribes and tongues and nations will look at their dead bodies for three and a half days, and will not permit

their dead bodies to be laid in a tomb. ^{10} *And those who dwell on the earth will rejoice over them and celebrate; and they will send gifts to one another, because these two prophets tormented those who dwell on the earth.*

^{11} *But after the three and a half days, the breath of life from God came into them, and they stood on their feet; and great fear fell upon those who were watching them.* ^{12} *And they heard a loud voice from heaven saying to them, "Come up here." Then they went up into heaven in the cloud, and their enemies watched them.* ^{13} *And in that hour there was a great earthquake, and a tenth of the city fell; seven thousand people were killed in the earthquake, and the rest were terrified and gave glory to the God of heaven.*

^{14} *The second woe is past; behold, the third woe is coming quickly.*

The Seventh Trumpet—Christ's Reign Foreseen

^{15} *Then the seventh angel sounded; and there were loud voices in heaven, saying,*

"The kingdom of the world has become the kingdom of our Lord and of His Christ; and He will reign forever and ever." ^{16} *And the twenty-four elders, who sit on their thrones before God, fell on their faces and worshiped God,* ^{17} *saying,*

"We give You thanks, O Lord God, the Almighty, who are and who were, because You have taken Your great power and have begun to reign. ^{18} *And the nations were enraged, and Your wrath came, and the time came for the dead to be judged, and the time to reward Your bond-servants the prophets and the saints and those who fear Your name, the small and the great, and to destroy those who destroy the earth."*

^{19} *And the temple of God which is in heaven was opened; and the ark of His covenant appeared in His temple, and there were flashes of lightning and sounds and peals of thunder and an earthquake and a great hailstorm.*

Notes on Revelation 11

Interlude: Rebuilding the Temple of God

The opening of chapter 11 continues the second part of our interlude of the second heptadic (sevenfold) preview. John is no longer in the throne room of God, but he is now on the earth where he is told to measure the Temple *"rise and measure the temple of God, and the altar, and those who worship in it."* However, Jerusalem and the Temple were destroyed in 70 AD by Titus and his Legions and John received his vision around 92 AD, a good twenty years after Herod's Temple was destroyed. Thus, this temple that John has to measure must be the "Third Temple."

With this new vision now appearing, it reveals some troubling inconsistencies with our understanding of the rebuilding of Solomon's Temple. Everyone puts the location of this third Temple on the Temple Mount, where the First (Solomon's) and Second (Zerubbabel's rebuilt temple which was later improved by Herod during Christ's time) Temple stood, and which is the holiest place to the people of Israel; the city of Jerusalem.

For generations this controversy has existed among Prophecy Buffs as to the exact location where Solomon's and Herod's Temples were located on the Temple Mount. In an article entitled *A New Muslim Vision: Rebuilding Solomon's Temple Together* by Sinem Tezyapar who is a Turkish news commentator; she suggests that both Islam and Judaism can exist together and each can have their own temple/mosque there on the Temple Mount and worship in unity and peace.

The recently formed Jewish Sanhedrin, having been absent for over 1600 years, is tackling this idea/question as one of its first priorities. Call me naïve but I think we've all been asking the wrong question. Yes, it's great to know the exact placement of these historical temples on the Temple Mount, but the real question which arises is, "Where will the next Temple be built?"

Many Prophesy Buffs believe the coming Third Temple will be desecrated by the Antichrist, which is known as the Abomination of Desolation and will take place during the Great Tribulation, it will then be destroyed as predicted in Daniel 9:27 and 2 Thessalonians 2:3–8. For this reason, they call it the Tribulation Temple, they also believe that another Temple, number 4, will be built at the beginning of the Millennium.

However, the only model we have for all of this is the desecration of the second Temple leading up to the Maccabean Revolt. Though Jesus points us toward the second desolation in the Olivet Discourse (Matt. 24:15) *"therefore when you see the Abomination of Desolation which was spoken of through Daniel the prophet, standing in the Holy Place..."* nowhere does he state that this third temple will be destroyed.

Historically, the Syrian ruler Antiochus Epiphanes stormed the second Temple and converted it into a pagan worship center in 167 BCE. He desecrated the temple by slaughtering a pig on the altar and erecting a statue of Zeus (Jupiter) in the holy place with his own face on it, thereby proclaiming himself to be God (*Epiphanes* means god made manifest) and required everyone to worship him on pain of death.

In 1 Maccabees 1:41–50, this desecration was called the Abomination of Desolation, the only event so named in history. It triggered the Maccabean revolt, a three-and-a-half-year battle to oust Antiochus from the Promised Land. The Jews thought this was the fulfillment of the Daniel 9:27 prophecy, but almost two hundred years later Jesus told Israel to look for it in the future as the sign that the Great Tribulation has begun, thereby identifying it as a Model for the End Times Abomination of Desolation. Yes, it's true that the Maccabean Revolt contains many remarkable similarities to what will be known as the Great Tribulation; however, this prophecy has not yet occurred nor has it been fulfilled.

My main point is this; the Israelites did not destroy the Temple after the Abomination of Desolation in 167 BCE. When they recaptured it, they destroyed the statue and replaced the altar. Then they subjected the Temple to the eight-day purification ceremony required by Law and began using it again. The purification is remembered to this day in the Feast of Chanukah.

If the model is accurate, then the Temple built during Daniel's seventieth week won't be destroyed either, but will become the Millennial Temple described in great detail by Ezekiel in chapters 40–48. The Jewish scribes call Ezekiel's Temple the "Third Temple," which I submit will not be built in Jerusalem because it does not line up with the rest of the prophecies concerning the Temple.

According to the prophecies in Daniel 9:27, Matthew 24:15, and 2 Thessalonians 2:4, a Temple will exist in Israel at the beginning of the Great Tribulation. This is confirmed in Revelation 11:1 by having John measure the Temple, court, and the worshipers there in shortly before the Tribulation begins. This can only be the Third Temple for the second was destroyed in 70 AD which is about 20+ years before John was given his revelation.

Now John is told to omit the outer court because it's been given over to the Gentiles (nonbelievers). Its location is given to be in the "Holy City," which will be trampled on by the Gentiles for forty-two months, which is the length of the time period given for the Great Tribulation. However, if we look at Revelation 11:8, Jerusalem is called *"the Great City which mystically is called Sodom and Egypt,"* but in verse 2 we find that the location given for this temple to be built is in the *"Holy City which will be trampled on by the nations for forty-two months,"* but certainly Christ said that Jerusalem would be trampled on by the Gentiles until the times of the Gentiles were fulfilled?

Chapter 11 also introduces the two witnesses who preach in the "Great City" and are ultimately killed there, their bodies left lying in the street. The Great City is thus identified as *"the place where the Lord was crucified,"* which we know is Jerusalem. Thus it has been trampled on by the Gentiles for about 1,500 years now. So the next question which arises is; are the Holy City and the Great City one in the same or are they different cities entirely?

According to Zechariah 14:4–8, on the Day of the Lord's return, an earthquake will split the Mount of Olives in two halves along an east-west line. This than creates a great valley through the center of Jerusalem and immediately a river will fill the valley creating a waterway from the Dead Sea to the Mediterranean Sea. This indicates that the Lord will return to the same area of the Mount of Olives from which He left as suggested by Acts 1:11, thus the earthquake creating this East-West valley will destroy Mount Zion; the current Temple Mount and anything that may be standing upon it, to include the Doom of the Rock.

In Ezekiel's vision found in Ezekiel 47:1–12, he describes a great river flowing from under the south side of the Temple and then eastward to the Dead Sea during a period of time that most scholars believe will occur during Revelation 22:1–2. If Ezekiel, Zechariah, and Revelation all describe the same river, then an interesting scenario begins to emerge.

This scenario requires a Temple to be present *"in that day"* when the Lord returns, but sense the current temple mount will have been destroyed by the earthquake mentioned above, this Temple must be somewhere else. The river originates under the Temple and flows from its south side in a southerly direction before heading east and west, so the temple must be north of the newly created valley.

When plotting the land grants for the twelve tribes of Israel on a map given in Ezekiel 48:10, it places the precincts of the Holy City about forty miles north of the current City of Jerusalem and gives its allotment in length and width to be 25,000 cubits in the north, 10,000 cubits in the west, 10,000 in the east and 25,000 in the south (thus forming a cross) with the Sanctuary/Tabernacle of the LORD in the center. This new location fits ideally with the ancient City of Shiloh, where the Tabernacle stood for nearly 400 years after the Israelites first conquered the Land. Shiloh was known as the Holy City and in Hebrew it is called *Adonai Shammah,* which means *"the LORD is here,"* according to Ezekiel 48:35.

Genesis 49:10 declares that *"the scepter shall not depart from Judah, nor the ruler's staff from between his feet, until Shiloh comes, and to him shall be the obedience of the peoples"* and Joshua 18:1 states *"then the whole congregation of the sons of Israel assembled themselves at Shiloh, and set up the tent of meeting* (the Tabernacle of the Lord) *there."* So if there is nothing new under the sun and if my interpretation is accurate, this location would meet all the requirements for the Temple mentioned in the above references. The current Temple Mount in Jerusalem would not.

Now, according to Ezekiel 44:6–9, this Temple must be defiled in a way never seen before in history and therefore it must take place sometime in the future and not in the past. A foreigner who is un-circumcised in heart and in flesh (neither Christian nor Jew) will take control of the sanctuary while offering sacrifices.

If we understand the chronology of Ezekiel, this will take place sometime after the re-gathering of the nation prophesied in Ezekiel 36–37 (which I believe took place in 1948) and the future national wake-up call prophesied in Ezekiel 38–39, but before the Millennial Kingdom begins in Ezekiel 40–48 with the rededication of the Temple. The only event we know of that fits within this time frame is the Great Tribulation. This is confirmed by Paul's prophecy of 2 Thessalonians 2:4 where the Antichrist sets himself up *"in the Temple of God displaying himself as being God."*

Here then is a rough outline of events: Following Israel's return to God after the Ezekiel 38–39 war, the Jewish people will reestablish their covenant (under the Old Law) with Him. This will require a return to the Levitical practices and thus a need for a new Temple to be built. This becomes the Third Temple spoken of in Daniel and Revelation. Following the instructions given by Ezekiel and avoiding the enormous problems that a Jerusalem Temple would create in the Islamic world; this Temple will be located north of Jerusalem in Shiloh. It thus will be defiled in the middle of the seven years as outlined in Daniel 9:24–27, Ezekiel 44:6–9, Matthew 24:15, and 2 Thessalonians 2:4 kicking off the Great Tribulation, but it won't be destroyed.

This Temple will be the source of the living water which begins flowing when the Lord returns and sets his feet on the Mount of Olives (Zechariah 14:8). After a cleansing and re-dedication similar to the one memorialized in the Feast of Chanukah, it will be used during the Millennium. This is the Third Temple, so vividly described in Ezekiel 40–48. Its purpose will be to recall the Lord's work at the cross and provide the perspective for children born during the Kingdom Age to choose salvation. If we look at Acts 15:14–16 we find that it confirms that after the Lord has chosen a people from among the gentiles called by his name (i.e., Christians), He will return and rebuild/restore David's fallen tent/house/Tabernacle (the Davidic Kingdom) so that the rest of mankind may see and understand that Christ Jesus is *"KING of Kings and LORD of Lords."*

Notes on Revelation 11

Interlude: The Two Witnesses

With the opening of chapter 11 John is told to measure the temple, *"rise and measure the temple of God, and the altar, and those who worship in it."* This marks the Third part of the interlude between the sixth and seventh Trumpet and is part of the *heptadic* (sevenfold) preview, which aligns with the seven seals, the seven trumpets, and the seven bowls all of which are depicting the same events, but only in different allegorical metaphors.

Between the six and seventh seal, trumpet, and bowl there are interludes that are not part of the sequences of events but are inserted to shed light on the overall theme of the book. In other words, it is information that helps the reader understand specific details of the revelation. *"He that has an ear, let him hear what the Spirit say to the churches."* This specific interlude does not follow chronologically after the sixth trumpet, but it is parallel to all six trumpets which are the increasing waves of the destructive delusion sent down upon mankind to get them to repent and turn from their wicked ways.

Thus verse 3 starts off with the 1,260 days or 3.5-year ministry of the Two Witnesses, which are not congruent with either half of Daniel's seventieth week but overlaps them. They start their ministry sometime after the seventieth week has started and ends sometime before the Second Coming of Christ. These two witnesses provide the ultimate fulfillment of Zechariah 4:11–14 and the *"two anointed ones"* prophecy, which was partially fulfilled by Zerubbabel and Joshua during the time of the Second Temple's construction.

What is interesting is that "Two Witnesses" denotes the complete legal testimony found in Deuteronomy 17:6, *"On the evidence of two witnesses…he who is to die shall be put to death."* It continues in verse 12 *"and the man who acts presumptuously by not listing to the priest who stands there to serve the Lord your God, nor to the judge, that man shall die; thus you shall purge the evil from Israel."* It is a clear principle in the Old Testament that the testimony of only one witness is not enough to convict a person of a capital crime. It takes a minimum of two witnesses to convict someone for the death penalty.

The Apostle Paul also makes it clear that this same principle is repeated in the New Testament: *"But if he does not listen to you, take one or two more with you, so that BY THE MOUTH OF TWO OR THREE WITNESSES EVERY FACT MAY BE CONFIRMED"* (Matthew 18:6) and *"This is the third time I am coming to you. EVERY FACT IS TO BE CONFIRMED BY THE TESTIMONY OF TWO OR THREE WITNESSES"* (2 Corinthians 13:1).

According to the Scriptures, there must be two witnesses to an act in order for the sentence of the Law to be carried out. Since those who accept the mark of the beast and worship him will *"drink of the wine of the wrath of God, which is poured out full strength into the cup of His indignation"* (Rev. 14:10), at least two witnesses to their sins will be necessary to convict and punish them. So these Two Witnesses then represent Mercy and Justice, the Priest and the Judge. One grants mercy only if repentance is found, the other executes judgment with the full penalty of the law if required.

These Two Witnesses are here at the end of the sixth trumpet so that their testimony cannot be legally set aside, in order that all who do not listen and set it aside will thereby legally condemn themselves. Hence, the testimony and prophecy concerning the Word Jesus Christ is rejected by those who *"tread underfoot the Holy City for forty-two months."*

Dates and times in scripture are always difficult to understand, but it is interesting that 42 months equal 1,260 days or 3.5 years, however if you convert the 1,260 days into years and add the date when Jerusalem became the center of Islamic worship for the Shia Muslims in 657, you end up with the date that Jerusalem was liberated from the Ottoman Empire and Islamic control in 1917. Is it a coincidence that Israel was controlled by Islamic forces for 1,260 years, I think not.

Now the Lord states that He will *"grant authority to my (His) two witnesses, and they will prophesy for twelve hundred and sixty days."* So our 42 months must be different than the 1,260 days that these two witnesses/prophets will prophecy or witness to in Jerusalem. They are dressed in sackcloth which is closely associated to a time of great mourning and distress according to scripture (Genesis 37:34, 2 Samuel 3:31, Esther 4:1–3, 2 Kings 19:1–2), it is also associated with penitence as we read in the book of Jonah 3:6, 8. So our two witnesses are to prophesy in great mourning and distress to bring about repentance during this time before the seventh trumpet sounds and God's judgment is poured out.

If we look at chapter 11 literally as many Prophecy Buffs teach today, there are three primary candidates for the identity of these two witnesses—Moses, Elijah, and Enoch. If we pair up Elijah and Enoch first, they are the only two in the Old Testament who did not die, but were taken into heaven alive. If we pair Moses and Elijah, we find that the powers of these two are identical to those exercised by Moses in the Plagues of Egypt and Elijah in his contention against idolatry in Israel. Remember, it climaxed in his spectacular defeat of the prophets of Baal on Mt. Carmel with fire from heaven coming down putting an end to the 3.5-year drought (1 Kings 18 and James 5:17).

Moses and Elijah were also on the Mount of Transfiguration with Jesus and the disciples (Matthew 17:1–13) and according to early church tradition they were also the two men in white who appeared to the disciples following the Lord's ascension (Acts 1:10–11).

Moreover, Moses and Elijah are two of the most highly revered figures in all of Israel's history; they were more able than anyone else whom God could send to convey His message. Moses was the Law Giver and Elijah was the greatest of Israel's Prophets. Their two names are all but synonymous with the Hebrew name for the scriptures, the Law and the Prophets, the *Torah and Novim.*

These two witnesses are attacked by the beast (see my notes on chapter 13) and are killed; their bodies are left where they fell in the streets of Jerusalem *"where also their Lord was crucified."* Through the technological advancements of satellite communications, their dead bodies will be visible to the whole world. For we are told that *"those of the people and tribes and tongues and nations will look at the dead bodies,"* these are those who dwell upon the earth, a constantly recurring expression throughout the Revelation, in reference to those unbelieving people who are afar from God and who reject him as their Lord and Savior; *"all whose names have not been written in the Book of Life of the Lamb slain from the foundation of the world."*

Attached to the subject "the people" *blepousi*, is the partitive *ek*, "of or from" phrase used as a noun and ties in the tribes and tongues and nations all belonging together with the use of the one article. Thus these nations, tribes, people and tongues have one thing in common, their hatred of the Living Word.

To better understand who these "people" are we need to have an understanding of Daniel 9:26, "the *Messiah will be cut off, but not for himself: and the people of the prince that shall come shall destroy the city and the sanctuary."* This event of course, was fulfilled when Jerusalem and the Temple were destroyed by the Roman Legions in 70 AD by Titus. Titus is the son of Titus Vespasian who left the siege in order to return to Rome to become Emperor in 69 AD.

This is also the main passage that our Prophecy Buffs believe indicate that this final world leader *"the prince that shall come"* (reference to Titus the younger, not Vespasian, who became Emperor in 79 AD after his father died, thus he was a prince during the sack of Jerusalem) will emerge out of the Roman Empire because it was the Roman Legions which sacked Jerusalem and destroyed the Temple.

However, the Prophecy Buffs are in error here, for they miss the meaning of the passage: *"the people of the prince that shall come shall destroy the city and the sanctuary."* This passage is not in reference to the Roman Legions themselves who destroyed the temple, which were of course under Roman authority, but it is in reference to the soldiers (the people) who made-up the legions.

The question which arises is who were these soldiers if not Romans? Well a quick look at Roman history will revile that the Roman legions under Titus were indeed made up *historically* of the following legions (the III *Cyrenaica [Gallica],* the V *Macedonia,* the X *Fretensis,* the XII *Fulminata,* the XV *Apollinaris and the XVIII*

Alexandrian), all of which were raised from people living in Ionia, Turkey, Syria and Egypt, not Western Europe, and definitely not Rome.

Thus the reference to *"of the people and tribes and tongues and nations"* in Revelation 11:9, which ties in with Daniel 9:26, is in reference to the historical enemies of Israel which today are all Islamic countries. These are the ones who will *"make war against them"* which implies that action against the two witnesses is much more involved than just having two men killed. The Greek word used here for "witnesses" is *martusin*, which our word "martyr" is derived from, these witnesses are also martyrs.

"And their dead bodies will lie in the streets…for three and half days, and will not permit their dead bodies to be laid in a tomb." In Islamic teaching and culture it is required to bury the dead within three days, so the greatest insult one can convey is to deny burial to one's enemy. Thus the deaths of these two witnesses prompt the only expression of joy on earth in the entire book. If you remember the Black Hawk Down incident in 1993, the Muslim Somalis drag around the dead bodies of our Soldiers for over a week celebrating over their demise. Again, we see the same sort of thing taking place on 9-11 where most of the Mid East celebrated the attack on the Twin Towers, just like what we will see when the two witnesses are killed, they will celebrate. But after 3.5 days, symbolic of the length of the Great Tribulation, the two witnesses will hear the same command that John heard in Revelation 4:1, *"Come up here!"* and will ascend into Heaven in full view of the whole world removing Mercy and Justice from the world, leaving only judgment and punishment.

Psalms 79:1–3 adds emphases to this scene, *"O God, the nations have invaded your inheritance; they have defiled your holy temple, they have reduced Jerusalem to rubble. They have given the dead bodies of your servants as food to the birds of the air, the flesh of your saints to the beasts of the earth. They have poured out blood like water all around Jerusalem, and there is no one to bury the dead."*

In the final climax with the removal of mercy and Justice, a catastrophic earthquake, *seismos*, takes place signifying the end (Matthew 24:14) whereas the survivors give glory to God. Here the Disciple

John does not mean that these survivors worshipped God or came to faith in Him or even repented, it means that they correctly attributed these miraculous events to God, just like the Egyptian priests did in explaining the cause of the plagues in Exodus 8:19. Thus when judgment descends, it is too late for repentance, but all will know who brought on the Judgments *"in that Day."*

Now if we look at chapter 11 allegorically, as we have been doing with our interpretation of all the six trumpets, we find that the Two Witnesses representing God's Word of Mercy and Judgment are rejected by those outside the temple. Those in the temple are those who have a heart toward God and are in fellowship with Him who heed and obey His Word.

The prophet Hosea adds to our understanding of what happens to those who disobey God when we look at the names of his three children. Hosea preached several decades before the fall of Israel to the Assyrians in 722 BCE. Although he addresses both the Southern Kingdom of Judah and the Northern Kingdom of Israel in his prophecies, his primary message is directed at the House of Israel, also known as Ephraim.

To graphically illustrate the kingdom of Israel's rebellion against Him, God commanded Hosea to take a harlot for a wife (Hosea 1:2). This harlot bore Hosea three children whom God had Hosea name. These names symbolically show us how He was going to deal with the kingdom of Israel. The children were named *Jezreel,* which means "God sows," *Lo-Ruhamah,* which means "no mercy," and *Lo-Ammi,* which means "no people."

All three of these names described God's punishment on the Northern Kingdom of Israel, as He explained to Hosea. *Jezreel* represented God's sowing of the House of Israel among the Gentile nations of the earth after they were carried away into captivity by the Assyrians (Hos. 8:8, Zech. 10:7–10). *Lo-Ruhamah* denoted the fact that God would no longer have mercy upon Israel, allowing them to be taken into captivity because of their sins (Hos. 1:6). And *Lo-Ammi* pictured the gradual loss of national identity by the House of Israel. After they were conquered by Assyria, they lost the knowledge of who they were because they were now scattered throughout the Gentile nations of the world (Hos. 1:9). Thus Israel forgot that they were part of the chosen people and eventually came to become Gentiles (those who are no longer God's people).

So our two witnesses are preaching to those who reject the Word of God and have not obeyed Him. For they are Not His People and they will receive No Mercy, which means they will ultimately experience God's Wrath because they believed the lie. *"They perish because they refused to love the truth and so be saved, For this reason God sends them a powerful delusion* (a false religion) *so that they will believe the lie and so that all will be condemned who have not believed the truth but have delighted in wickedness"* (2 Thess. 2:10–12).

What better way to reveal those who delight in wickedness then by understanding *"those who dwell on the earth will rejoice over and make merry; and they will send gifts to one another, because these two prophets* (the Word of God representing both the law and prophets) *tormented those who dwell on the earth,"* by convicting them of their evil thoughts and deeds.

Now that mercy and justice are removed from the world God will be able to pour out His Judgment and Wrath on those who dwell upon the earth on; *"all whose names have not been written in the Book of Life of the Lamb slain from the foundation of the world."*

Revelation

CHAPTER 12

New American Standard Bible (NASB)

The Woman, Israel

12 A great sign appeared in heaven: a woman clothed with the sun, and the moon under her feet, and on her head a crown of twelve stars; 2 and she was with child; and she *cried out, being in labor and in pain to give birth.

The Red Dragon, Satan

3 Then another sign appeared in heaven: and behold, a great red dragon having seven heads and ten horns, and on his heads were seven diadems. 4 And his tail *swept away a third of the stars of heaven and threw them to the earth. And the dragon stood before the woman who was about to give birth, so that when she gave birth he might devour her child.

The Male Child, Christ

5 And she gave birth to a son, a male child, who is to rule all the nations with a rod of iron; and her child was caught up to God and to His throne. 6 Then the woman fled into the wilderness where she *had a place prepared by God, so that there she would be nourished for one thousand two hundred and sixty days.

The Angel, Michael

⁷ And there was war in heaven, Michael and his angels waging war with the dragon. The dragon and his angels waged war, ⁸ and they were not strong enough, and there was no longer a place found for them in heaven. ⁹ And the great dragon was thrown down, the serpent of old who is called the devil and Satan, who deceives the whole world; he was thrown down to the earth, and his angels were thrown down with him. ¹⁰ Then I heard a loud voice in heaven, saying,

"Now the salvation, and the power, and the kingdom of our God and the authority of His Christ have come, for the accuser of our brethren has been thrown down, he who accuses them before our God day and night. ¹¹ And they overcame him because of the blood of the Lamb and because of the word of their testimony, and they did not love their life even when faced with death. ¹² For this reason, rejoice, O heavens and you who dwell in them. Woe to the earth and the sea, because the devil has come down to you, having great wrath, knowing that he has only a short time."

¹³ And when the dragon saw that he was thrown down to the earth, he persecuted the woman who gave birth to the male child. ¹⁴ But the two wings of the great eagle were given to the woman, so that she could fly into the wilderness to her place, where she *was nourished for a time and times and half a time, from the presence of the serpent. ¹⁵ And the serpent poured water like a river out of his mouth after the woman, so that he might cause her to be swept away with the flood. ¹⁶ But the earth helped the woman, and the earth opened its mouth and drank up the river which the dragon poured out of his mouth. ¹⁷ So the dragon was enraged with the woman, and went off to make war with the rest of her children, who keep the commandments of God and hold to the testimony of Jesus.

Notes on Revelation 12

Understanding the Symbolism of Seven Heads and Ten Horns

The scene in heaven changes with the opening of chapter 12. John is no longer witnessing the *seismos* in the temple/throne room of God where the *"flashes of lightning, peals of thunder, rumblings and shaking"* emanate. These occurrences are brought about by the sounding of the seventh trumpet which ushers in *"the Day of the Lord's Wrath,"* however now John witness' *"a great and wondrous sign in heaven."*

This new vision which now appears has nothing to do with the sounding of the seventh trumpet or the pouring out of the seven bowls. This vision is a flashback if you will of all history/time/space, which reveals the ancient struggle between God's chosen people Israel represented by the woman and God's adversary (one of his own creations who rebelled) represented by the dragon. It traverses the same ground covered throughout scripture from the beginning of time to the incarnation and ascension of Christ. It also takes us forward in time to show us the overall picture of what will take place up to and including the *parousia*, Christ's return.

This insight is revealed to us in two parallel, but separate set of interwoven visions which take place both in heaven and on Earth. Both sets of visions start with a broad overall picture of what will take place, then the picture is refined with more detail, and finally the picture is brought into focus.

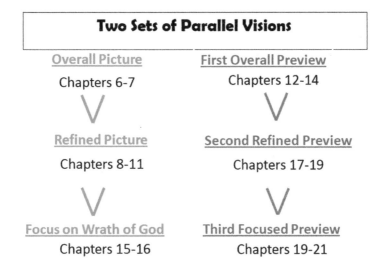

The first set of visions are depicted in the Seven Seals, Seven Trumpets, and the Seven Bowls, which culminates the focus on the Wrath of God. The second set of visions which I call the First, Second, and Third Previews depict the struggle between the forces of God and Satan and finally focuses with the Third Preview on the Victorious Christ.

It is important to remember that prophetic scripture through symbolic metaphor can represent past, present, or future all at the same time, or any combination thereof. So the vision before John not only tells us about the past and present, it also reveals to us the future. Now in this First Preview of the overall picture (see outline of the Book) we are witnesses to Israel's Travail, Rev. 12:1–17; the Beast, Rev. 13:1–10; the Antichrist, Rev. 13:11–18; and finally the Victorious Christ, Rev. 14:1–20.

Now as we look at Israel's travail, many think and believe that the woman represents the Church or Mary herself; however symbolically she represents Israel from which the Messiah will come forth to save the world. For John and the early church this understanding would be unmistakable and any discussion to the contrary would be unnecessary. So like the early Church we need to discard our presuppositions and let scripture speak to us through scripture, thus acknowledging the fact that this woman represents Israel is of utmost importance for then we are able to understand the struggle between God and Satan.

The term *"dragon"* is also symbolic, however we are told exactly who it represents in v. 9 where he is called *"the devil and Satan."* Again no mistake as to who the dragon represents and no discussion necessary to try to allegorize. The symbolism of the seven heads and ten horns are also evident as we compare Daniel's image of the statue in chapter 2 and the four beasts in chapter 7 to these heads and horns found in Revelation 12:3 and 13:1, so let us look at these scriptures.

The four parts of Daniel's statue corresponds to the four beasts in his later vision. They all rise out of the sea of humanity and become great kingdoms/empires (Dn. 7:17). However, this last empire with its iron teeth and bronze claws is *"different from all the other empires"* for it crushes and devours its victims and tramples everything else underfoot, vv. 19 and 23. This fourth beast wages war against the saints (the Christian believers) and will have power over them for *"a time, times and half a time"* (3.5 years) according to verse 25, which represents the last days before *"the Day of the Lord's Wrath"* is poured out.

The ten horns corresponds to the ten toes in Daniel's statue which represent ten kings/nations that will all arise from this last empire to assist in the war against the saints. The arrogant little horn which arise among the other ten horns, which speaks blasphemous things against God, becomes an eleventh horn, which will uproot three of its own type in order to *"change the set times and the laws,"* which God has ordained, vv. 20–22 and 24–25.

However, when we are in doubt, scripture has a way of coming to our rescue to tell us exactly what is implied through the symbolism here. So if we look at Revelation 17:9–14 we are given the answer to what the seven heads and ten horns represent. For *"this calls for a mind with wisdom,"* in order to understand the symbolism found here for *"the seven heads are seven mountains,"* and mountains throughout scripture always represent Kingdoms or in reality Empires. When we think of the Babylon Empire or the Persian Empire or even the Greek Empire, we think of more than a kingdom, we think of all the territory/nations that were conquered to make up the vast empire.

So it is here, the mountains represent many hills which make up this huge kingdom, hence the term empire is appropriate to apply here to each of the seven heads.

What confuse the reader are the next two sentences which describe the seven mountains as seven kings. *"They are also seven kings. Five have fallen, one is, the other has not yet come; but when he does come, he must remain for a little while."* When a king dies, the kingdom does not die with him, most of the time there is a transition from one king unto another, thus the kingdom continues; however kingdoms cease to exist when they are conquered. So what we have here is a metaphor or comparison to the symbolism of the mountains, for mountains don't die or fade away they remain, thus John needs to lead the reader to the understanding that these mountains/empires have fallen and are completely done away with, thus the metaphor of kings.

The five fallen kings/mountains/empires represent: Egypt, Assyria, Babylon, Persia, and Greece. The one that is will take place in the future sometime after the Revelation/vision was recorded by John. It does not equate to the present time that John was living in, hence as our Prophecy Buffs interpret (representing the Roman Empire) but some future empire that conquers the same territories as the Babylonian, Persian, and Greek empires controlled. Rome does not fit the paradigm, for it did not conquer the city of Babylon itself or any of the territories beyond the Euphrates River, which made up the largest portion of the empire. So just based on geography itself, Rome did not conquer the last empire of Greece, for Greece reached all the way to India and the Himalayan Mountains.

Now let us look at the ten horns found in Revelation 17:12–14 and see what they represent and how they relate back to Daniel chapters 2, 4, and Revelation 12. We are told in v. 12 that *"the ten horns you saw are ten kings who have not yet received a kingdom, but who for one hour will receive authority as kings along with the beast."* These ten horns which also correspond to the ten toes in Daniel's statue are a continuation of the metaphor found in v. 10 representing kings/leaders/nations that will all arise from this last empire with one purpose only, and that is to assist the Antichrist in the war against Christ *"the Lamb"* of God.

These kings are the leaders of nations which will join together with the Antichrist, for they receive their power and authority from the Beast and lead their nations to unite with the Antichrist in rebellion against God. Both the nations and the empires belong to the seven headed Beast and are part of the Beast, though they function differently. We are also told that they belong together and will ultimately be destroyed together when *"the Day of the Lord's Wrath"* is poured out.

The metaphor of *"the beast who once was, and now is not, is an eighth king. He belongs to the seven and is going to his destruction"* (v. 11), helps us the reader distinguish between the horns as individual nations within the larger context of the heads symbolizing empires. However, this eighth king who belongs to the seven headed Beast, also represented by the little horn which arises among the ten horns, is the Antichrist himself; who belongs to the Beast and exercises all the authority and power of the Beast, but is not the Beast. For the Beast itself is an empire made up of an all-encompassing religious, political, socio-economic, militaristic entity in which the Antichrist will be its leader/king.

I submit that this is played out in chapter 13 as follows: Satan who desires to *"make himself like the Most High,"* creates a destructive religious delusion which will deceive and torment mankind. This lie *"rises out of the sea"* of humanity, *"every tribe, people, language and nation,"* in the form of a beast which is unlike anything known. This beast is a conglomeration of all the historical enemies of Israel for *"the dragon gave the beast his power and his throne and great authority."* Its seven heads represent seven specific empires which throughout time have propagated the lie of this religious delusion.

We understand that the first five heads represent Egypt, Assyria, Babylon, Persia, and Greece; however the last two heads are debated among Prophecy Buffs and most believe that they are Rome in two parts. I believe however that they represent the Islamic/Ottoman Empire. The Ottoman Empire and the seat of Islamic control (the Caliphate) ceased to exist after World War 1 in 1924; hence *"one of the heads has been slain unto death."* Though recently the "Arab Spring" has called to reestablish a world-wide Caliphate which ultimately favors *shari'a* law for the whole world, *"and his fatal wound was healed and the whole world was amazed and followed after the beast."*

Satan does not have the power to create like our God, but he can duplicate what has been created through a counterfeit creation. God raised the nation of Israel from the dead, so Satan has to raise his counterfeit satanic empire from the dead. Thus we have the symbolism of one of the heads being slain unto death and being resurrected so that the nations would be amazed. What confuses the Prophecy Buffs is that they believe this metaphor represents a person being raised from the dead, thus a counterfeit to the resurrection of Christ; however Satan does not have the power to raise an actual person from the dead, his miracles are false and meant to deceive only. All he can do is plant the lie in men's minds to recreate/resurrect his counterfeit government/empire so that those who are deceived will think it is something wonderful and god inspired. If Satan had the power to resurrect he would have already resurrected Nero or Hitler or a hundred other evil leaders all through history in order to propel his satanic agenda. But he can't; only God has the ability and power to resurrect a person from death.

Thus, the world will be deceived and by doing obeisance and bowing in admiration before the power of this beast (this ungodly governmental power of the Caliphate) men really stoop before the dragon himself for *"men worshiped the dragon because he had given authority to the beast, and they also worshiped the beast and asked, 'Who is like the beast? Who can make war against him?"* The question which arises is how can you fight an idea/religion which is bent on the complete submission of mankind? The question becomes rhetorical at this point and no answer can be given because we can't fight this satanic idea.

"Then I saw another beast rising out of the earth," those who have rejected God as their rightful Lord and Savior are *"those who dwell on the earth."* This beast is not like the first for it appears innocent and harmless *"like a Lamb"* but *"he deceives the inhabitants of the world."* This beast is the Antichrist himself, appearing as a Lamb, but *"exercising all the authority of the first beast on his behalf...whose fatal wound*

had been healed," thus the dragon in disguise. This is the Antichrist (a.k.a. the Assyrian) who will be an actual man who will take the reestablished seat of the "Caliph of Islam" in the newly revised Ottoman Empire and *"he will perform great and miraculous signs,"* with the intent to deceive and lead astray all those of the earth (the godless world) who are not followers of the beast of Islam.

After he has established his governmental power, he will point to the beast and tell us that we must pay homage to the beast, *"saying to those who dwell on the earth to make an image of the beast...and cause all who refused to worship* (bow down) *the image to be killed."* Then he will *"force everyone...to receive a mark on his right hand or on his forehead, so that no one could buy or sell unless they had the mark."*

One unique and not highly known aspects of *shari'a* law is that if you are not a Muslim (a believer of Islam) you are not able to buy or sell in the common market place. Nonbelievers fall under *Dhimmitude,* which applies to all non-Muslim populations who were vanquished by a *jihad*-war and governed by *shari'a* law encompassing all theological, social, political, and social-economical levels. Thus when the Antichrist forces the nonbeliever to receive the mark of the beast either on their right hand or forehead, he is in complete compliance with established governmental authority of *shari'a* law.

Stay tuned for more information on the numbering of the beast *"Here is wisdom! If anyone has insight, let him calculate the number of the beast, for it is a man's number. His number is 666,"* or is it?

Revelation

CHAPTER 13

New American Standard Bible (NASB)

The Beast from the Sea

¹³ *And the dragon stood on the sand of the seashore.*

Then I saw a beast coming up out of the sea, having ten horns and seven heads, and on his horns were ten diadems, and on his heads were blasphemous names. ² *And the beast which I saw was like a leopard, and his feet were like those of a bear, and his mouth like the mouth of a lion. And the dragon gave him his power and his throne and great authority.* ³ *I saw one of his heads as if it had been slain, and his fatal wound was healed. And the whole earth was amazed and followed after the beast;* ⁴ *they worshiped the dragon because he gave his authority to the beast; and they worshiped the beast, saying, "Who is like the beast, and who is able to wage war with him?"* ⁵ *There was given to him a mouth speaking arrogant words and blasphemies, and authority to act for forty-two months was given to him.* ⁶ *And he opened his mouth in blasphemies against God, to blaspheme His name and His tabernacle, that is, those who dwell in heaven.*

⁷ *It was also given to him to make war with the saints and to overcome them, and authority over every tribe and people and tongue and nation was given to him.* ⁸ *All who dwell on the earth will worship him,*

everyone whose name has not been written from the foundation of the world in the book of life of the Lamb who has been slain. [9] *If anyone has an ear, let him hear.* [10] *If anyone is destined for captivity, to captivity he goes; if anyone kills with the sword, with the sword he must be killed. Here is the perseverance and the faith of the saints.*

The Beast from the Earth

[11] *Then I saw another beast coming up out of the earth; and he had two horns like a lamb and he spoke as a dragon.* [12] *He exercises all the authority of the first beast in his presence. And he makes the earth and those who dwell in it to worship the first beast, whose fatal wound was healed.* [13] *He performs great signs, so that he even makes fire come down out of heaven to the earth in the presence of men.* [14] *And he deceives those who dwell on the earth because of the signs which it was given him to perform in the presence of the beast, telling those who dwell on the earth to make an image to the beast who *had the wound of the sword and has come to life.* [15] *And it was given to him to give breath to the image of the beast, so that the image of the beast would even speak and cause as many as do not worship the image of the beast to be killed.* [16] *And he causes all, the small and the great, and the rich and the poor, and the freemen and the slaves, to be given a mark on their right hand or on their forehead,* [17] *and he provides that no one will be able to buy or to sell, except the one who has the mark, either the name of the beast or the number of his name.* [18] *Here is wisdom. Let him who has understanding calculate the number of the beast, for the number is that of a man; and his number is six hundred and sixty-six.*

Notes on Revelation 13

The First Beast

I submit that Revelation 13:1–10 is played out as follows: Satan who desires to *"make himself like the Most High,"* creates a destructive religious delusion which will deceive and torment mankind. This lie *"rises out of the sea"* of humanity, *"every tribe, tongue, people, and nation,"* in the form of a beast which is unlike anything known. This beast is a conglomeration of all the historical enemies of Israel for *"the dragon gave the beast his power and his throne and great authority."* Its seven heads represent seven specific empires which throughout time have propagated the lie of this religious delusion.

As mentioned in the proceeding chapter, we understand that the first five heads represent Egypt, Assyria, Babylon, Persia, and Greece; however, the last two heads are debated among prophecy buffs and most believe that they are Rome in two parts. However, I maintain that they represent the Islamic/Ottoman Empire. The Ottoman Empire and the seat of Islamic control (the Caliphate) ceased to exist after World War I in 1921; hence *"one of the heads has been slain unto death."* Though recently the "Arab Spring" has called to reestablish a world-wide Caliphate which ultimately favors *shari'a* law for the whole world and the PM of Turkey is calling for the reestablishment of the old Ottoman Empire, *"and his fatal wound was healed and the whole world was amazed and followed after the beast."* (See the article "Islamist Super-Bloc Begins Forming in the Middle East" by Ryan Mauro.)

Satan does not have the power to create like God, because he himself is a created being (an angel), but Satan can duplicate what has been created through a counterfeit creation. God raised the nation of Israel from the dead, so Satan has to raise his counterfeit Satanic Empire from the dead. Thus, we have the symbolism of one of the heads being slain unto death and being resurrected so that the nations would be amazed.

What confuses the Prophecy Buffs is that they believe this metaphor represents a person being raised from the dead, thus a counterfeit to the resurrection of Christ; however, Satan does not have the power to raise an actual person from the dead, his miracles are false and meant to deceive only. All he can do is plant the lie in men's minds to recreate/resurrect his counterfeit religious governmental empire so that those who are deceived will think it is something wonderful and god-inspired. If Satan had the power to resurrect he would have already resurrected Nero or Hitler or hundred other evil villainous leaders all throughout history in order to propel his satanic agenda. But he can't; only God has the ability and power to resurrect a person from death.

Thus, the world will be deceived and by doing obeisance and bowing in admiration or homage before the power of this beast (the ungodly governmental power of the Caliphate) thus men really stoop before the dragon himself for *"men worshiped the dragon because he had given authority to the beast, and they also worshiped the beast and asked, 'Who is like the beast? Who can make war against him?"* The question which arises is how can you fight a religious ideology which is bent on the complete submission of mankind? The question becomes rhetorical at this point and no answer can be given because we can't fight this satanic ideology with our own power. It is a spiritual fight that must take place daily.

The argument from our Prophecy Buffs that this first beast could not be a religious governmental entity, because the pronouns refer to this beast as a person, are explained easily way through the use of metaphors. Metaphorically speaking, Uncle Sam has been regarded as the universal symbol of the United States, while Great Britain enjoys the national symbol of John Bull who is sometimes pictured as a lion, or with a lion, analogous to the American eagle, which is sometime shown with Uncle Sam. Thus, the metaphor of this first beast being a horrible dragon type beast with the feet of a bear, the body of a leopard, and seven heads each having the mouth of a lion is pure symbolism representing this resurrected religious governmental entity of the revised Islamic/Ottoman Empire and not a person.

However, this Beast is *"given power to make war against the saints and to conquer them."* How does he make war and conquer the saints if he is not a person but a religious governmental entity? Through the deceptive power of a governmental idea, i.e., Islam which is a religious, militaristic, social-economic and political system all rolled into one and is a direct contradiction of what the Word of God states. This religious governmental power is able to wage war through deception. One such way of waging war is by deceiving the saints to believe that we worship the same loving god of peace and thus we can become good Christians and good Muslims at the same time by combining our religions into one called Chrislam!

A Common Word between Us and You is a carefully crafted Muslim document, bridging the gap between Christianity and Islam which was originally addressed to Pope Benedict XVI, the Patriarchs of the Orthodox Churches, and the leaders of the larger Christian denominations, as well as to leaders of Christians everywhere.

The response *Loving God and Neighbor Together, A Christian Response to 'A Common Word Between Us and You'* has over three hundred signatories of leading pastors, ministers, and professors who have signed onboard with this movement to include: Rick Warren, Saddleback Church; Bill Hybels, Willow Creek Community Church; Dr. Robert Schuller, Crystal Cathedral and Hour of Power; R. Charles Lewis Jr., First Presbyterian, Vintage Faith Church; Robert K. Johnston, Fuller Theological Seminary; Paul Knitter, Union Theological Seminary; Dr. Mari Thorkelson, Bethel Lutheran Church; Dr. Mark Rutledge, Duke University; J. Dudley Woodberry, Fuller School of International Studies; Clifton Kirkpatrick, Presbyterian Church (USA); David Coffey, Baptist World Alliance; Mark S. Hanson, Lutheran World Federation, Rowan Williams, Archbishop of Canterbury, are just a few of those who think it is a good idea; hence, even the elect will be deceived, because it is a spiritual fight not a physical one that we are in.

"For our struggle is not with flesh and blood but against the rulers of the authorities, against the powers of the world forces of this present darkness, with spiritual forces of wickedness in the heavenly places." (Ephesians 6:12)

This idea (the religious governmental entity) then takes shape as people rally behind it. For we are told that *"every tribe, tongue, people, and nation,"* those who dwell upon the earth in reference to those unbelieving people who are afar from God by rejecting him as their Lord and Savior; *"all whose name have not been written in the Book of Life of the Lamb slain from the foundation of the world."* These are the ones who will support and back this idea. Thus, every nonbeliever will succumb to the authority of this beast, because their names were not found written in the Book of Life. They will believe the lie and the delusion and they will fight and make war against the saints even to the point of believing that they will go to paradise if they kill the Christian and the Jew.

Verse 9 now changes the tone of this horrific vision for the Disciple John now admonishes us faithful believers (whose names are written in the Book of Life) as Christ himself has already done, to heed this call, *"if anyone has an ear, let him hear!"* For what follows next does not apply to the believers but to the earth dwellers/nonbelieving followers of the beast. Thus, the believers are given hope in-order to persevere in the tribulation which will come, for *"here is the endurance and faith of the saints!"*

Our hope is found in the word "captivity" *aigmaloosia*, which does not mean imprisonment for the saints, but to the followers of the beast, who choose to out of their own free will, go into the "captivity of hell." Why do I make such a statement, because the only other place this word is found in the New Testament is in Ephesians 4:8 and refers to those in hell who Christ visited when he died and descended into hell to preach to the captives (see also 1 Peter 3:18–21). So here *"if anyone goes into captivity, into captivity he goes,"* should be translated to really mean *"for those who are destine to hell, then into hell they will go."*

Our endurance for suffering is also strengthened for *"if anyone shall kill with the sword, it is necessary that he with the sword be killed."* This is not a warring to the saints to become pacifists and not defend themselves against the followers of the beast, but it is in reference to those who use the sword to help exterminate the saints. Here we have God's *Lex Talionis* or Law of Retribution played out against the admirers of the beast who do physical harm against his saints, *"for we know the one who said, Vengeance is mine. I will repay those who deserve it,"* Hebrews 10:30. They are the ones who will perish by the sword in the end. Thus, our hope in the midst of tribulation is twofold; for those who will get what they deserve and *"go away into eternal punishment, but* (for those who are) *the righteous into eternal life"* (Matthew 25:46).

"Then I saw another beast rising out of the earth..." Satan just does not want to give up; now he uses an actual individual human being (this is now the Antichrist) in conjunction with the religious governmental entity to carry out his *"evil plan."*

Notes on Revelation 13

The Second Beast

Now Revelation 13 makes it clear that the Dragon stands on the sands of the shore, where the earth and sea meet. He has one beast on one side of him coming up out of the sea of humanity and the second on his other side coming out of the unbelieving people of the earth, thus they become like two arms extended from the Grand Puppet Master.

This Grand Puppeteer is none other than Satan himself (a.k.a. the Dragon) who desires to *"make himself like the Most High,"* he has created this destructive religious delusion which has deceive and torment mankind throughout history. This lie *"rises out of the sea"* of humanity, which envelopes all the unbelievers of *"every tribe, tongue, people, and nation,"* in the form of a beast which is unlike anything known. This first beast is a conglomeration of all the historical enemies of Israel for *"the dragon gave the beast his power and his throne and great authority."* The dragon gave *edwke* this beast all his power, throne and authority v. 2 and 4. The beast was also given *edothe* a mouth to utter blasphemies, authority to dominate for forty-two months, ability to do battle with the saints, and authority over all those who do not follow after Christ.

Its seven heads represent seven specific empires which throughout time have propagated the lie of this religious delusion and now come together in a final empire which I believe is the reemergence of the religious governmental entity of the sixth empire, the Islamic/Ottoman Empire which now becomes a seventh empire here at the end.

"Then I saw another beast rising out of the earth..." this is the second beast which rises out of the earth in reference to *"those dwelling in it"* who are apart or separated from God through their own unbelief v. 11. Hence, out of the unbelieving mankind throughout the world, Satan will raise up an actual individual human being in conjunction with the religious governmental entity represented by the first beast to carry out his "evil schemes." This is the Antichrist who will act just like Antiochus Epiphanes and fulfills the prophecies of Daniel 8:11 and 11:29–45. (A little known fact is that the Israelites called Antiochus *"Epimanes"* which is a word play on his title Epiphanes and means the "Mad One.") Is the Antichrist now a repeat of the true Mad One? I would say yes.

Now this second beast (a.k.a. the Antichrist) operates *"all the authority of the first beast on his behalf."* The word *enwpion* in v. 12, means in the presence of or in sight of...in relationship to the first beast. Thus this first beast does not have the ability to do anything on its own. It requires the second beast to carry out or perform what the first beast designs. The second beast is distinguished by his actions whereas the first is distinguished by its authority. Both beasts are personifications of Satan, the first is the ferocious power and the second is the deceptive activity.

The Greek word *poiei* means works or effects, which is the action carried out on behalf of the first beast through the second beast. This second beast wheels the authority of the first beast and works to affect or carries out that which the dragon has ordained. The second beast does all the action, the first beast does nothing at all; it is the entity from which the second beast derives his power. An example of this is the President of the United States; he does not have any power in his own right except that which is bestowed to the Office of the President on behalf of the people through the Government which is the entity of control. So the President acts with the full authority of the US Government behind him.

The first beast is the religious governmental entity which gives the second beast (a.k.a. the Antichrist) the power and authority to carry out the evil intentions of the dragon (a.k.a. Lucifer) to get man to bow down and worship him. Satan does this through deception;

by deceiving mankind into believing that he can perform miracles. His exhibition of some sort of phenomenal pyrotechnics found in verse 13, will be nothing more than a sham meant to deceive mankind; remember all Satan can do is to imitate the true miracles of God. *"And he performs great signs so that even fire comes down out of the heaven to the earth before men,"* why? In order to get men to accept the deception of the raising of his counterfeit Satanic Empire from the dead, *"so that they shall do obeisance* (bow down) *to the first beast whose death stroke was healed,"* thus making the deception legitimate in the eyes of the world so that men will clamor after this first beast.

Through the deceptive power of this reemerging seventh empire (Islam which is a religious, militaristic, socio-economic, and political system all rolled into one under the auspicious of the Ottoman Empire, which will be led by the Caliph) this religious governmental power will utter blasphemies against the Trinity, will have authority to dominate the holy lands for seven years (forty-two months), will waged war on the saints (the Christians), and will have authority to lead astray all the nonbelievers who do not follow after Christ in order to do the bidding of this first beast.

If we look at scripture we find that Satan does nothing more than imitate what God does. An example of Satan's deception is found in Moses miracles in Exodus 7 where Jannes and Jambres compete against him with their false miracles, yet though they were a poor exhibition, Pharaoh believed the sorcerers and denied God's power. So it will be with the world, they will believe the false miracles of the second beast (a.k.a. the Antichrist) and will set up an image of the first beast to pay homage to, because *"he ordered them to set up an image in honor of the beast that was slain with the sword and yet lived."*

This whole scene is a repetition of Daniel 3 where Nebuchadnezzar set up a golden image of himself and commanded the people to bow down to it on pain of death. However, here our new image is given breathe *pneuma* or spirit and speaks unlike Daniel's statute. Again this is a deception which is meant to dupe the earth dwellers (infidels/unbelievers) into believing the works of their own hands.

This second beast (a.k.a. the Antichrist) is also the false prophet (the religious leader/Caliph), an agent of Satan who points to the beast and orders these earth dwelling infidels to bow down to this created image. He operates like a wolf in sheep's clothing deceiving mankind in to believing the lie of Satan. *"And he causes all, the small and the great…to receive a mark on their right hand or on their foreheads, so that no one could be able to buy or to sell unless he had the mark, which is the name of the beast…"*

With the reemergence of the Ottoman Empire and the seat of the Caliph there will be a cry to establish *shari'a* law in the land. (Oh, we are already hearing this throughout the "Arab Spring" and the term *spring* in Arabic means *shari'a*.) What is interesting and not highly known is the unique aspects of *shari'a* law; if you are not a Muslim (a believer in Islam) you are not able to buy or sell in the common market place. Nonbelievers fall under *Dhimmitude* which is slavery and applies to all non-Muslim populations who were vanquished by a *jihad*-war and governed by pure Islamic *shari'a* law encompassing all theological, social, political and socio-economical levels. In other words, you are considered a slave (*dhimmi*) and have no rights under Islam, thus you cannot even feed your family without the permission from the Muslim authorities and you are also forced to pay the (*jizya*) tax, which under the strict Islamic *shari'a* doctrine, all non-Muslims (*dhimmi*) living under Muslim sovereignty must pay in return for protection.

Thus when the second beast (a.k.a. the Antichrist/False Prophet) forces the nonbeliever to receive the mark of the beast either on their right hand or forehead, he is in complete compliance with established governmental authority of *shari'a* law according to Islamic theology by requiring everyone to submit to Islam.

The mark *charagma* is given in opposition to the seal *sphragis*, which sets aside God's remnant the 144,000 in Revelation 7:2–17. Thus this mark is Satan's counterfeit, meant to single out those who do not follow after the beast and make it easier to persecute. Yet we need to understand the difference in order to make any since of the significance of 666. Both the mark and the seal are in reference to a name; the former is the beast's name, the latter is Christ's name. Each identifies who the one sealed or marked belongs to, one to God the other to Satan.

Verse 18 now changes the tone of this second vision for the Disciple John now admonishes us to use our mind in order to understand the hidden meaning behind the number of the beast. *"Here is wisdom! If anyone has insight, let him calculate the number of the beast, for it is a man's number. His number is 666."* The Greek phrase *arithmos anthropou* should be translated as *"for it is a human multitude"* and not *"for it is a man's number,"* because it is an indefinite genitive with no article attached or associated with the passage. If it was in reference to "a man" or some individual man, it would be written as a normative predicate with the article as such, *os anthropos*, which means "a man," however, what is written is *anthropou* with no article which should be translated as "human" as in human beings.

Also the word *arithmos* can be translated as "number" or many numbers as in a "multitude," which changes the meaning of the context of the passage from a human number in reference to an individual, to a human multitude which is in reference to a lot of people. If it had the article attached it would mean a certain number such as 666 or 616 (which some early manuscripts record) or a certain multitude of people totaling 666/616. However, what we have is *arithmos* without the article which I maintain should be translated as "multitude."

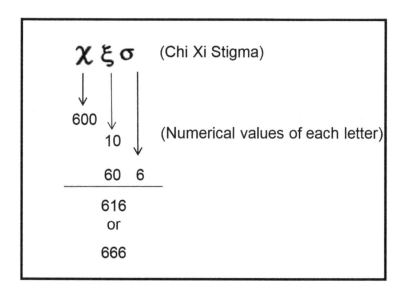

Henceforth, what John is telling us is that this mark belongs to the human multitudes of people who bear the name of the beast; in other words, all the follows of the beast will have this mark of their god on their heads or arms/hand which will separate them from the nonbeliever (i.e., Christians and Jews). It is interesting that the Qur'an states that the beast of the earth will mark all Muslims on their forehead in order to distinguish them from non-Muslims.

Walid Shoebat, a former Muslim and Palestinian terrorist, noted in his book *God's War on Terror; Islam, Prophecy and the Bible*, and makes a compelling argument that when he examined the Greek text of the Codex Vaticanus, he found that the "supposed Greek letters (*chi xi sigma*) that are used to translate to the number 666 very much resemble the most common creed of Islam—the Bismillah (or Basmallh) written in Arabic. Bismillah literally means 'In the Name of Allah,' and is followed by the symbol of crossed swords, which is used universally throughout the Muslim world to signify Islam."[41]

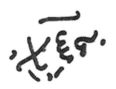

(Writing found in the Codex Vaticanus)

So to finish Walid's thought "is it possible that the Disciple John, while receiving his divine revelation, did not see Greek letters, but instead was supernaturally shown Arabic words and an Islamic symbol, which he then faithfully recorded?" And "could it be that years after John recorded these images; scribes commissioned to copy the text were unable to recognize the foreign words and symbols and thus thought them to be Greek letters?"[42]

[41.] Walid Shoebat and Joel Richardson, *God's War on terror; Islam, Prophecy and the Bible* (United States: Walid@Shoebat.com, 2008), 370.

[42.] Ibid., 369–372.

This would explain why we misinterpret this passage, because we are looking for the number of a man's name to equate to 666 or 616 and not to a multitude of people that bear the name of Allah. I would submit that this passage should be translated as: *"Here is wisdom! If anyone has insight, let him count the multitudes of the beast, for it is a human multitude and this multitude bears the name of Allah"* followed by crossed "X" swords showing that these are militant followers of the beast which represents Islam and the Ottoman Empire.

Now as we look back at the interlude between the six and seventh seal in Revelation 7:9–17, we are able to understand what the Christian multitudes suffer and endure in maintaining their faith as they go through the Great Tribulation. This multitude are those coming out of the tribulation, *ek tas phlipeoos*, who are being refined by fire. They are not spared the trials but have to endure them and come out the far side with their faith intact. What most Prophecy Buffs miss is the statements following the fact that the multitudes are serving the Lord in his sanctuary. *"They shall not hunger any more, nor shall they thirst any more, nor shall the sun beat down upon them, nor any heat."*

The context of the passage is clear and is used to recall hardship and suffering, trials and afflictions, pain, and weariness, etc....something they are going through which is just like what *shari'a* law calls for. The multitudes can't buy or sell anything, i.e., food and drink, nor do they have any shelter to keep the sun off their backs because they can't buy homes or rent living places, thus they are at the mercy of their oppressors because they have not received the mark of the beast, *"And he* (the Antichrist) *causes all, the small and the great...to receive a mark on their right hand or on their foreheads, so that no one could be able to buy or to sell unless he had the mark, which is the name of the beast..."*

However, as they experience and suffer through the tribulation, the Lord will *"shepherd them and lead them to springs of living water,"* where God will ultimately *"wipe away every tear from their eyes,"* as he embraces' them and welcomes them into heaven at the rapture which is post-tribulation.

Now if we look further back at Revelation 6 and the four horsemen of the apocalypse, we see our scriptures translate this passage as *"authority was given to them over a fourth of the earth, to kill with sword and with famine and with pestilence and by the wild beasts of the earth."* Again, I submit to you that this passage is mistranslated and should be changed with regard to the last portion of the passage *"by the beast of the earth."*

The Greek rendering for Revelation 6:8b is written as

kai	*upo*	*twn*	*therion*	*tes*	*ges*
and	by	the	beast	the	earth
			(brute)		

This passage is commonly translated *"and by the wild beasts of the earth"* as mention above to make it fit in with the preceding part of the passage associated with famine and pestilence which occurs because of the result of war. Thus after famine and pestilence take place; wild animals will come forth and kill mankind as well. However, I believe this is a mistranslation and rendering of the passage and should be translated as *"and by the beast of the earth,"* because if we compare it to Revelation 13:11 we get a different conception.

The Greek rendering for Revelation 13:11 is written as

kai	*eidon*	*therion*	*anabainon*	*ek*	*tes*	*ges*
and I saw		beast	from beneath	out	the	earth
		(brute)	(come up)			

When translating this passage it will mean *"and I saw a beast come up out of the earth."* So I will submit to you that the two passages are the same and refer to this second beast who comes up out of the earth. Thus as we look back to Revelation 6 we have a new understanding of the passage, *"authority was given to them* (all four horsemen) *over a fourth of the earth, to kill with sword and with famine and with pestilence and by the beast* (who is the Antichrist) *of the earth."* Even if you make *twn therwn* plural, it refers to both the first and second beast and not to wild animals. The four colors of the four horsemen, white, red, black, and green; are also the four holy colors of Islam. Do you see the picture.

The Greek rendering for Revelation 13:1 is written as
kai eidon   ek   tes thalasses therion   anabainon
and I saw out the   sea   beast   from beneath
                                  (brute) (come up)

Now Revelation 13:1 is translated as *"and I saw out of the sea a beast coming up,"* which correlates with the rest of the chapter 13 regarding this first beast that comes up out of the "sea of humanity," which is *"every tribe, tongue, people, and nation,"* and *"those dwelling in it,"* which is indicated clearly in the text. So in reality both passages refer to the beasts (Islam and the Antichrist/Caliph) of the earth that in chapter 6 will kill one fourth of mankind.

Just some more food for thought.

Notes on Revelation 13

The Second Beast, a.k.a.
The Antichrist

It is apropos to stop here and take a look at why I believe this second *"Beast from the earth"* is *"the Antichrist."* So let's look at what Scripture teaches us about the one whom we will call the Antichrist. Please remember it is essential that we stand back from our presumptions and prejudices and listen carefully to what Scripture is teaching us, for the only certain barrier to truth is the presumption that we already have the truth and there is no other. Thus, we need to be diligent in our study of God's Word and what it reveals to us.

Our Prophecy Buffs claim that the Antichrist is the first "beast who raises out of the sea" and that the second "beast who comes out of the earth" is the False Prophet. That the Antichrist will come from the European Union and that the False Prophet is the Pope of Rome. However, as we look closer we will see this presumption is inaccurate and leads us to look in the wrong direction, thus allowing the church to be taken off guard when the actual Antichrist does appear on the scene. Remember that Satan is the Grand Puppeteer who wants us to watch only one area while he is working in another. In other words, watch the smoke and mirrors in front of you and pay no attention to what's happening behind the curtain.

It is interesting that the term *Antichrist* is not found in the Book of Revelation, however it is found several other places in Scripture, seven times to be exact in 1 and 2 John. Christ Himself even warns us to be aware of being misled, *"And Jesus answered and said to them, "See to it that no one misleads you. For many will come in My name,* saying, *'I am the Christ,' and will mislead many"* (Matthew 24:4–5). Jesus goes on to say:

> *Many false prophets will arise and will mislead many. Because lawlessness is increased, most people's love will grow cold. But the one who endures to the end, he will be saved... Then if anyone says to you, 'Behold, here is the Christ,' or 'There He is,' do not believe him. For false Christs and false prophets will arise and will show great signs and wonders, so as to mislead, if possible, even the elect. Behold, I have told you in advance.* (Matthew 24:11–25)

Now how do we know that we are being misled and who are we to believe? Well, the Disciple John makes it clear to us when we are being misled when he wrote, *"Who is the liar but the one who denies that Jesus is the Christ? This is the antichrist, the one who denies the Father and the Son. Whoever denies the Son does not have the Father..."* (1 John 2:22). The Disciple John continues to let us know who we can trust and believe in, for the next verse 23 states, *"the one who confesses the Son has the Father also."* So whoever confesses that Jesus is the Christ/Messiah, their Lord and Savior can be trusted and followed! But, whoever denies that Jesus is the Son of God has the spirit of antichrist and are untrustworthy.

It is interesting that the Greek word *antichristo* has a dual meaning, for it means *"against Christ"* as well as *"in-place of Christ."* Normally when we hear the word *anti*, we think about being against something or opposed to something, but it also carries the meaning of being in place of something. So in our Scriptures when we hear about this Antichrist we need to see this person not only as opposed to what Christ has done, but also acting in Christ's place as if he were the world's leader and messiah himself (by the way, the Greek word *Christ* and the Hebrew word *Messiah* are interchangeable and mean the same thing, *"the Anointed One"*).

This leader will be accepted by the world *"every tribe, tongue, people, and nation,"* as the Christ/Messiah; however, we know him to be a false messiah. This leader will also set himself up as God which will replace the notion of having a Messiah as the redeemer of the world, for we will now have "God" dwelling among us. Ultimately there will be no need for the Christ/Messiah who is found in the pages of our Bibles because he is now here in the flash.

We now need to look at what our Scriptures teach us about the one whom we will call *"the Antichrist."* One of the most fundamental passages concerning eschatology today is the famous "Seventy Weeks" prophecy contained in the last four verses of Daniel 9, which describes this coming world leader. So, after the Messiah is killed *"cut off,"* the *"people of the Prince that shall come will destroy the city and the sanctuary"* (Daniel 9:26). This event was fulfilled when Jerusalem and the Temple were destroyed by Titus and the Roman legions in 70 AD. However, *"The Prince that shall come"* is also a reference to a future leader who will be prominent in our end-time scenario.

This is also the main passage that our Prophecy Buffs believe indicate that this final world leader *"the prince that shall come"* will emerge out of the Roman Empire (i.e., the European Union) because it was the Roman Legions that sacked Jerusalem and destroyed the Temple. However, our Prophecy Buffs are in error here, for they miss the true meaning of the passage: *"the people of the prince that shall come shall destroy the city and the sanctuary."* This passage is not in reference to the Roman Legions themselves who destroyed the temple, which were of course under Roman authority, but it is in reference to the soldiers (*the people*) who made up the legions. If Daniel wanted the reader to understand that he was referring to the legions than I am sure he would have written (*the army*) instead of (*the people*). Which were all raised from people living in Ionia, Turkey, Syria, Egypt, and Arabia where these six legions and auxiliary troops were garrisoned. They were not from Western Europe, and definitely not Rome, so the Antichrist can't be from the European Union which has more than ten signatory countries affiliated with it (the Antichrist will lead the "ten horn" nations against Israel) as our Prophecy Buff's teach.

Under this future leader's watch *"War will continue until the end, and desolations have been decreed"* at which time:

> *He* (the Antichrist) *will confirm a covenant with many for one 'seven'* (seven years). *In the middle of the 'seven'* (three and a half years) *he* (the Antichrist) *will put an end to sacrifice and offering. And at the temple he* (the Antichrist) *will set up an abomination that causes desolation, until the end that is decreed is poured out on him* (the Antichrist). (Daniel 9:26b–27)

Historically, the Syrian ruler Antiochus IV Epiphanes conquered Israel and stormed the second Temple converting it into a pagan worship center in 167 BC. He slaughtered a pig on the altar and erected a statue of Zeus (Jupiter) in the holy place with his own face on it, thereby proclaiming himself to be God (Epiphanes means god made manifest) and he required everyone to worship him on pain of death. So in Antiochus Epiphanes we have the forerunner or archetype of this end-times Antichrist who will, just like Antiochus cause the temple to be desecrated and claim that he is God.

"Therefore when you see the Abomination of Desolation which was spoken of through Daniel the prophet, standing in the Holy Place..." (Matthew 24:15). Here, Christ Himself is pointing us toward this second desolation thereby identifying the first event as the archetype or model for the future Abomination of Desolation event found in the Olivet Discourse prophecy. The Apostle Paul also declares in his epistle to the Thessalonians that the Antichrist will ultimately set himself to be worshiped in the third Temple which will be rebuilt in Israel:

> *That man of sin be revealed, the son of perdition;* (the Antichrist) *who oppose and exalts himself above all that is called God, or that is worshipped; so that he as God sits in the temple of God, showing himself that he is God.* (2 Thessalonians 2:4)

Here again we have the model or archetype of Antiochus being fulfilled by one who is like Antiochus. It is important here to understand that Antiochus was the king of the Seleucid Empire, and he was known as ("the king of the north") which is modern day Syria and Eastern Turkey. Now it is also interesting that in the Old Testament prophesies, the Prophet Micah refers to this future leader, *"the prince that shall come"* as the Assyrian:

> *And this One* (the Messiah) *shall be our peace. When the Assyrian* (the Antichrist) *shall come into our land: and when he shall tread in our palaces, then shall we* (the Trinity) *raise against him seven shepherds, and eight principal men. And they shall waste the land of Assyria with the sword, and the land of Nimrod in the entrances thereof: thus shall he* (the Messiah) *deliver us from the Assyrian* (the Antichrist), *when he comes into our land, and when he tramples within our borders.* (Micah 5:5–6)

As we continue to carefully examine the many references in the Old Testament, we discover a surprising number of allusions to this dominant leader who is known as *"the Assyrian."* Isaiah 10:24 states, *"Therefore thus says the Lord GOD of hosts, "O My people who dwell in Zion, do not fear the Assyrian* (the Antichrist) *who strikes you with the rod and lifts up his staff against you, the way Egypt did."* This and other passages like Isaiah 10:5, 24; 14:25; 30:31; and Ezekiel 31:3f, all seem to focus on the region that we know today as Turkey, Syria and Iraq. Now with the current world tensions over this very region, it seems quite timely to re-examine some of our presumptions regarding the potential role of this geographical region in the climactic end-times scenario and the re-establishment of the Caliphate by Turkey!

Today, the Muslim nations have been calling for the re-establishment of the Caliphate through the Arab Spring, and their position has been defined by Jordanian columnist Hussein Al-Ruwashdeh in a recent article entitled "*Muslims Need a Spiritual Leader like the Pope to Unite Them*":

> The Muslims are in dire need of an esteemed moral leadership…at a time when others scrutinize every possible word [the Muslims say, looking for an excuse] to include them on the terror list, and while the only thing left for the Islamic world to do is call for tolerance and justice, and persuade others that we are equal and that our religion is not based on the sword and does not believe in violence and blood.

Please remember that the Antichrist (a.k.a. *the Assyrian*, or *the Arrogant One*) will be the master of deceit, "*and through his shrewdness he will cause deceit to succeed by his influence; And he will magnify himself in his heart, and he will destroy many while they are at ease. He will even oppose the Prince of princes…*" (Daniel 8:25). Even Jesus warned us as I stated earlier that if it were possible he would deceive the very elect, "*for false Christs and false prophets will arise and will show great signs and wonders, so as to mislead, if possible, even the elect*" (Matthew 24:24).

Hence this Caliph/Leader will unit all Islam into an Islamic state known as a Caliphate and he will deceive the rest of the world into believing that Islam is a "*Religion of Peace.*" A *Caliph* is a political and religious leader who is a successor to the Islamic prophet Muhammad. The Caliph's power and authority is absolute, for he is both the political leader (i.e., the Antichrist) and the religious leader (i.e., false prophet), for they are one in the same person. Remember in Antiochus we have the archetype of the Antichrist. Antiochus was only one person and he did not have a religious man working with him when he desecrated the temple, so the Antichrist will be only one person when he fulfills the same type of prophecies.

Our First Beast is not a person but a religious governmental entity as I have stated earlier. This religious governmental entity is Islam, for it is a religious, militaristic, socio-economic, and political system all rolled into one. Our Second Beast will control this religious governmental entity through the office of the Caliph who is both the political leader and the religious leader who holds absolute authority over the First Beast. Keep in mind that both beasts are personifications of Satan, the first is the ferocious power and the second is the deceptive activity.

> *For many deceivers have gone out into the world, those who do not acknowledge Jesus Christ as coming in the flesh. This is the deceiver and the antichrist. Watch yourselves, that you do not lose what we have accomplished, but that you may receive a full reward. Anyone who goes too far and does not abide in the teaching of Christ, does not have God; the one who abides in the teaching, he has both the Father and the Son. If anyone comes to you and does not bring this teaching, do not receive him into your house, and do not give him a greeting; for the one who gives him a greeting participates in his evil deeds* (2 John 1:7–11).

Now according to the Qur'an and Islamic teachings, *"Allah has no sons,"* and Isa the Islamic Jesus is not the son of God. So whoever denies that Jesus is the Son of God has the spirit of antichrist and should be considered untrustworthy and evil. Thus, I submit to you that Islam is the single greatest challenge that the Christian Church will face before the return of Christ. For many in the church will believe the false claim of this religion because they have no knowledge of what our Scriptures truly teaches, thus they will fall away from the One True Faith, for *"My people perish for lack of knowledge."*

Revelation

CHAPTER 14

New American Standard Bible (NASB)

The Lamb and the 144,000 on Mount Zion

¹⁴ *Then I looked, and behold, the Lamb was standing on Mount Zion, and with Him one hundred and forty-four thousand, having His name and the name of His Father written on their foreheads.* ² *And I heard a voice from heaven, like the sound of many waters and like the sound of loud thunder, and the voice which I heard was like the sound of harpists playing on their harps.* ³ *And they *sang a new song before the throne and before the four living creatures and the elders; and no one could learn the song except the one hundred and forty-four thousand who had been purchased from the earth.*

⁴ *These are the ones who have not been defiled with women, for they have kept themselves chaste. These are the ones who follow the Lamb wherever He goes. These have been purchased from among men as first fruits to God and to the Lamb.* ⁵ *And no lie was found in their mouth; they are blameless.*

Vision of the Angel with the Gospel

⁶ *And I saw another angel flying in midheaven, having an eternal gospel to preach to those who live on the earth, and to every nation and*

tribe and tongue and people; ⁷ and he said with a loud voice, "Fear God, and give Him glory, because the hour of His judgment has come; worship Him who made the heaven and the earth and sea and springs of waters."

⁸ And another angel, a second one, followed, saying, "Fallen, fallen is Babylon the great, she who has made all the nations drink of the wine of the passion of her immorality."

Doom for Worshipers of the Beast

⁹ Then another angel, a third one, followed them, saying with a loud voice, "If anyone worships the beast and his image, and receives a mark on his forehead or on his hand, ¹⁰ he also will drink of the wine of the wrath of God, which is mixed in full strength in the cup of His anger; and he will be tormented with fire and brimstone in the presence of the holy angels and in the presence of the Lamb. ¹¹ And the smoke of their torment goes up forever and ever; they have no rest day and night, those who worship the beast and his image, and whoever receives the mark of his name." ¹² Here is the perseverance of the saints who keep the commandments of God and their faith in Jesus.

¹³ And I heard a voice from heaven, saying, "Write, 'Blessed are the dead who die in the Lord from now on!'" "Yes," says the Spirit, "so that they may rest from their labors, for their deeds follow with them."

The Reapers

¹⁴ Then I looked, and behold, a white cloud, and sitting on the cloud was one like a son of man, having a golden crown on His head and a sharp sickle in His hand. ¹⁵ And another angel came out of the temple, crying out with a loud voice to Him who sat on the cloud, "Put in your sickle and reap, for the hour to reap has come, because the harvest of the earth is ripe." ¹⁶ Then He who sat on the cloud swung His sickle over the earth, and the earth was reaped.

[17] And another angel came out of the temple which is in heaven, and he also had a sharp sickle. [18] Then another angel, the one who has power over fire, came out from the altar; and he called with a loud voice to him who had the sharp sickle, saying, "Put in your sharp sickle and gather the clusters from the vine of the earth, because her grapes are ripe." [19] So the angel swung his sickle to the earth and gathered the clusters from the vine of the earth, and threw them into the great wine press of the wrath of God. [20] And the wine press was trodden outside the city, and blood came out from the wine press, up to the horses' bridles, for a distance of two hundred miles.

Notes on Revelation 14

The 144,000

In order to understand chapter 14, we need to recognize that Revelation chapters 12–14 belongs together and depicts the First Preview of the overall picture of the coming end (see outline of the book). Chapter 12 contains two signs, *sameion*, dealing with Israel's Travail and Struggle—Revelation 12:1–17; chapter 13 reveals, *kai horao*, The Beast—Revelation 13:1–10 and The Antichrist—Revelation 13:11–18; and chapter 14 contains the three visions, *kai eidon*, of The Victorious Christ—Revelation 14:1–20, which now completes this preview that John saw starting in heaven and finishing up on earth.

The 144,000 who have the name of God written on their foreheads here at the beginning of chapter 14 also tie in chapter 7, which deals with the fifth seal and the martyrs under the altar of chapter 6 and completes the thought of those who have been martyred, those who are sealed, and those who now in heaven. However, they are placed in this order because they show the chronological progression of what will take place at the end of days.

First on the scene will be the Four Horsemen of the Apocalypse; that of war, famine, and death, brought on by the Antichrist. Followed by those who will be martyred during the Antichrist's rule. Then comes the sealing of the 144,000 in which the four winds of destruction are held back. After the sealing now comes the cataclysmic (four winds of destruction) events of God getting mankind's attention here on earth culminating with the rapture where the multitudes are then taken up to heaven. As the multitudes ascend, they will witness the Second Coming of Christ (for they pass each other in the clouds) who now returns to earth to pour out the Wrath of God.

The multitudes have to suffer through the Great Tribulation. They wash their robes *himatia* through what they have had to experience in order to maintain their faith, before their robes are made white in heaven. The martyrs under the altar are given white robes *stoles*, which are considered Robes of State because of what they have endured, i.e., they were beheaded in Revelation 20:4 for their testimony in Jesus Christ for which they gave the ultimate sacrifice, their lives.

Now here in Revelation 14:1–5 we glean more detail as to who these 144,000 sealed ones are: There is no falseness *peudos* found in their months for they are honorable in their speech and conduct v. 5, as opposed to those dwelling on the earth that are wicked and deceitful who follow after the beast and his ways. They are men who have not defiled themselves with women *meta gunaikwn*, v. 4; they are male virgins *parthenoi*, v. 4b. They are singing a military type song *ode* that the angels have taught them which no one on earth knows, v. 3; and they are encamped on Mount Zion following the Lord Jesus Christ wherever He goes, v. 1. Remember that Christ has now returned to earth with the Second Advent or *parousia*, which means "an arrival and a continuing presence." Thus, Christ is here on earth and will continue to be here through the millennium.

The question which arises is; if these are men who are chaste and sexually pure, who are honorable with no deceit found in them, and who sing a military type song that was taught to them only; are the 144,000 a type of bodyguard as some would ask? I would have to say no, not bodyguards, but they are soldiers/valiant warriors of the Lord. For *"these* (the followers of the Antichrist) *will wage war against the Lamb, and the Lamb will overcome them, because He is Lord of lords and King of kings, and those who are with Him* (the 144,000 a.k.a. the remnant) *are the called and chosen and faithful"* (Rev. 17:14).

A look at the Old Testament will reveal much about who these remnants are. Starting in the Book of Zephaniah 3:13 we see how it confirms Revelation 14:5, for *"The remnant of Israel will do no wrong and tell no lies, nor will a deceitful tongue be found in their mouths; For they shall feed and lie down with no one to make them tremble."* They eat and lie down with no one to bother them, because the King is with them. Who will stir up trouble when they know the Lord is there. They are principled *men of honor* preparing to go into battle with the Lord against the deceitful enemies of Israel who follow after the lies of the Antichrist.

The Book of Micah 2:12–13 continues to tell us that the Lord will *"gather the remnant of Israel"* and *"will put them together like sheep in a fold: Like a flock in the midst of its pasture they will be noisy with men. The breaker* (Christ) *goes up before them; they break out, pass through the gate, and go out by it. So their king* (Christ) *goes on before them, and the Lord at their head."* This passage is telling us that the remnant will be camped together and will cry out singing a military style song ready to break out through the gates of Jerusalem with the Lord leading the attack.

Reading on a little further in Micah 5:7–15 we are again told that the remnant will be *"like a lion among the beast of the forest, like a young lion among flocks of sheep, which, if he passes through, tramples down and tears, and there is none to rescue. Your hand will be lifted up against your adversaries, and all your enemies will be cut off."* It goes on to say in that day the Lord will *"execute vengeance in anger and wrath on the nations which have not obeyed."* The imagery is clear that these are the valiant warriors/soldiers who are destroying the enemies of Israel who have attacked and trampled their land and territory.

The question that arises is, who is the enemy? If we look back at the proceeding passages we find that the enemy is the army of the Antichrist for both passages each uses one of the thirty-three names of the Antichrist in their description. The first is *"the Apostate"* who takes their fields, and the second is *"the Assyrian"* who invades their land.

The Prophet Jeremiah adds to our understanding of how the Lord will use His 144,000 remnant against Israel's enemies, for he calls them His War-Club:

> *"For the Maker of all is He, and of the tribe of His inheritance; The LORD of hosts is His name. He says, "You* (the 144,000) *are My war-club, My weapon of war; and with you* (the 144,000) *I shat-*

ter nations, and with you (the 144,000) *I destroy kingdoms. "With you* (the 144,000) *I shatter the horse and his rider, and with you* (the 144,000) *I shatter the chariot and its rider, and with you* (the 144,000) *I shatter man and woman, and with you* (the 144,000) *I shatter old man and youth, and with you* (the 144,000) *I shatter young man and virgin, and with you* (the 144,000) *I shatter the shepherd and his flock, and with you* (the 144,000) *I shatter the farmer and his team, and with you* (the 144,000) *I shatter governors and prefects."* (Jer. 51:19–23)

In the Book of Ecclesiastes 1:9–11 we are reminded *"That which has been is that which will be, and that which has been done is that which will be done. So there is nothing new under the sun....Already it has existed for ages which were before us. There is no remembrance of earlier things; and also of the later things which will occur, there will be for them no remembrance among those who will come later still."*
So I submit to you that the 144,000 are to the Lord what the three hundred were to Gideon in Judges 7:19–8:26. Gideon is an archetype of Christ who leads his people in victory over the Midianites, Amalekites and the kings of the east (the same enemy that Christ must deal with in the last days) for raiding and terrorizing the people and the land. Gideon does it with a chosen few (only three hundred men), least Israel boasts that they delivered themselves and God's hand was not involved. Christ will deliver Israel with His chosen (144,000 men), for again least anyone should boast that God was not involved in the victory.
A further look reveals that after Gideon defeated (Zeba and Zalmunna) the kings of Midia in the valley of Jezreel (which is the same location as Armageddon), he then chased them across the Jordan River where he finally caught up with them in Edom. After he had killed them he then took the ornaments that were on their necks and on their camel's necks, melted them down and made an ephod out of them. So, what were these ornaments you ask? Verse

21 and 26 tell us that they were crescent shaped ornaments, i.e., the crescent moon and star design for the god that the Midianites as well as the kings of the east worshiped.

So the question now arises, who are the gods that they worshiped? Well, the Babylonians worshiped *Sin*, the Assyrians worshiped *Bel*, the Canaanites worshiped *Baal*, and the Midianites worshiped *Allah*. These are different names for the same god, the moon and war god, whose symbol happens to be the crescent moon. The star represents the moon god's daughter (*Ishtar*—Babyonian and Assyrian, *Asherah*—Canaanite, and *Allot*—Midianite) who happens to be the goddess of sex and fertility.

Now the nations surrounding Israel today are all Islamic who worship this same god whose symbol again happens to be the crescent moon and star. Is this just another coincidence or what!

It is interesting that Satan is the great counterfeiter, he cannot create but he can duplicate. Thus, he has created his own trinity through the imagery of the dragon and the two beasts. If we take the thirty-three names of the Antichrist found in the scriptures and multiply it by three for the false trinity, we come up with ninety-nine, which is exactly the number for the *"ninety-nine beautiful names of Allah."*

The prophet Isaiah tells us that on the *"Day of the Lord,"* God will pour out His vengeance on His enemies and we will see Him (Christ) return from Edom with His robes dripping in blood:

"Who is this who comes from Edom (the Arabian Peninsula)... *Why is Your apparel red, and Your garments like the one who treads in the wine press?* "*I* (Jesus) *have trodden the wine trough... I also trod them in My anger and trampled them in My wrath; and their lifeblood is sprinkled on My garments, and I stained all My raiment.* "*For the day of vengeance was in My heart, and My year of redemption has come... I trod down the peoples in My anger and made them drunk in My wrath, and I poured out their lifeblood on the earth"* (Isaiah 63:1–6)

Is this just another coincidence, that both Gideon and Christ defeat their enemies in Edom? Is it also a coincidence that what was, will be again. God will carry out His Judgment so all the world will know that He is God and He is Just, hence it has to be God's wrath which will destroy Islam in the end for striking terror against Israel and His elect.

Revelation

CHAPTER 15

New American Standard Bible (NASB)

A Scene of Heaven

¹⁵ *Then I saw another sign in heaven, great and marvelous, seven angels who had seven plagues, which are the last, because in them the wrath of God is finished.*

² And I saw something like a sea of glass mixed with fire, and those who had been victorious over the beast and his image and the number of his name, standing on the sea of glass, holding harps of God. ³ And they *sang the song of Moses, the bond-servant of God, and the song of the Lamb, saying,

> *"Great and marvelous are Your works,*
> *O Lord God, the Almighty;*
> *Righteous and true are Your ways,*
> *King of the nations!*
> *⁴ "Who will not fear, O Lord, and glorify Your*
>   *name?*
> *For You alone are holy;*
> *For ALL THE NATIONS WILL COME AND WORSHIP*
>   *BEFORE YOU,*
> *For YOUR RIGHTEOUS ACTS HAVE BEEN REVEALED."*

[5] After these things I looked, and the temple of the tabernacle of testimony in heaven was opened, [6] and the seven angels who had the seven plagues came out of the temple, clothed in linen, clean and bright, and girded around their chests with golden sashes. [7] Then one of the four living creatures gave to the seven angels seven golden bowls full of the wrath of God, who lives forever and ever. [8] And the temple was filled with smoke from the glory of God and from His power; and no one was able to enter the temple until the seven plagues of the seven angels were finished.

Notes on Revelation 15

The Victorious Saints

In John's Revelation, he is taken up into heaven and is standing in the throne room of God where he is given insight into what will happen in the last days leading up to and including what will take place on the *"Day of The Lord."* This insight is revealed to us in two parallel, but separate set of interwoven visions which take place both in heaven and on Earth. Both sets of visions start with a broad overall picture of what will take place, then the picture is refined with more detail, and finally the picture is brought into focus.

The first set of visions is depicted in the Seven Seals, Seven Trumpets, and the Seven Bowls, which culminates the focus on the Wrath of God. The second set of visions which I call the First, Second, and Third Previews depict the struggle between the forces of God and Satan and finally focuses with the Third Preview on the Victorious Christ.

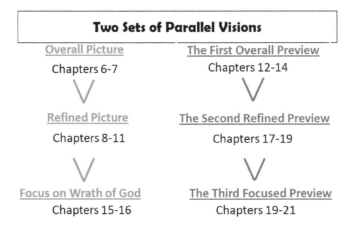

Two Sets of Parallel Visions	
Overall Picture	The First Overall Preview
Chapters 6-7	Chapters 12-14
Refined Picture	The Second Refined Preview
Chapters 8-11	Chapters 17-19
Focus on Wrath of God	The Third Focused Preview
Chapters 15-16	Chapters 19-21

Here in chapter 15, John now see *kai horao* another scene taking place in Heaven, only this time it seems to be a Celebration of Praise before God's Wrath is poured out by the Angel's holding the Seven Bowls. *"And I saw something like a sea of glass mixed with fire, and those who had been victorious* (the Tribulation Saints) *over the beast and his image and the number of* (the multitudes who wear) *his name, standing on the sea of glass, holding harps of God. And they sang the song of Moses, the bond-servant of God, and the song of the Lamb..."* (Rev. 15:2–3a)

So who are these who were *"victorious over the beast"* and why are they now celebrating in Heaven? These are the Tribulation Saints who have been raptured to Heaven and who are now singing praises to the Lord. They are the ones who suffered and endured for their faith as they went through the Great Tribulation. This multitude are those coming out of the tribulation *"ek tas phlipeoos"* who have been refined by fire. They were not spared the trials but had to endure them and come out with their faith intact.

Even Christ Jesus himself asked the Father to *"not take His* (Jesus') *disciples from the earth, but to keep them from the evil one"* (John 17:15–16). In other words, Jesus asked our Heavenly Father to assist and help the saints (believing Christians) through the tribulation so they could endure all that the beast and the Antichrist brought upon them. These are the ones that *"shall not hunger any more, nor shall they thirst any more, nor shall the sun beat down upon them, nor any heat."*

The imagery of this passage recalls the hardship and suffering, trials and afflictions, pain and weariness, etc., something they have gone through. Thus, the multitudes can't buy or sell anything, i.e., food and drink, nor do they have any shelter to keep the sun off their backs because they can't buy homes or rent living places, so they are at the mercy of their oppressors because they have not received the mark of the beast, *"And he* (the Antichrist) *causes all, the small and the great...to receive a mark on their right hand or on their foreheads, so that no one could be able to buy or to sell unless he had the mark, which is the name of the beast..."*

Keep in mind 2 Thessalonians 2:1–8, where the Apostle Paul reveals what will take place leading up to Christ's Second Coming:

> *"Now, brethren, concerning the coming of our Lord Jesus Christ and our gathering together* (rapture) *to Him, we ask you, not to be quickly shaken in mind or disturbed either by a spirit or a message or a letter as if from us, as to the effect that the day of Christ had come. Let no one deceive you, for it* (the rapture) *will not come unless the apostasy comes first and the man of lawlessness is revealed* (the Antichrist), *the son of destruction, who opposes and exalts himself above every so-called god or object of worship* (just like Antiochus Epiphanes), *so that he takes his seat in the temple of God, displaying himself as being God. Do you not remember that when I was still with you, I told you these things? And now you know what restrains him now, so that in his time he may be revealed. For the mystery of lawlessness is already at work; only He* (Christ) *who now restrains will do so until he* (the Antichrist) *is taken out of the way. And then that lawless one* (Satan) *will be revealed whom the Lord will slay with the breath of His mouth* (the Sword of the Spirit) *and bring to an end* (the tribulation) *by the appearance of His coming."*

Combine this with what Christ told the Disciples about His Second Coming in the Book of Matthew:

> *"But immediately after the tribulation of those days the sun shall be darkened, and the moon shall not give its light, and the stars shall fall from heaven, and the powers of the heavens shall be shaken: and then shall appear the sign of the Son of man* (Christ Himself) *in heaven: and then shall all the tribes*

of the earth mourn, and they shall see the Son of man (Jesus) *coming on the clouds of heaven with power and great glory. And He shall send forth His angels with a great sound of a trumpet, and they shall* (rapture) *gather together His elect from the four winds, from one end of heaven to the other."* (Matthew 24:29–31)

In other words, the Rapture is a Post-Tribulation event. The *rapture* and *parousia* (Christ returning to earth) all happens just before the angels pours out the Wrath of God on the remaining earth dwellers.

The Apostle Paul makes it clear that *"the Lord* (Jesus) *Himself will descend from heaven with a shout, with the voice of the archangel, and with the trumpet of God; and the dead* (those who were martyred) *in Christ shall rise first. Then we who are alive and remain* (having endured the tribulation) *shall be caught up* (raptured) *together with them in the clouds, to meet the Lord* (Jesus) *in the air, and thus we shall always be with the Lord* (God)*"* (1 Thess. 4:13–17).

Hence, these Victorious Tribulation Saints are now standing in Heaven in the presence of God in celebration for keeping their faith and being raptured and removed from the Wrath of the God which will now be poured out on the followers of the Beast. Now Revelation 15:5–16:1 continues:

"After these things I looked, and the temple of the tabernacle of testimony in heaven was opened, and the seven angels who had the seven plagues came out of the temple, clothed in linen, clean and bright, and girded around their chests with golden sashes. Then one of the four living creatures gave to the

seven angels seven golden bowls full of the wrath of God…Then I heard a loud voice from the temple, saying to the seven angels, "Go and pour out on the earth the seven bowls of the wrath of God."

Now it's too late for repentance.

Revelation

CHAPTER 16

New American Standard Bible (NASB)

Six Bowls of Wrath

¹⁶ *Then I heard a loud voice from the temple, saying to the seven angels, "Go and pour out on the earth the seven bowls of the wrath of God."*

The First Bowl

² *So the first angel went and poured out his bowl on the earth; and it became a loathsome and malignant sore on the people who had the mark of the beast and who worshiped his image.*

The Second Bowl

³ *The second angel poured out his bowl into the sea, and it became blood like that of a dead man; and every living thing in the sea died.*

The Third Bowl

⁴ *Then the third angel poured out his bowl into the rivers and the springs of waters; and they became blood. ⁵ And I heard the angel of the waters saying, "Righteous are You, who are and who were, O Holy One, because You judged these things; ⁶ for they poured out the blood of saints*

and prophets, and You have given them blood to drink. They deserve it."
⁷ And I heard the altar saying, "Yes, O Lord God, the Almighty, true and righteous are Your judgments."

The Fourth Bowl

⁸ The fourth angel poured out his bowl upon the sun, and it was given to it to scorch men with fire. ⁹ Men were scorched with fierce heat; and they blasphemed the name of God who has the power over these plagues, and they did not repent so as to give Him glory.

The Fifth Bowl

¹⁰ Then the fifth angel poured out his bowl on the throne of the beast, and his kingdom became darkened; and they gnawed their tongues because of pain, ¹¹ and they blasphemed the God of heaven because of their pains and their sores; and they did not repent of their deeds.

The Sixth Bowl

¹² The sixth angel poured out his bowl on the great river, the Euphrates; and its water was dried up, so that the way would be prepared for the kings from the east.

Armageddon

¹³ And I saw coming out of the mouth of the dragon and out of the mouth of the beast and out of the mouth of the false prophet, three unclean spirits like frogs; ¹⁴ for they are spirits of demons, performing signs, which go out to the kings of the whole world, to gather them together for the war of the great day of God, the Almighty. ¹⁵ ("Behold, I am coming like a thief. Blessed is the one who stays awake and keeps his clothes, so that he will not walk about naked and men will not see his shame.") ¹⁶ And they gathered them together to the place which in Hebrew is called Har-Magedon.

Seventh Bowl of Wrath

[17] *Then the seventh angel poured out his bowl upon the air, and a loud voice came out of the temple from the throne, saying, "It is done."* [18] *And there were flashes of lightning and sounds and peals of thunder; and there was a great earthquake, such as there had not been since man came to be upon the earth, so great an earthquake was it, and so mighty.* [19] *The great city was split into three parts, and the cities of the nation's fell.*

Babylon the great was remembered before God, to give her the cup of the wine of His fierce wrath. [20] *And every island fled away, and the mountains were not found.* [21] *And huge hailstones, about one hundred pounds each, *came down from heaven upon men; and men blasphemed God because of the plague of the hail, because its plague *was extremely severe.*

Notes on Revelation 16

"The Wrath of God" a.k.a.
"The Day of the Lord"

Zephaniah 1:14–18 states that

> *"the great day of the Lord* (when God pours out His Wrath on mankind) *is near—near and coming quickly. Listen! The cry on the day of the Lord will be bitter, the shouting of the warrior* (the 144,000) *there. That day will be a day of Wrath, a day of distress and anguish, a day of trouble and ruin, a day of darkness and gloom, a day of clouds and blackness, a day of trumpet and battle cry* (the 144,000) *against the fortified cities and against the corner towers. I* (Christ) *will bring distress on the people and they will walk like blind men, because they have sinned against the Lord* (God). *Their blood will be poured out like dust and their entrails like filth. Neither their silver nor their gold will be able to save them on the day of the Lord's Wrath. In the fire of His* (God's) *jealousy the whole world will be consumed, for He* (God) *will make a sudden end of all who live in the earth."*

When we come to Scriptures passages like this we need to view it, not in our western American-centric worldview, but on an eastern Jerusalem-centric Hebraic worldview of the first century AD. Thus the reference to *"the whole world will be consumed,"* deals specifically with the Middle East. This mind set helps us to visualize the audience to whom John's Revelation was given and how it would be interpreted.

Though John was writing to the Seven Churches in Asia Minor, his vision like the other prophets of the Old Testament and Christ as well, is specifically Jerusalem-centric, and deals with the nations surrounding Israel, hence the phrase *"Go and pour out the seven bowls of the wrath of God into the earth"* (Rev. 16:1), does not mean the whole earth as we know it. It is a symbolic/metaphorical representation of the middle-east and the nations surrounding Israel, for she is the apple of God's eye and the center of the world.

All the prophecy's against all the nations involved in God's Wrath found throughout the Old Testament in Isaiah 13–23, Jeremiah 46–51, and especially Ezekiel 25–39, are still waiting to be fulfilled. Since these judgments have not been completed through historical events, they must then be fulfilled when Christ return's on *"the Day of the Lord."* So who are these nations which God will punish in Revelation 16:1–21?

1. Assyria—*Eastern Turkey*: They will go down to Sheol (Hell), Ez. 31:15; They will feel God's blazing wrath, Ez. 38:19–23; God will enter into judgment against them, Joel 3:2–4; God will destroy Assyria, Zeph. 2:13; Meshech and Tubal (Asia Minor/Turkey), are cast into Hell, Ez. 32:26; They are punished for striking terror against Israel and the believers, Ez. 32:22–24, 27.

   Greece/Ionia, *Western Turkey*: They will go down to Sheol, Ez. 31:15; They will feel God's blazing wrath, Ez. 38:19–23; God will enter into judgment against them, Joel 3:2–4; God will destroy Ionia, Zeph. 2:13; Meshech and Tubal (Asia Minor), are cast into Hell, Ez. 32:26; Punished for striking terror against Israel and the believers, Ez. 32:22–24, 27.

2. Babylon, *Iraq*: Everlasting desolation, Jer. 25:12; She will not be inhabited, but she will be completely desolate; everyone who passes by Babylon will be horrified, Jer. 50:13,

39; God will enter into judgment against them, Joel 3:2–4; Disaster will fall on you for which you cannot atone, and destruction about which you do not know will come on you suddenly, Is. 47:11; Prophecy against, Jer. 50:1–51:58; Other prophecies show Asshur (Iraq/Syria), are cast into Hell, Ez. 32:22–23; They are punished for striking terror against Israel and the believers, Ez. 32:22–24, 27.

3. Persia/Elam, *Iran*: They will feel God's blazing wrath, Ez. 38:19–23; God will enter into judgment against them, Joel 3:2–4; Prophecy against, Jer. 49:28–33; Elam is cast into Hell, Ez. 32:24–25; Punished for striking terror against Israel and the believers, Ez. 32:22–24, 27.

4. Egypt—*Egypt*: Become a desolation and waste, Ez. 29:8; Summoning a sword against them, Jer. 25:19–38; Enter into judgment against them, Joel 3:2–4; Will be a waste because of the violence done to the sons of Israel, Joel 3:19.

5. Edom—*Arabia*: They will know my vengeance, Ez. 25:14; I will make you a desolation and a waste Ez. 35:3,14; Summoning a sword against them, Jer. 25:19–38; Enter into judgment against them, Joel 3:2–4; Edom will become a desolate wilderness because of the violence done to the sons of Israel, Joel 3:19; A perpetual desolation, Zeph. 2:9; trod them in His anger, trampled them in His wrath, Is. 63:3; Prophecy against, Jer. 49:7–22. Edom is cast into Hell, Ez. 32:29; Punished for striking terror against Israel and the believers, Ez. 32:22–24, 27; Will flee from battle, Is. 21:13–17.

6. Moab/Ammon—*Jordan*: God will execute His judgment against them, Ez. 25:11; Summoning a sword against them, Jer. 25:19–38; Enter into judgment against them, Joel 3:2–4; A perpetual desolation, Zeph. 2:9; Prophecy against, Jer. 48:1–47; Destroyed in a night, Is. 15:1–9.

7. Philistia, *Gaza*: God will execute great vengeance on them, Ex. 25:17; Summoning a sword against them, Jer. 25:19–38; Enter into judgment against them, Joel 3:2–4; Gaza will be abandoned, Zeph. 2:4; Consumed with fire, Zech.

9:4; Prophecy against, Jer. 47:1–7; God will punished for striking terror against Israel and the believers, Ez. 32:22–24, 27; Destroyed by famine, Is. 14:28–32.

8. Damascus, *Syria*: I shall destroy you, Ez. 25:7; God Himself will enter into judgment against them, Joel 3:2–4; A perpetual desolation, Zeph. 2:9; Prophecy against, Jer. 49:23–27; The are punished for striking terror against Israel and the believers, Ez. 32:22–24, 27; Will become a heap of ruins, Is. 17:1–14.

9. Tyre/Sidon, *Lebanon*: You will never be found again, Ez. 26:21; The sword will be against her on every side, Ez. 26:22–23; Summoning a sword against them, Jer. 25:19–38; Enter into judgment against them, Joel 3:2–4; Consumed with fire, Zech. 9:4; Punished for striking terror against Israel and the believers, Ez. 32:22–24, 27; Their fortress will be destroyed, Is. 23:1–18.

10. Cush—*Sudan, Somalia*: Will fall by the sword, Ez. 30:5; They will feel God's blazing wrath, Ez. 38:19–23; God will enter into judgment against them, Joel 3:2–4; Slain by the sword, Zeph. 2:12; Cush and Phut, Lydia (Turkey) and all Arabia, and Libya will fall by the sword along with Egypt, Ez. 30:5; They will be lead away into captivity, Is. 20:1–5.

   Phut, *Libya*: Will fall by the sword, Ez. 30:5; They will feel God's blazing wrath, Ez. 38:19–23; God will enter into judgment against them, Joel 3:2–4; Slain by the sword, Zeph. 2:12; Cush and Phut, Lydia (Turkey) and all Arabia, as well as Libya twill fall by the sword along with Egypt, Ez. 30:5; God will cut of the shoots with pruning knives, Is. 18:5–7.

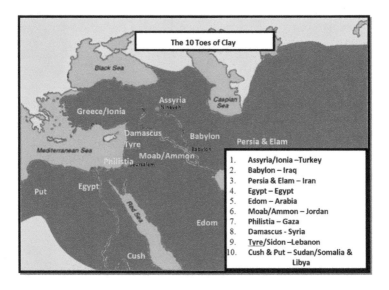

If we incorporate both Assyria and Ionia (East and West Turkey) as one nation for their judgments mirror each other, as well as Cush and Phut for the same reason, then we have a total of ten nations which God will judge. These nations than correspond to the ten toes of Daniel's prophecy (Dan. 2:31–35), which *"a stone was cut out without hands* (Christ)*,"* will destroy on *"the day of the LORD."* Nowhere does scripture indicate that Europe, America, or the Far East will be judged, it's all Middle-East centric. To try to spiritualize these countries into becoming the whole world today, to include America, is preposterous and is just bad hermeneutics and exegesis.

Scholars are unanimous in their agreement that Christ's second coming must happen *after* the Antichrist appears on the scene. Thus Christ's mission will be to destroy the Antichrist and establish His Millennium kingdom. The "European-Roman Model" of eschatology as our Prophecy Buff's claim has the religion of Islam destroyed before the Tribulation period. However, scriptures show that Jesus Himself deals with these nations when He returns. These nations all happen to be Muslim today and the likely hood of the religion of Islam (which is the fastest growing religion in the world today) being destroyed or going away in the near future and no-longer existing is again preposterous.

In every portrayal of Christ's return to the earth, He is fighting a nation that is today an Islamic nation! The significance of this statement is enormous, for the Wrath of God is poured out *on the people who had the mark of the beast and who worshiped his image* (Rev. 16:2). For it is against the ungodly that practice this false religion and who will not obey God's laws. Make no mistake, that the religion of Islam is a counterfeit to all that which is Holy.

It is important to also understand that these nations are all punished for striking terror against Israel and the elect. Thus, Islam as a destructive religious delusion created by Satan joins terror by way of the sword with that of hatred for all that is Holy of God into a powerful weapon against all nonbelievers (those who worship something other than Allah).

The Qur'an states that all people will submit to the religion of Islam one way or another, and Mohammad claimed that the greatest way to submission is by the use of the sword, *"For they poured out the blood of saints and prophets"* (Rev. 16:6). And how did they accomplish this? *"And I saw the souls of those who had been beheaded Because of their testimony of Jesus and because of the word of God, and those who had not worshiped the beast or his image, and had not received the mark on their forehead and on their hand"* (Rev. 20:4). So can there be any doubt as to who God will Judge.

A look at Jeremiah 25:15–26 specifically spells out to whom the cup of God's Wrath is poured out upon. The focus of this wrath is on the Middle East and those who have oppressed His chosen people, and *"the fifth angel poured out his bowl on the throne of the beast"* (Rev. 16:10), those who have embraced this false religious delusion of Islam, which envelopes *"every tribe, tongue, people, and nation."*

Yes, the nations of the world will be judged according to how they treated Israel, but the wrath is directed against these ten nations whom from ancient times have hated and plotted to destroy God's Holy people and whom have done violence to the sons of Israel throughout history, to include today. *"All of them are slain* (these 10 nations), *fallen by the sword* (of Christ), *whose graves are set in the remotest parts of the pit* (hell) *and her company is round about her grave.*

All of them are slain, fallen by the sword, who spread terror in the land of the living (Israel)*"* (Ez. 32:22–23).

With that said, it is important to understand that we as Christians are not called to suffer the Wrath of God, but we will suffer man's wrath which takes place during the seven year tribulation period, which has been called the Great Tribulation or the Time of Jacobs troubles.

The Wrath occurs after Christ returns to the earth and we are raptured for *"the Lord* (Jesus) *Himself will descend from heaven with a shout, with the voice of the archangel, and with the trumpet of God; and the dead* (those who were martyred) *in Christ shall rise first. Then we who are alive and remain* (having endured the tribulation) *shall be caught up* (raptured) *together with them in the clouds, to meet the Lord* (Jesus) *in the air, and thus we shall always be with the Lord* (God)*"* (1 Thess. 4:13–17).

1 Thessalonians 5:9: *For God did not appoint us to wrath, but to obtain salvation through our Lord Jesus Christ.*

Romans 1:18: *For the wrath of God is revealed from heaven against all ungodliness and unrighteousness of men, who suppress the truth in unrighteousness.*

John 3:36: *He who believes in the Son has everlasting life; and he who does not believe the Son shall not see life, but the wrath of God abides on him.*

1 Peter 2:9: *Then the Lord knows how to deliver the godly out of temptations* (the rapture) *and to reserve the unjust under punishment* (wrath) *for the day of judgment.*

Ephesians 5:6: *Let no one deceive you with empty words, for because of these things the wrath of God comes upon the sons of disobedience.*

Revelation 15:1: *Then I saw another sign in heaven, great and marvelous: seven angels having the seven last plagues, for in them the wrath of God is complete. God wraps up all of His wrath.*

Luke 17:26–30: *And as it was in the days of Noah, so it will be also in the days of the Son of Man: They ate, they drank, they married wives, they were given in marriage, until the day that Noah entered the ark, and the flood came and destroyed them all. Likewise as it was also in the days of Lot: They ate, they drank, they bought, they sold, they planted, they built; but on the day that Lot went out of Sodom it rained fire and brimstone from heaven and destroyed them all. Even so will it be in the day* (the Day of the Lord) *when the Son of Man is revealed.*

2 Thessalonians 1:5–8: *Which is manifest evidence of the righteous judgment of God, that you may be counted worthy of the kingdom of God, for which you also suffer* (through the tribulation); *since it is a righteous thing with God to repay with tribulation those who trouble you, and to give you who are troubled rest* (by being removed during the rapture) *with us when the Lord Jesus is revealed* (the Second Coming) *from heaven with His mighty angels, in flaming fire taking vengeance* (pouring out God's Wrath) *on those who do not know God, and on those who do not obey the gospel of our Lord Jesus Christ.*

It is interesting to note that the Redemption of the believers and the Wrath of God all happen on the same day. To me this indicates that the Rapture will take place when Christ returns to pour out God's anger and vengeance on those who do not believe that Jesus is the son of God.

According to Islamic teachings, Isa (the Muslim Jesus) who is not the same as our Jesus, for the Muslim believe that Isa is not Allah's son (for Allah has no sons according to the Qur'an) and that he did not die on the cross, a counterfeit took his place and died while Isa was taken to heaven by Allah and he will return again after the Mahdi (the Muslim Messiah) has established himself as the Caliph of Islam (the new world leader). Isa will then tell the Christians that they were never to worship him and that we got it wrong, he is not Allah's son and we are only to worship Allah and out of obligation we are to fight against the Jews; at which point the Qur'an states that the rocks and the trees will cry out that there is a Jew hiding behind me come and kill him. Thus the Christian's who convert to Islam will be among those killing the Jews and if you don't convert then Isa and his followers will kill you along with the Jews.

So here again we see the counterfeit tactics of Satan in the perversion of our Scriptures and in the creation of his, the Qur'an. We worship one God, they worship one god; we have Jesus as the Messiah, they have Isa working with the Mahdi who is their messiah; we have two beast who will mislead people and be thrown into the pit, they have two beast who will mislead the infidels and be thrown into the pit, etc.... So I do not see God allowing the religion of Islam to just fade off into oblivion or be destroyed by man as some of our church fathers and Prophecy Buffs teach. Even today, there are many followers of John Calvin who taught that the sound of the great trumpet carries Islam into the Great Tribulation where he believed Islam would be removed (destroyed) prior to Christ's second coming and thus the Muslims are not the ones who feel God's wrath.[43]

However, God will have to have a hand in the demise of this counterfeit false religion, so all the world will know that He is God and He is Just, hence it has to be God's wrath which will destroy Islam. Just as Luther taught "The Turks are certainly the last and most furious raging of the devil against Christ...after the Turk comes the judgment."[44] Thus according to Luther the Turks would be allowed dominion for a time, but then would be destroyed on the "Day of the Lord" when God pours out His Wrath and Judgment, for these nations are all punished for striking terror against Israel and His elect.

> "*And the beast* (the false religion of Islam) *was seized, and with him the false prophet* (the Antichrist) *who performed the signs in his presence, by which he deceived those* (every tribe, tongue, people, and nation) *who had received the mark of the beast and those who worshiped his image; these*

---

43. *Calvin's Commentary on the Bible, Revelation* (Philadelphia: Westminster Press, 1958).

44. *Luther's Works, Volume 46* (Minneapolis: Augsburg Publishing House, 1959), 170.

two were thrown alive into the lake of fire which burns with brimstone. And the rest were killed with the sword which came from the mouth of Him (Christ) *who sat on the horse."* (Rev. 19:20–21)

So now you know "the rest of the story" as Paul Harvey use to say.

Notes on Revelation 16

The Seven Bowels

In John's Revelation, he is taken up into heaven and is standing in the throne-room of God where he is given insight into what will happen in the last days leading up to and including what will take place on the *"Day of His Fierce Wrath."* As I have stated before, this insight is revealed to us in two parallel, but separate set of interwoven visions, which take place both in heaven and on Earth. Both sets of visions start with a broad overall big picture of what will take place as we have seen in chapters 6 and 12. Then the picture is refined with more detail, which we find in chapters 8 and 9, as well as what we will see in chapters 17–19. Finally the picture is brought into focus here in chapter 16 with the first set of parallel visions and as we well see, in chapters 19–21, which will complete the second set of parallel visions.

The Seven Seals are a literal, chronological series of events leading up to the return of the Lord. The Seven Trumpets should be viewed as allegory (an indirect method representing truths or ideas) depicting the false religious dilution, which has swept over mankind. The Seven Bowls on the other hand, need to be taken literally, for they act as a reminder of what happened when the Israelites were held in captivity and they are a foreshadowing of things to come for the followers of the beast. *"What was will be again, nothing is new under the sun."*

Now these events/plagues depicted through these Seven Bowls, while similar to the ten plagues, are not a repeat of them. Because these plagues are much more severe than the original plagues. While they are a depiction of what Egypt went through with the ten plagues of Moses (yet Pharaoh's heart was hardened, just like the Antichrist and his follower's hearts will be) for *"they did not repent of their deeds."* These plagues completes the vision by focusing in on what God will do to mankind to get their attention and yet *"they still blasphemed God."*

The key to understanding the Seven Bowls of plagues is identifying to whom they are poured out on. Well, these plagues are directed against *"the people who had the mark of the beast."* The followers of the beast who received the mark, *chragma*, these are the tormentors of mankind, for inflicting their terror on those who do not worship their god. Thus the Lord God will inflict them with these plagues, which correlate with what they had inflected on the Jewish/Christian believer, the ones who did not take the mark of the beast. In other words, what the followers of the beast did to the believers, God will do back to them only more severely.

So what did the followers of the beast do to the believer other than behead them? Well if the believer did not submit to the religion of the beast (by the way, *Islam* means submission) or take *"the mark of the beast,"* than they were not *"able to buy or to sell"* anything in order to sustain life and live. Revelation 7:14–17 states that *"These are the ones* (the believers) *who come out of the great tribulation... They* (the believers) *will hunger no longer, nor thirst anymore; nor will the sun beat down on them, nor any heat."* The accompanying clause to the passage indicates that the believers have to endure something. They have to go through the tribulation, for they are not able to buy or sell because they did not receive the mark. They are NOT able to buy or sell anything (i.e., food and drink, nor do they have any shelter to keep the sun off their backs because they can't buy homes or rent living places), and so they are at the mercy of their oppressors (they fall under *Dhimmitude*) because they have not received the mark of the beast.

Dhimmitude applies to all non-Muslim populations who were vanquished by a *jihad*-war and governed by pure Islamic *shari'a* law encompassing all theological, social, political, and economic levels. In other words, you are considered a slave (*dhimmi*) and have no rights under Islam, thus you cannot even feed your family without the permission from the Muslim authorities and you are also forced to pay the (*jizya*) tax, which under the strict Islamic *shari'a* doctrine, all non-Muslims (*dhimmi*) living under Muslim sovereignty must pay in return for protection.

Thus it will also be with the followers of the beast, they will suffer hunger and thirst and the sun will scorch them with fire and heat, which correlates with the second, third, and fourth bowls. However, God pays back much more and make these plagues severer than what the Egyptians experienced. Not only will these followers of the beast suffer hunger and heat and have loathsome and malignant sores on their bodies, but they also experience a darkness in which *"they gnawed their tongues because of the pain."* Then, cataclysmic events take place, which will make the followers of the beast hate and blaspheme God even more. For *"THE SUN WILL BE DARKENED, AND THE MOON WILL NOT GIVE ITS LIGHT, AND THE STARS WILL FALL from the sky, and the powers of the heavens will be shaken"* and will descend upon those who have taken the mark of the beast.

These followers of the beast, from *"every tribe, tongue, people, and nation,"* will ultimately seek refuge in the rock and caves to hide themselves from the Wrath of God which will soon be poured out on them:

> *And there was a great earthquake; and the sun became black as sackcloth made of hair, and the whole moon became like blood; and the stars of the sky fell to the earth... The sky was split apart like a scroll when it is rolled up, and every mountain and island were moved out of their places. Then the kings of the earth and the great men and the commanders and the rich and the strong and every slave and free man* (those who had the mark of the beast) *hid themselves in the caves and among the rocks of the mountains; and they *said to the mountains and to the rocks, "Fall on us and hide us from the presence of Him* (God) *who sits on the throne, and from the wrath of the Lamb* (Jesus); *for the great day of their* (the Holy Trinity) *wrath has come, and who is able to stand?"* (Rev. 6:12–17)

Revelation

CHAPTER 17

New American Standard Bible (NASB)

The Doom of Babylon

¹⁷ Then one of the seven angels who had the seven bowls came and spoke with me, saying, "Come here, I will show you the judgment of the great harlot who sits on many waters, ² with whom the kings of the earth committed acts of immorality, and those who dwell on the earth were made drunk with the wine of her immorality." ³ And he carried me away in the Spirit into a wilderness; and I saw a woman sitting on a scarlet beast, full of blasphemous names, having seven heads and ten horns. ⁴ The woman was clothed in purple and scarlet, and adorned with gold and precious stones and pearls, having in her hand a gold cup full of abominations and of the unclean things of her immorality, ⁵ and on her forehead a name was written, a mystery, "BABYLON THE GREAT, THE MOTHER OF HARLOTS AND OF THE ABOMINATIONS OF THE EARTH." ⁶ And I saw the woman drunk with the blood of the saints, and with the blood of the witnesses of Jesus. When I saw her, I wondered greatly. ⁷ And the angel said to me, "Why do you wonder? I will tell you the mystery of the woman and of the beast that carries her, which has the seven heads and the ten horns.

⁸ "The beast that you saw was, and is not, and is about to come up out of the abyss and go to destruction. And those who dwell on the earth, whose name has not been written in the book of life from the foundation of the world, will wonder when they see the beast, that he was and is not and will come. ⁹ Here is the mind which has wisdom. The seven heads are seven mountains on which the woman sits, ¹⁰ and they are seven kings; five have fallen, one is, the other has not yet come; and when he comes, he must remain a little while. ¹¹ The beast which was and is not, is himself also an eighth and is one of the seven, and he goes to destruction. ¹² The ten horns which you saw are ten kings who have not yet received a kingdom, but they receive authority as kings with the beast for one hour. ¹³ These have one purpose, and they give their power and authority to the beast.

Victory for the Lamb

¹⁴ These will wage war against the Lamb, and the Lamb will overcome them, because He is Lord of lords and King of kings, and those who are with Him are the called and chosen and faithful."

¹⁵ And he *said to me, "The waters which you saw where the harlot sits, are peoples and multitudes and nations and tongues. ¹⁶ And the ten horns which you saw, and the beast, these will hate the harlot and will make her desolate and naked, and will eat her flesh and will burn her up with fire. ¹⁷ For God has put it in their hearts to execute His purpose by having a common purpose, and by giving their kingdom to the beast, until the words of God will be fulfilled. ¹⁸ The woman whom you saw is the great city, which reigns over the kings of the earth."

Notes on Revelation 17

Understanding the Mother of all Harlots

Chapters 17 and 18 are part of the Second Preview which gives the reader a closer look at God's triumph over Babylon. This second preview of the interwoven visions, becomes the refined picture which culminates in chapter 19 with the Victory and Marriage of the Lamb. However, here in chapters 17 and 18 we are given a glimpse into the *"judgment of the great harlot"* and to whom *"fallen Babylon"* refers to.

So Satan who desires to be *"like the Most High,"* creates a destructive religious delusion which will deceive and torment mankind. This deception is portrayed through John's vision here in chapter 17 as *"the great harlot."* The Greek word used is *porna* from which we get the word pornography from. It is closely linked to the word *eros,* which is one of the three major types of love. *Agapa* is God-centered unconditional love, *philio* is brotherly love shown to our fellow man, *eros* is sexual intimate love between man and wife, and *porna* is erotic sex outside the confines of marriage.

Metaphorically, she is called *"the great harlot who sits on many waters,"* because as we have already discovered in Revelation 13, this lie *"rises out of the sea"* of humanity, which is described as *"every tribe, tongue, people, and nation."* They are represented as *"many waters"* because of the countless waves that ebb and flow which are always moving and surging and are seldom at rest. So there can be no doubt here, God tells us actually what the waters represent; *"The waters which you saw where the harlot sits, are peoples and multitudes and nations and tongues"* (Rev. 17:15).

She sits on them because she has control over them, thus the symbolism is one sitting on a throne controlling the movement all around her throne. The image that comes to mind is the Kaaba in Mecca during the Hajj with the masses of people flowing around the Kaaba in a counter-clockwise direction moving in and out trying to touch the black stone on the eastern corner in order to gain Allah's favor.

This harlot is not a bride and is not called an "adulteress" thought she does *"commit acts of immorality"* with the kings of the earth and those who dwell on the earth. The metaphor of the Harlot is in opposition to the Woman Israel found in Revelation 12:1–5, *"A great sign appeared in heaven: a woman clothed with the sun, and the moon under her feet, and on her head a crown of twelve stars; and she was with child... And she gave birth to a son, a male child, who is to rule all the nations with a rod of iron; and her child was caught up to God and to His throne."* Now many think and believe that the Woman represents the Church or Mary herself; however symbolically she represents Israel from which the Messiah will come forth to save the world.

The Harlot on the other hand is a counterfeit to the Women; she is also a daughter and sits on a throne as queen, however her reign will come to an end. *"O virgin daughter of Babylon... Your nakedness will be uncovered, your shame also will be exposed... Sit silently, and go into darkness, O daughter of the Chaldeans, for you will no longer be called the queen of kingdoms"* (Isaiah 47:1–5).

Her acts of immorality are not sexual in nature as some Prophecy Buffs teach, but they are used to draw someone into idolatry to worship a false god. The Greek word *porneuō*, meaning immorality (see Strong's G4203) is described as a *Hebraism* in Thayer's Greek Lexicon and is used throughout Revelation 17 and 18, as to permit oneself to be drawn away by another into idolatry. 1 Chronicles 5:25 states: *"But they* (the people of Israel) *acted treacherously against the God of their fathers and played the harlot after the gods of the peoples of the land, whom God had destroyed before them."* The expression of being a harlot is used throughout the Old Testament to symbolize worshiping false gods/idolatry and so it should be applied here as well (see Psalms 73:27, Jeremiah 3:6, Ezekiel 23:19, Hosea 9:1).

The *"Kings of the earth"* represents those who are in power ruling over nations, while *"those who dwell on the earth"* represent those who are separated from God through their own unbelief, they are caught up in idolatry and false worship. *"Then you will see and be radiant, and your heart will thrill and rejoice; because the abundance of the sea will be turned to you, the wealth of the nations will come to you"* (Isaiah 60:5).

The vision changes at v. 3 and John sees the harlot seated upon *"a scarlet beast, full of blasphemous names, having seven heads and ten horns."* This beast is the virtual image of the dragon, who is Satan, whom he bestows with all authority and power (see notes on Revelation 17:9–14 to understand the seven headed beast). The harlot is adorned with purple and scarlet robes and every kind of gold and silver trinket which represents the wealth of the nations. She holds a golden *"cup full of abominations and of the unclean things of her immorality."*

The Apostle Timothy supplies us with a clue to what these are when he wrote *"in later times some will fall away from the faith, paying attention to deceitful spirits and doctrines of demons,"* thus her abominations and immorality is the destructive religious delusion which deceives mankind.

What clear image is there for us readers of John's revelation then the name written on the forehead of this harlot, *"Babylon the Great, the Mother of Harlots and of the Abominations of the Earth,"* for this statement tells us exactly who we are dealing with. The term *"Mother of"* is a Middle Eastern expression of a superlative, representing the biggest, bad-est, worst, or most significant! Just like when Saddam Hussein claimed that at the end of the first Gulf War that Iraq had won the *"Mother of all Battles."*

So this harlot represents the most significant religious delusion that there is (which Satan has created to be a counterfeit of God's perfect work) and it is found within the conglomeration of all the historical enemies of Israel. She also represents the most destructive force against the followers of God. *"And I saw the woman drunk with the blood of the saints, and with the blood of the witnesses of Jesus."*

This is not just a superlative statement, it a factual statement, for Revelation 20:4 makes it very clear who we are dealing with; *"And I saw the souls of those who had been beheaded because of their testimony of Jesus and because of the word of God, and those who had not worshiped the beast or his image, and had not received the mark on their forehead and on their hand."*

Now what could that be but the Religion of Islam for who else today takes pleasure in beheading people. We saw this recently on the news with what ISIL/S (the Islamic State of Iraq and Levant/Syria) was doing to their enemies. Islam teaches that the use of the sword is the greatest form of submission, for all will submit to Islam in one way or another.

Notes on Revelation 17

The Key to Understanding Revelation 17:9–14

Now the term *"Babylon the Great"* does not refer to ancient Babylon itself, but it refers to a type of Babylon which is a religious governmental entity emanating from the geographical area of what was once the territory controlled by Babylon, Persia and Greece. Which today is all Islamically controlled.

This harlot who is sitting on the Beast with the seven heads and ten horns, *"And I saw a woman sitting on a scarlet beast, full of blasphemous names, having seven heads and ten horns"* (Rev. 17:3), is none other than Daniel's four beasts combined. For the four parts of Daniel's statue in chapter 2 corresponds to the four beasts in his later vision found in chapter 7. They all rise out of the sea of humanity and become great kingdoms/empires (Daniel 7:17). However, this last empire with its iron teeth and bronze claws is *"different from all the other empires"* for it crushes and devours its victims and tramples everything else underfoot, vv. 19 and 23.

This fourth beast wages war against the saints (the Christian believers) and will have power over them for *"a time, times and half a time"* (3.5 years) v. 25, which represents the last days before *"the Day of the Lord's Wrath"* is poured out.

The ten horns corresponds to the ten toes in Daniel's statue, which represent ten kings/nations that will all arise from this last empire to assist in the war against the saints. The arrogant little horn which arise among the other ten horns which speaks blasphemous things against God, becomes an eleventh horn which will uproot three of its own type in order to *"change the set times and the laws,"* which God has ordained, vv. 20–22 and 24–25, this is the Antichrist himself.

However, when we are in doubt, scripture has a way of coming to our rescue to tell us exactly what is implied through the symbolism here. So if we look at Revelation 17:9–14 we are given the answer to what the seven heads and ten horns represent. For *"this calls for a mind with wisdom,"* in order to understand the symbolism found here for *"the seven heads are seven mountains,"* and mountains throughout scripture always represent Kingdoms or in reality Empires. When we think of the Babylonian Empire or the Persian Empire or even the Greek Empire, we think of more than a kingdom, we think of all the territory/nations that were conquered to make up the vast empire. So it is here, the mountains represent many hills which make up this huge kingdom, hence the term empire is appropriate to apply here to each of the seven heads.

What confuse our Prophecy Buffs are the next two sentences which describe the seven mountains as seven kings. *"They are also seven kings. Five have fallen, one is, the other has not yet come; but when he does come, he must remain for a little while."*

When a king dies, the kingdom does not die with him, most of the time there is a transition from one king unto another, thus the kingdom continues. However, kingdoms cease to exist when they are conquered. So what we have here is a metaphor or comparison to the symbolism of the mountains, for mountains don't die or fade away they remain, thus John needs to lead us to the understanding that these mountains/empires have fallen and are completely done away with, thus the metaphor of kings.

The five fallen kings/mountains/empires represent: Egypt, Assyria, Babylon, Persia, and Greece. The one that is, will take place in the future sometime after the Revelation/vision was recorded by John. It does not equate to the present time that John was living in, hence as many Prophecy Buffs interpret (representing the Roman Empire), nor is it describing a city build on seven hills (i.e., Rome) but some future empire that conquers the same territories as the Babylonian, Persian, and Greek Empires controlled.

So let's look at the following maps of the territories which comprise these empires to gain a better understanding of what I have been talking about:

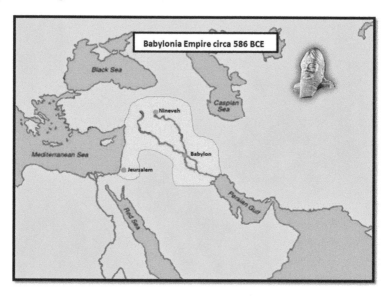

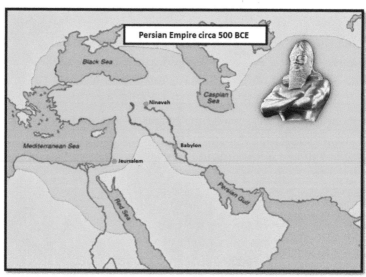

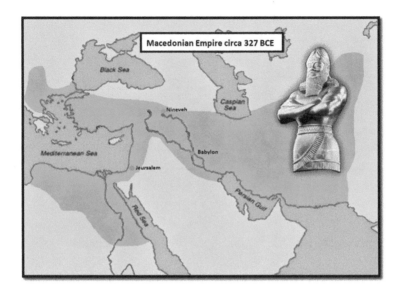

Rome does not fit the paradigm, for it did not conquer the city of Babylon itself or any of the territories beyond the Euphrates River which made up the largest portion of the empire. So just based on geography itself, Rome did not conquer the last empire of Greece, for Greece reached all the way to India and the Himalayan Mountains. Rome focused on conquering the Mediterranean world and up into northern Europe and England. The Romans were afraid of the Parthians who lived beyond the Euphrates River.

First century readers would have made the connection to the Parthians immediately and would have realized that Rome was not this empire that John was prophesizing about. Because in 103 AD the Emperor Trajan would launch a campaign against the Parthians who had been moving steadily into Roman territories west of the Euphrates River. However, the Roman Legions were defeated one hundred miles from Babylon and never went any further, nor did they even attempt to cross the Tigris River to push eastward.

The Parthians were fierce warriors who were also expert horse-men and equally efficient with the war bow. It is a said that they could shoot an arrow behind them with supreme accuracy at an enemy as they rode way. Hence, the Parthian shot has become known as "the parting shot." The Roman Empire never again ventured further east to Babylon.

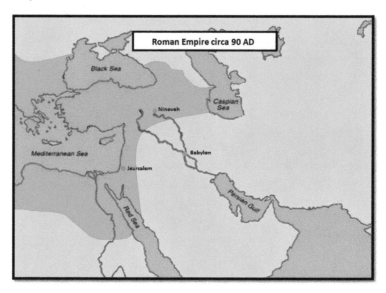

The only empire that conquered the same territory that Babylon, Persia, and Greece conquered is the Islamic Empire. This empire became the six empire which ceased to exist after 1917 with the fall of the Ottoman Empire at the end of World War 1. And as I have stated before, this empire will be resurrected during the latter days and will become the future seventh empire from which the Antichrist will emerge. For *"one is, the other has not yet come; but when he does come, he must remain for a little while."*

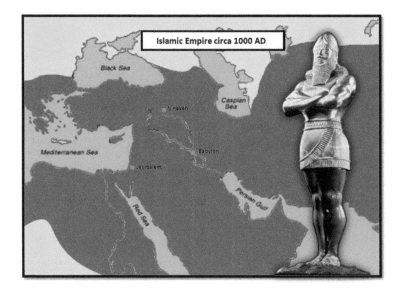

Now let us look at the ten horns found in Revelation 17:12–14 and see what they represent and how they relate back to Daniel chapters 2, 4, and Revelation 12. We are told in v. 12 that *"the ten horns you saw are ten kings who have not yet received a kingdom, but who for one hour will receive authority as kings along with the beast."* These ten horns which also correspond to the ten toes in Daniel's statue are a continuation of the metaphor found in v. 10 representing kings/leaders/nations that will all arise from this last empire with one purpose only, and that is to assist the Antichrist in the war against Christ *"the Lamb"* of God.

These kings are the leaders of nations which will join together with the Antichrist, for they receive their power and authority from the Beast and lead their nations to unite with the Antichrist in rebellion against God. Both the nations and the empires belong to the seven headed Beast and are part of the Beast, though they function differently. We are also told that they belong together and will ultimately be destroyed together when *"the Day of the Lord's Wrath"* is poured out.

The metaphor of *"the beast who once was, and now is not, is an eighth king. He belongs to the seven and is going to his destruction"* (v.

11), helps us the reader distinguish between the horns as individual nations within the larger context of the heads symbolizing empires. However, this eleventh king who belongs to the seven headed Beast, also represented by the little horn which arises among the ten horns, is the Antichrist himself; who belongs to the Beast and exercises all the authority and power of the Beast, but is not the Beast. For the Beast itself is an empire made up of an all-encompassing religious, political, socio-economic, militaristic entity in which the Antichrist will be its leader/king. If this leader is to control the Islamic world, than this leader/Antichrist must also be the Caliph of Islam. For that is the only way he will be able to control the ten toe nations surrounding Israel.

Revelation

CHAPTER 18

New American Standard Bible (NASB)

Babylon Is Fallen

¹⁸ After these things I saw another angel coming down from heaven, having great authority, and the earth was illumined with his glory. ² And he cried out with a mighty voice, saying, "Fallen, fallen is Babylon the great! She has become a dwelling place of demons and a prison of every unclean spirit, and a prison of every unclean and hateful bird. ³ For all the nations have drunk of the wine of the passion of her immorality, and the kings of the earth have committed acts of immorality with her, and the merchants of the earth have become rich by the wealth of her sensuality."

⁴ I heard another voice from heaven, saying, "Come out of her, my people, so that you will not participate in her sins and receive of her plagues; ⁵ for her sins have piled up as high as heaven, and God has remembered her iniquities. ⁶ Pay her back even as she has paid, and give back to her double according to her deeds; in the cup which she has mixed, mix twice as much for her. ⁷ To the degree that she glorified herself and lived sensuously, to the same degree give her torment and mourning; for she says in her heart, 'I SIT AS A QUEEN AND I *AM NOT A* WIDOW, *and will never see mourning.' ⁸ For this reason in one day her plagues will come, pestilence and mourning and famine, and she will be burned up with fire; for the Lord God who judges her is strong.*

Lament for Babylon

⁹ *"And the kings of the earth, who committed acts of immorality and lived sensuously with her, will weep and lament over her when they see the smoke of her burning,*
¹⁰ *standing at a distance because of the fear of her torment, saying, 'Woe, woe, the great city, Babylon, the strong city! For in one hour your judgment has come.'*

¹¹ *"And the merchants of the earth weep and mourn over her, because no one buys their cargoes anymore—¹² cargoes of gold and silver and precious stones and pearls and fine linen and purple and silk and scarlet, and every kind of citron wood and every article of ivory and every article made from very costly wood and bronze and iron and marble,* ¹³ *and cinnamon and spice and incense and perfume and frankincense and wine and olive oil and fine flour and wheat and cattle and sheep, and cargoes of horses and chariots and slaves and human lives.* ¹⁴ *The fruit you long for has gone from you, and all things that were luxurious and splendid have passed away from you and men will no longer find them.* ¹⁵ *The merchants of these things, who became rich from her, will stand at a distance because of the fear of her torment, weeping and mourning,* ¹⁶ *saying, 'Woe, woe, the great city, she who was clothed in fine linen and purple and scarlet, and adorned with gold and precious stones and pearls;* ¹⁷ *for in one hour such great wealth has been laid waste!' And every shipmaster and every passenger and sailor, and as many as make their living by the sea, stood at a distance,* ¹⁸ *and were crying out as they saw the smoke of her burning, saying, 'What city is like the great city?'* ¹⁹ *And they threw dust on their heads and were crying out, weeping and mourning, saying, 'Woe, woe, the great city, in which all who had ships at sea became rich by her wealth, for in one hour she has been laid waste!'* ²⁰ *Rejoice over her, O heaven, and you saints and apostles and prophets, because God has pronounced judgment for you against her."*

²¹ *Then a strong angel took up a stone like a great millstone and threw it into the sea, saying, "So will Babylon, the great city, be thrown down with violence, and will not be found any longer.* ²² *And the sound*

of harpists and musicians and flute-players and trumpeters will not be heard in you any longer; and no craftsman of any craft will be found in you any longer; and the sound of a mill will not be heard in you any longer; 23 and the light of a lamp will not shine in you any longer; and the voice of the bridegroom and bride will not be heard in you any longer; for your merchants were the great men of the earth, because all the nations were deceived by your sorcery. 24 And in her was found the blood of prophets and of saints and of all who have been slain on the earth."

Notes on Revelation 18

Understanding Metaphor of Fallen Babylon

The scene in this preview changes at the opening of chapter 18 with *"After these things I saw another angel coming down from heaven..."* which now describes the fall of Babylon and completes the victory over Satan. Chapters 17 and 18 mark this Second Preview of the refined picture displaying God's triumph over Babylon and the Harlot. However, the term *meta tauta, "After these things,"* points us back to the seven churches and the *"end of the church age"* and not to the preceding chapter where the harlot is revealed.

The phrase *"After these things,"* does not follow chronologically after Revelation 17:18, but moves the reader back to the beginning of the book where Christ himself tells the Disciple John to write down what he see in the past, the present, and in the future. *"Write, therefore, what you have seen* (past), *what is now* (present) *and what will take place after these things* (future)"* (Rev. 1:19).

The Greek word *meta tauta,* after these things, denotes that these future events become one significant event which John is instructed to record. Revelation 4:1 continues with a dual emphasis of *meta tauta,* by stating *"After these things I looked...and the voice... said...I will show you what must take place after these things."* Thus *"these things"* in the present become *"these things"* in the future (prophetic) which must happen before Christ is seated on the throne with His Father.

Thus the keys to understanding how the *prophetic application of this scene* fits into the Book of Revelation can be found in chapters 4:1, 7:9, 18:1, and 19:1. They all point the reader back to chapters 2 and 3, which deals with the seven churches whom prophetically become the *"Church age."* Hence, the term applied here means that *"after"* the *"end of the church age"* and the *"great falling away" "these things"* will take place. What things you ask, well the destruction of Babylon.

The Metaphor of *"Fallen, fallen is Babylon the great"* here in verse 2, helps the reader distinguish between the women riding the beast (the Mother of all Harlots) and the beast itself in the larger context symbolizing the empire of Babylon. For the Beast (the first Beast of Revelation 13), is an empire made up of an all-encompassing religious, political, socio-economic, and militaristic entity. The Harlot then represents the leading nation who controls and directs this evil empire. However, as we have just seen in chapter 17, the other nations of the empire will *"hate the harlot and will make her desolate and naked, and will eat her flesh and will burn her up with fire"* (Rev. 17:16). In other words, they will make war against this one nation and do away with her, because they are tired of being controlled and manipulated by her, do to her influence, power, and wealth.

> *"Therefore, behold, I will gather all your lovers with whom you took pleasure, even all those whom you loved and all those whom you hated. So I will gather them against you from every direction and expose your nakedness to them that they may see all your nakedness... I will also give you into the hands of your lovers, and they will tear down your shrines, demolish your high places, strip you of your clothing, take away your jewels, and will leave you naked and bare. They will incite a crowd against you and they will stone you and cut you to pieces with their swords. They will burn your houses with fire and execute judgments on you... Then I will stop you from playing the harlot"* (Ez. 16:37–41).

With the fall of the Ottoman Empire at the end of World War I in 1918, there was a resurgence of nationalism in which many separate ethnic groups pushed to form their own countries. However in the Middle East, the Sykes-Picot Agreement (a secret agreement between the governments of the United Kingdom, France, and Russia) defined their proposed spheres of influence and control. This agreement effectively divided the Ottoman Empire and the provinces of Arabia, Mesopotamia, and Persia, into the modern-day countries of Saudi Arabia, Jordon, Lebanon, Palestine, Iraq, and Iran with Turkey breaking away and effectively fighting for their own independence from British, Italian, and Greek control in 1923.

With the discovery of vast oil reserves in the Persian Gulf in 1938, Saudi Arabia now had economic prosperity and developed substantial political leverage over all the other Mid-East nations. *"For all the nations have drunk of the wine of the passion of her immorality, and the kings of the earth have committed acts of immorality with her, and the merchants of the earth have become rich by the wealth of her luxury"* (Rev. 18:3). Saudi Arabia also held control over the religion as well due to the fact that it contains the two holiest sites, the cities of Mecca and Medina which are of the cradle of Islam. Control of Mecca has always been vital for the control of the religion, for it is the destination of the only pilgrimage required in the Qur'an.

The Five Pillars of Islam are the framework of Islamic life, they are (1) The testimony of faith which states that there is no other god but Allah, (2) praying five times a day, (3) giving zakat (support of the needy), (4) fasting during the month of Ramadan, and (5) the pilgrimage to Mecca. Now according to this fifth pillar, the obligatory Islamic pilgrimage, called the *hajj*, has to be performed during the Islamic month of Dhu al-Hijjah in the city of Mecca and every able-bodied Muslim who can afford it must make the pilgrimage to Mecca at least once in his or her lifetime. That's a lot of people and money flowing into Saudi Arabia which gives them almost complete control and influence over the followers of the religion.

However, there was a split in the religion back in the eighth century between the Sunni-Umayyad dynasty and the Shiite—'Abbasid dynasty, which according to some Muslim historians, claim that 'Abd al-Malik of the 'Abbasid dynasty, built the Dome of the Rock (in 691 AD) as an attempt to relocate the site of the Muslim hajj from Mecca to Jerusalem.

Why you ask, because the Sunni's controlled the Ka'bah and have had a substantial influence on everyone making the hajj. Changing the location of the pilgrimage from Mecca to Jerusalem would effectively change the balance of power to the Shiite. Thus, this split has continued to be the cause of contention within the Mid-east today. I submit to you that this split is the reason for the hatred of the Harlot (Saudi Arabia) whom they will destroy to make Jerusalem the new center of Islam. *"For she says in her heart, 'I SIT AS A QUEEN AND I AM NOT A WIDOW, and will never see mourning'"* (Rev. 18:7).

Isaiah 47:8–10 also states, *"Now, then, hear this, you sensual one, who dwells securely, who says in your heart, 'I am, and there is no one besides me. I will not sit as a widow, nor know loss of children.' "But these two things will come on you suddenly in one day: Loss of children and widowhood. They will come on you in full measure In spite of your many sorceries, In spite of the great power of your spells. "You felt secure in your wickedness and said, 'No one sees me,' your wisdom and your knowledge, they have deluded you; for you have said in your heart, 'I am, and there is no one besides me.'"*

However her boasts are for naught, for the prophet Jeremiah tells us that the Assyrians and the Medes will come against the Harlot,

"For a nation has come up against her out of the north; it will make her land an object of horror, and there will be no inhabitant in it... Lift up a signal in the land, blow a trumpet among the nations! Consecrate the nations against her, summon against her the kingdoms of Ararat, Minni and Ashkenaz; appoint a marshal against her, bring up the horses like bristly locusts. Consecrate the nations against her, the kings of the Medes, their governors and all

their prefects, and every land of their dominion"
(Jer. 51:27–28).

These nations are Turkey, from the north and Iran and Iraq from the east who also happen to be Islamic nations who will wage war against her to fulfill God's purpose. *"So the land quakes and writhes, for the purposes of the LORD against Babylon stand, To make the land of Babylon a desolation without inhabitants"* (Jer. 51:29).

Even Ezekiel prophesied against the Harlot; *"I will make you a desolation. As you rejoiced over the inheritance of the house of Israel because it was desolate, so I will do to you. You will be a desolation, O Mount Seir, and all Edom, all of it. Then they will know that I am the LORD"'* (Ez. 35:15). God causes the nations to rise up against their own and make her cities desolate because of what she has done to the house of Israel.

Now, it is important to remember how scripture is used here in the Book of Revelation, so understanding the literary style of Allegory, Metaphor, and Symbolism is vital to interpreting each verse and each chapter as a whole, especially here in chapters 17 and 18.

Allegory is the method of indirect representation of ideas or truths. It is a literary form where abstract ideas and principles are described in terms of characters, figures and events to tell a story with a purpose of teaching or explaining an idea or a principle (i.e., Revelation 13:1, *"Then I saw a beast coming up out of the sea, having ten horns and seven heads"* or here in Revelation 18:2, *"Fallen, fallen is Babylon the great! She has become a dwelling place of demons and a prison of every unclean spirit, and a prison of every unclean and hateful bird"*).

Metaphor is the literary form of expressing an analogy or simile. It is a way to compare two different things to make an interesting connection in the reader's mind like a word-picture (i.e., Revelation 20:2, *"The dragon, the serpent of old, who is the devil and Satan"* or in Revelation 8:3, *"For all the nations have drunk of the wine of the passion of her immorality, and the kings of the earth have committed acts of immorality with her, and the merchants of the earth have become rich by the power of her luxury"*).

Symbolism is the method of comparison whereby something stand for something else by reason of relationship or association (i.e., the lion is used as the symbol of courage or kingship; Revelation 5:5, *"Behold, the Lion that is from the tribe of Judah."* Also in Revelation 17:5, we understand that Babylon symbolizes all that which is evil; *"Babylon the Great, the Mother of Harlots and of the Abominations of the Earth"*).

So as we read chapters 17 and 18 we find all the literary forms of allegory, metaphor and symbolism entwined here to paint a picture for the reader that will be memorable. One that is not easily forgotten and one that is sure to bring hope to the reader:

> *"Then a strong angel took up a stone like a great millstone and threw it into the sea, saying, So will Babylon, the great city, be thrown down with violence, and will not be found any longer."* (Rev. 18:21)

Revelation

CHAPTER 19

New American Standard Bible (NASB)

The Fourfold Hallelujah

¹⁹ *After these things I heard something like a loud voice of a great multitude in heaven, saying,*

"Hallelujah! Salvation and glory and power belong to our God; ² BECAUSE HIS JUDGMENTS ARE TRUE AND RIGHTEOUS; *for He has judged the great harlot who was corrupting the earth with her immorality, and* HE HAS AVENGED THE BLOOD OF HIS BOND-SERVANTS ON HER." ³ *And a second time they said, "Hallelujah!* HER SMOKE RISES UP FOREVER AND EVER." ⁴ *And the twenty-four elders and the four living creatures fell down and worshiped God who sits on the throne saying, "Amen. Hallelujah!"* ⁵ *And a voice came from the throne, saying,*

"Give praise to our God, all you His bond-servants, you who fear Him, the small and the great." ⁶ *Then I heard something like the voice of a great multitude and like the sound of many waters and like the sound of mighty peals of thunder, saying,*

"Hallelujah! For the Lord our God, the Almighty, reigns.

Marriage of the Lamb

7 Let us rejoice and be glad and give the glory to Him, for the marriage of the Lamb has come and His bride has made herself ready." 8 It was given to her to clothe herself in fine linen, bright and clean; for the fine linen is the righteous acts of the saints.

9 Then he *said to me, "Write, 'Blessed are those who are invited to the marriage supper of the Lamb.'" And he *said to me, "These are true words of God." 10 Then I fell at his feet to worship him. But he *said to me, "Do not do that; I am a fellow servant of yours and your brethren who hold the testimony of Jesus; worship God. For the testimony of Jesus is the spirit of prophecy."

The Coming of Christ

11 And I saw heaven opened, and behold, a white horse, and He who sat on it is called Faithful and True, and in righteousness He judges and wages war. 12 His eyes are a flame of fire, and on His head are many diadems; and He has a name written on Him which no one knows except Himself. 13 He is clothed with a robe dipped in blood, and His name is called The Word of God. 14 And the armies which are in heaven, clothed in fine linen, white and clean, were following Him on white horses. 15 From His mouth comes a sharp sword, so that with it He may strike down the nations, and He will rule them with a rod of iron; and He treads the wine press of the fierce wrath of God, the Almighty. 16 And on His robe and on His thigh He has a name written, "KING OF KINGS, AND LORD OF LORDS."

17 Then I saw an angel standing in the sun, and he cried out with a loud voice, saying to all the birds which fly in midheaven, "Come, assemble for the great supper of God, 18 so that you may eat the flesh of kings and the flesh of commanders and the flesh of mighty men and the flesh of horses and of those who sit on them and the flesh of all men, both free men and slaves, and small and great."

¹⁹ And I saw the beast and the kings of the earth and their armies assembled to make war against Him who sat on the horse and against His army.

Doom of the Beast and False Prophet

²⁰ And the beast was seized, and with him the false prophet who performed the signs in his presence, by which he deceived those who had received the mark of the beast and those who worshiped his image; these two were thrown alive into the lake of fire which burns with brimstone. ²¹ And the rest were killed with the sword which came from the mouth of Him who sat on the horse, and all the birds were filled with their flesh.

Notes on Revelation 19

The Marriage of the Lamb

The scene on earth changes at the opening of chapter 19 with *meta tauta*, *"After these things,"* where the reader is directed back to the major event that John described in chapters 2 and 3, which deals with the seven churches whom prophetically become the "Church age." So just like in chapter 18 the term applied here means that *"after"* the end of the church age and the destruction of Babylon *"these things"* will take place. Again, what things you ask? Well, after the destruction of Babylon there is a Victory Celebration.

This new vision that now appears here in Revelation 19:1, John is no longer witnessing the destruction of Babylon and the Harlot, but he is witnessing a celebration in heaven where the multitudes sing out *"Hallelujah! Salvation and Glory and power to our God... Hallelujah! For the Lord our God, the Almighty, reigns."* For the victory is complete and Christ has defeated his foe and He is now reigning supreme!

Verse 19:2 is in the past tense aorist meaning that His just judgments have recently occurred and *"He has avenged the blood of His bond-servants..."* Thus he has completely avenged the martyred saints who lost their lives during the tribulation. The Harlot along with the Beast/Babylon who corrupted the earth with their false religion and idolatry will no longer be able to do so, for they have been judged and sentenced:

> *"I kept looking until thrones were set up, and the Ancient of Days took His seat...the court sat, and the books were opened...until the beast was slain,*

and its body was destroyed and given to the burning fire." (Dan. 7:1–11)

Not only is the beast slain but also the Antichrist is cast into the sea of fire. Remember that this sea or lake if fire is literal and not some metaphor, *"And the beast was seized, and with him the false prophet* (a.k.a. the Antichrist*)…these two were thrown alive into the lake of fire which burns with brimstone"* (Rev. 19:20).

This celebration scene is the Coronation Ceremony found in Daniel 7:13–14 where Christ is crowned *"King of Kings and Lord of Lords"* and then sits on the thrown of heaven and earth to reign over them. *"But when the Son of Man comes in His glory, and all the angels with Him, then He will sit on His glorious throne. All the nations will be gathered before Him; and He will separate them from one another, as the shepherd separates the sheep from the goats; and He will put the sheep on His right, and the goats on the left"* (Mt. 25:31–33).

Christ will then reign for a thousand years until such time when Satan is released (Rev. 20:7–10) and finally defeated. The Coronation scene follows the Great White Throne of Judgment scene (Rev. 20:11–15), which is depicted in the proper order in Daniel 7:9–14, but is out of sequence here in Revelation 19 for verses 11–21 precedes verse 1–10, which follows after Revelation 20:11–15.

The celebration of Christ's Coronation becomes two fold here because it moves into the Marriage Ceremony of the Lamb. *"Let us rejoice and be glade and give glory to Him, for the marriage of the Lamb has come…"* (Rev. 19:7). The marriage now takes place following on the heels of His coronation *"And His bride has made herself ready."*

However, here again John is describing an event that has already taken place, past tense. Notice that while the clothing represents the bride's righteousness, it's not her clothing, *"It was given to her."* Thus we are not righteous by our own works, but our righteousness is given to us by the Lord. The Apostle Paul makes this clear by stating that, *"He made Him who knew no sin to be sin on our behalf, that we might become the righteousness of God in Him"* (2 Cor. 5:21). The Greek word here in 19:8, *dikaiomata*, literally means righteousness rather than righteous acts.

Isaiah 61:10 describes this scene even more clearly.

> *"I rejoice greatly in the Lord, my soul will exult in my God; For He has clothed me with garments of salvation, He has wrapped me in a robe of righteousness, as a bridegroom decks himself with a garland, and as a bride adorns herself with her jewels."*

Now the marriage celebration is not depicted in this vision/revelation of John's, nor is the marriage feast, though they are self-evident. To attempt to separate the two means to depart from the imagery of the ancient wedding. First came the betrothal, which was made public; no priest or official were needed; only the heads of the two families sufficed. Second Corinthians 11:2 clearly states, *"For I am jealous for you with a godly jealousy; for I betrothed you to one husband, so that to Christ I might present you as a pure virgin."*

The betrothal was followed by an interval until the day when the groom led a festal procession to the bride's home, where she was waiting. *"Then the kingdom of heaven will be comparable to ten virgins, who took their lamps and went out to meet the bridegroom... But at midnight there was a shout, 'Behold, the bridegroom! Come out to meet him.' The bridegroom came, and those who were ready went in with him to the wedding feast"* (Mt. 25:1–10).

Then the groom brought the bride to his own home (the one he built for her) *"And I saw the holy city, new Jerusalem, coming down out of heaven from God, made ready as a bride adorned for her husband,"* where the festivities continued for a week or longer. This is what is being depicted here in this vision, the celebration, where the bride is brought to the groom's home.

John then changes to the present tense in speaking of those who are invited to the wedding banquet in verse 9. The guests are in reference to the believing survivors of the tribulation here on earth, who will soon to be invited into the Kingdom as described in the parable of the marriage feast (Mt. 22:1–14). Though the invitation is extended to all, however, it is not accepted by many and although they were invited, they are not allowed to enter the feast. *"But he (the bridegroom, i.e., Christ) answered, 'Truly I say to you, I do not know you'" (Mt. 25:12).* The perfect participle does not designate all who are invited, but only those who are blessed are welcome. For *"Blessed are those who are invited to the marriage supper of the Lamb."* These are the tribulation saints who are welcome, both living and dead, who are invited to the marriage feast.

The question that now arises is who is the Bride of Christ if it is not the Church? If God wants us to know then He will reveal it to us, so read down a couple of chapters and you find that God comes to our rescue and specifically tells us who the Bride is, *"Come here, I shall show you the bride, the wife of the Lamb... And He carried me away in the Spirit to a great mountain, and showed me the holy city, Jerusalem, coming down out of heaven from God..."* (Rev. 21:10–27). Now if we back up to verse 2, God again reveals to us new insights into the identity of the holy city, *"And I saw the holy city, new Jerusalem, coming down out of heaven from God, made ready as a bride adorned for her husband."*

Jerusalem is a metaphor for Israel like Babylon is a metaphor for the Beast. Israel is the Bride, the wife of the Lamb. And according to the Apostle Paul in Romans 11; the Church is grafted into the vine of Judaism not the other way around as our Replacement Theologians and Prophecy Buffs would have us believe, thus the Bride is Israel, not the church. The Bride is also not a bunch of invited guests, nor even a group of bridesmaids as many believe Matthew 25:1–12 describes.

Like the Church, Israel is one body and the church is a member of that body, *"the body is a unit, though it is made up of many parts; and though all its parts are many, they form one body...and each one of you is a part of it"* (1 Cor. 12:12–27). So Israel does not need an invitation to her own wedding banquet, because she's the main attraction, for without her there would be no wedding, nor banquet.

The scene now changes again in verse 11 with John witnessing a white horse coming out of heaven, *kai eidon, "and I saw."* This scene is not in sequential order and does not follow the celebration in heaven; it follows (Rev. 16:21) (which is the pouring out of the seventh bowl) and precedes or takes place before the celebration just described above. Like most of John's revelation the scenes are not in sequential order and do not follow one another, so it is important to watch for the key phrases (i.e., after these things, *meta tauta*, and I saw, *kai eidon*, and I heard, *kai nkousa*, then I saw, *kai horao*, etc.…). These phrases denote scene changes.

Thus, like Proverbs 25:2 states, *"It is the glory of God to conceal a matter, but the glory of kings is to search out a matter."* We as joint heirs with Christ must seek out the hidden manna/phrase and place them in the correct order to complete each vision, *"for those who have insight will understand"* (Daniel 12:10).

He who sits upon the white horse has several names which takes the reader back to chapters 2 and 3 and the names revealed in the sevenfold (*heptadic*) structure of each church and the seven key elements. Now, the second of the seven key elements is the title of Jesus, each one is chosen to be relevant to the message of that particular church. In Revelation 3:7 and 14—He *"is called Faithful and true."* In Revelation 1:14, 2:18—His *"eyes are a flame of fire"* and in Revelation 2:17 *"He has a name written on Him which no one knows except Himself."*

Verse 13 changes the mix by giving the reader insight into what will come. For "He is clothed with a robe dipped in blood." Why are His robes dipped in blood you might ask? Well the prophet Isaiah tells us that on the *"Day of the Lord,"* God will pour out His vengeance on His enemies.

> *"Who is this who comes from Edom* (Arabia)…? *Why is Your apparel red, and Your garments like the one who treads in the wine press? "I* (Jesus) *have trodden the wine trough… I also trod them in My anger and trampled them in My wrath; and their lifeblood is sprinkled on My garments, and I stained all My raiment. "For the day of vengeance was in My heart, and My year of redemption has come… I trod down the peoples* (those who received the mark of the beast) *in My anger and made them drunk in My wrath, and I poured out their lifeblood on the earth"* (Isaiah 63:1–6).

This passage is a very graphic image of what will happen when Christ returns and pours out His Wrath. What follow next is another title to remind the reader of what God has said throughout scripture, that the *"Anointed One"* (i.e., Messiah/Christ) *"is The Word of God"* (John 1:1) now coming to bring judgment on all those who received the mark of the beast and fell into idolatry. God is long-suffering, but His patients have come to an end!

"And the armies which are in heaven, clothed in fine linen, white and clean, were following Him on white horses." Verse 14 does not represent the raptured believers, for they are on their way to heaven to be purified and made ready for the marriage (v. 7). So who are these armies? In Hebrew its *tsaba'*, in Greek its *strateuma,* which is in reference to host of angels, God's heavenly army. It is NOT the saints!

I heard a pastor recently claim the he hopes when he comes back that he will be riding a pony because he does not like horses. This is just pure absurdity, for if we are the bride of Christ, we are to be spotless, and righteous, not covered and stained with sin/blood. Christ does not need our help nor does He want it. We pass Him in the air on our way up when He is coming down, 1 Thessalonians 4:13–17 is taken out of context for:

> *"The Lord* (Jesus) *Himself will descend from heaven with a shout, with the voice of the archangel, and with the trumpet of God; and the dead* (those who were martyred) *in Christ shall rise first. Then we who are alive and remain* (having endured the tribulation) *shall be caught up* (raptured) *together with them in the clouds, to meet the Lord* (Jesus) *in the air, and thus we shall always be with the Lord* (God, not Christ for He is on His way to battle). *"*

Just because these armies are clothed in white linen does not make it the saints who received robes, *himatia* or *stoles,* of white do to what the churches overcame throughout the prophetic Church Age (see notes on Revelation 7—the Interlude between the Sixth and Seventh Seal for more information). These garments that the armies wear are called *byssinos* and there is nothing distinct about them other than they are fine linen, clean and white. Hence, no spot or blemish on them unlike us before we will be clothed in righteousness, as stated above.

Remember that many armies in history wore white, i.e., the Crusaders and the Teutonic Knights, so it only makes sense that God's army of angels ware white as well, white represents holiness, purity, and righteousness for the brilliance of Christ and His Army will not be undone by Satan and his forces. *"And I saw the beast and the kings of the earth and their armies assembled to make war against Him who sat on the horse and against His army."*

The last image of Christ here in this passage is of Him wheeling a *"sharp sword, so that with it He may strike down the nations,"* which is also related to the title of Christ found in Revelation 2:12. The sword that Christ is wheedling is the *rhomphaia,* which is a great, long, heavy sword, almost as tall as a man (about 41 inches long with a curved blade with only the inside curve sharpened) that is wielded with both hands. This sword was a weapon used by the Thracian Cavalry in Alexander's great Macedonian Army. The Roman Cavalry used a similar weapon for their cavalry, called the *spathe,* of which brought sudden death.

For when the cavalry appears out of nowhere, it suddenly strikes terror by slashing and cutting at all in its path. This mayhem and killing spree can only be achieved by the use of a long cavalry type sword, *rhomphaia or spatha,* which can reach to the ground to slash at those lying on the ground from which there is no escape. The symbolism is quite clear, for there is no escaping God's wrath.

Then *"He will rule them with a rod of iron."* The rod is the *rhabdos which is* a royal scepter not a club as Revelation 2:27, 12:5 confirms. The Apostle Paul makes it clear when he says in Hebrews 1:8 in reference to the second coming that: *"Your Throne, O God, is Forever and Ever, and the Righteous Scepter is the Scepter of His* (Christ's) *Kingdom."* It is with this scepter, Hebrew *shebet,* that *"You* (Christ) *shall break them with a rod* (scepter) *of iron, You* (Christ) *shall shatter them like earthenware,"* Psalms 2:9. Even Balaam the son of Beor, prophesied in Numbers 24:15–19 that Christ would have dominion over His enemies:

"I see him (the Lord), *but not now; I behold him* (the Lord), *but not near; a star shall come forth from Jacob, a scepter shall rise from Israel, and shall crush through the forehead of Moab* (Southern Jordan), *and tear down all the sons of Sheth* (Jebusites). *Edom* (Arabia) *shall be a possession, Seir* (the West Bank), *its enemies, also will be a possession, while Israel performs valiantly. One from Jacob* (Christ) *shall have dominion, and will destroy the remnant from the city."*

Now after Christ has defeated His enemies He will be crowned *"King of Kings and Lord of Lords,"* however His robes already bare this title. Why? Because His dominion is an everlasting one. He was with God from the beginning, Genesis 1:1, and He will be with God through eternity, hence there is no beginning nor end of His reign.

"And to Him was given dominion, glory and a kingdom, that all the peoples, nations and men of every language might serve Him. His dominion is an everlasting dominion which will not pass away; and His kingdom is one which will not be destroyed." (Daniel 7:14)

So it should come as no surprise that the last passage of verses 20–21, now deals with the defeat of Christ's enemies whom there is no escape. *"And the beast* (the false religion of Islam) *was seized, and with him the false prophet* (the Antichrist) *who performed the signs in his presence, by which he deceived those* (every tribe, tongue, people, and nation) *who had received the mark of the beast and those who worshiped his image; these two were thrown alive into the lake of fire which burns with brimstone. And the rest were killed with the sword which came from the mouth of Him* (Christ) *who sat on the horse."*

So now you know "the rest of the story" as Paul Harvey use to say. Christ WINS!

Revelation

CHAPTER 20

New American Standard Bible (NASB)

Satan Bound

²⁰ *Then I saw an angel coming down from heaven, holding the key of the abyss and a great chain in his hand. ² And he laid hold of the dragon, the serpent of old, who is the devil and Satan, and bound him for a thousand years; ³ and he threw him into the abyss, and shut it and sealed it over him, so that he would not deceive the nations any longer, until the thousand years were completed; after these things he must be released for a short time.*

⁴ *Then I saw thrones, and they sat on them, and judgment was given to them. And I saw the souls of those who had been beheaded because of their testimony of Jesus and because of the word of God, and those who had not worshiped the beast or his image, and had not received the mark on their forehead and on their hand; and they came to life and reigned with Christ for a thousand years. ⁵ The rest of the dead did not come to life until the thousand years were completed. This is the first resurrection. ⁶ Blessed and holy is the one who has a part in the first resurrection; over these the second death has no power, but they will be priests of God and of Christ and will reign with Him for a thousand years.*

Satan Freed, Doomed

⁷ When the thousand years are completed, Satan will be released from his prison, ⁸ and will come out to deceive the nations which are in the four corners of the earth, Gog and Magog, to gather them together for the war; the number of them is like the sand of the seashore. ⁹ And they came up on the broad plain of the earth and surrounded the camp of the saints and the beloved city, and fire came down from heaven and devoured them. ¹⁰ And the devil who deceived them was thrown into the lake of fire and brimstone, where the beast and the false prophet are also; and they will be tormented day and night forever and ever.

Judgment at the Throne of God

¹¹ Then I saw a great white throne and Him who sat upon it, from whose presence earth and heaven fled away, and no place was found for them. ¹² And I saw the dead, the great and the small, standing before the throne, and books were opened; and another book was opened, which is the book of life; and the dead were judged from the things which were written in the books, according to their deeds. ¹³ And the sea gave up the dead which were in it, and death and Hades gave up the dead which were in them; and they were judged, every one of them according to their deeds. ¹⁴ Then death and Hades were thrown into the lake of fire. This is the second death, the lake of fire. ¹⁵ And if anyone's name was not found written in the book of life, he was thrown into the lake of fire.

Notes on Revelation 20

The Thousand Years

Revelation 20:1 starts off with a scene change *kai eidon*, *"and I saw,"* where John now views Satan being bound and thrown into the abyss for a thousand years. The question that now arises; is John in heaven, on earth, or somewhere in between? Wherever he is, he is able to view the dragon being locked away so that the devil cannot deceive the nations any longer until the thousand years are over.

There is no mistake in our understanding of who is bound and thrown into the abyss in verse 2, for it is an exact repeat of Revelation 12:9, *"and the great dragon was thrown down, the serpent of old who is called the devil and Satan, who deceives the whole world."* Only in chapter 12 Satan is thrown out of heaven to earth where he then deceives mankind, but now here in chapter 20, Satan is thrown into the abyss and can no longer deceive mankind until the millennium (a thousand years) are over.

However, in our understanding of how Satan deceives the whole world we need to look back at chapters 13, 17, and 18 together which reveal to us that the dragon is compelled to work through such agencies as the two beasts and the great harlot. The two beasts represent the authority and the power behind Satan's deception. The harlot represents the seduction of mankind and their willingness to be led astray into idolatry.

Dates and times in scripture are always difficult to understand, but it is interesting that six times in verses 1–7 the term *chilia eta*, *"one thousand years"* occurs, three times in verses 1–3 and 7 and three times in verses 4–6. Is this significant, marking a one one-thousand-year period or does the repartition indicate that there are six, one-thousand-year periods totaling six thousand years?

The term *chilia eta* is where we get the Latin phrase *"millennium,"* which depicts a futuristic event that will last for a one thousand year period. However many count the six references as six workdays in a week and then add one millennium for the Sabbath rest at the end of the week thus coming up with seven thousand literal years. The six thousand years of creation will be up soon according to some Prophecy Buffs and then will come the one-thousand-year Sabbath rest where Christ rules supreme.

Here we have to be careful not to resort to literalism and remember that what is depicted here, *chilia eta*, as a thousand years is only symbolic. For there will be a period of time in which mankind will no longer be deceived by Satan himself, but once that time is over (950 years or 1,000 years does not matter) Satan will again deceive mankind once more until God says enough is enough and puts an end to it all.

Verses 1–3 and 7–10 belong together as a whole; verses 1–3 has Satan thrown into the abyss for a thousand years and verses 7–10 completes the defeat of Satan after he has been released and finishes the victory by throwing Satan into the lake of fire *"forever and ever."*

Verses 4–6 and 11–15 are a different scene that completes the thought of the first scene as to what happens to the saints during the thousand years. Here again John moves us to a different picture within this chapter by stating *kai eidon, "and I saw,"* which takes us back to Revelation 19:2 and completes the prophecy of Daniel 7:1–11.

These thrones are royal thrones *"ebasileusan,"* which symbolize power, rule and dominion. The imagery is that of a king sitting on his throne in his *praetorium* (judgment hall) exercising judgment and righteousness as he delivers his verdicts to those who come before him, like King Solomon in 1 Kings 3:16–28. These thrones are related to *"the throne"* which becomes an extension of Christ's throne, *"I will grant to him to sit down with Me on My throne, as I also…sat down with My Father on His throne"* (Rev. 3:21).

Once again the scene changes with John proclaiming *kai eidon*, *"and I saw,"* in verse 4b, where he looks back to Revelation 6:9, *"I saw beneath the altar the souls of those who had been slain because of the Word of God, and because of the testimony which they maintained."* Now Johns tells us what happened to those who maintained the Testimony of Jesus Christ; they were beheaded!

These martyrs and only these martyrs will be the ones who will rule with Christ during the *chilia eta, "one thousand years."* Not all faithful Christian believers who have died or were raptured will be included in this group who will rule, for John clearly states that those who had been beheaded, *twn pepelekismenwv*, which is the perfect participle and belongs to the nominative finite aorist verb, will *"reign"* with Christ.

This first thrown room scene in verses 1–3 will become what will be known as the judgment of nations. For all nations will be judged according to how they treated Israel:

> *"For behold, in those days and at that time, when I restore the fortunes of Judah and Jerusalem, I will gather all the nations and bring them down to the valley of Jehoshaphat. Then I will enter into judgment with them there on behalf of My people and My inheritance, Israel, whom they have scattered among the nations; and they have divided up My land...because of the violence done to the sons of Judah, in whose land they have shed innocent blood"* (Joel 3:1–19).

However, those who have died in their sins, who are unbelievers who did not take part in persecuting Israel will not be resurrected, *anastasis*, and judged until the final defeat of Satan after the thousand years are complete. These souls will be judged at the time of the Great White Throne of Judgment, when the earth and the sea give up their dead along with Death and Hades, verses 11–15.

This judgment is God's alone, for the saints of v 4, are not involved. These souls will not receive eternal life, *zwa*, for their names are not found in the Book of Life, but will be condemned to be separated from God for eternity in the lake of fire, Luke 16:19–31. The Disciple Peter also informs us:

> *"For if God did not spare angels when they sinned, but cast them into hell and committed them to pits of darkness, reserved for judgment; and did not spare the ancient world…and to keep the unrighteous under punishment for the day of judgment, and especially those who indulge the flesh in its corrupt desires and despise authority"* (2 Peter 2:4–10).

They will also experience the *"second death"* for the Spirit of God will not be found in them, *"but for the cowardly and unbelieving and abominable and murderers and immoral persons and sorcerers and idolaters and all liars, their part will be in the lake that burns with fire and brimstone, which is the second death"* (Rev. 21:8).

Now, if we are trying to place chapters 19 and 22 in some sort of chronological order, they would follow as such:

> Revelation 19:11–19: Second Coming of Christ
> Revelation 19:20–21: Defeat of the two Beasts
> Revelation 20:1–3: Satan bound for one thousand years
> Revelation 20:4–6: Judgment of the Nations
> Revelation 19:1–6: Coronation Celebration
> Revelation 19:7–10: Marriage of the Lamb
> Revelation 21:1–9: Bride of Christ
> Revelation 21:10–22: New Jerusalem
> Revelation 22:1–9: River and Tree of Life
> Revelation 22:10–17: Second Chance
> Revelation 20:7–10: Satan freed and final defeat
> Revelation 20:11–15: Great White Throne Judgment
> Revelation 22:18–22: Final Message

Notes on Chapter 20

The Armageddon Campaign

There are two major events that take place in Revelation 16–20, which most Prophecy Buffs seem to confuse. The Second major event (which I will discuss first); takes place after a period of *chilia eta, "one thousand years"* of Christ's reign is completed. This is when Satan is released to deceive the nations one last time. Satan will gather the same nations he did prior to his defeat the first time, in an attempt to usurp the throne of God one more time. God however, does not play games anymore and defeats Satan in one quick swoop which is recorded in Revelation 20:7–10.

It is during this one-thousand-year reign that we find the Martyred Saints ruling with Christ. These martyrs and only these martyrs will be the ones who will rule with Christ during the *chilia eta, "one thousand years."* Note, that not all faithful Christian believers will be included in this group who will rule, for John clearly states that those who were beheaded, *twn pepelekismenwv*, which is the perfect participle and belongs to the nominative finite aorist verb, will *"reign"* with Christ, Revelation 20:4: *"and they* (those who lost their heads, i.e., the martyrs) *came to life and reigned with Christ for a thousand years."*

Whom do they reign over, you might ask? Well, they reign over the *"outsiders."* For *"Outside the city* (the New Jerusalem) *are the dogs and the sorcerer's and the immoral persons and the murderers and the idolaters, and everyone who loves and practices lying"* (Rev. 22:15). When the New Jerusalem comes down from heaven, only the Bride of Christ will be allowed inside, for there is a stipulation as to who can enter the New Jerusalem: *"Nothing unclean and no one who practices abomination and lying, shall ever come into it"* (Rev. 21:27).

So you see that these subjugated outsiders will be the ones deceived when Satan is released from his prison the last time:

> *"When the thousand years are completed, Satan will be released from his prison, and will come out to deceive the nations which are in the four corners of the earth, Gog and Magog, to gather them together for war."* (Rev. 20:7–9)

These outsiders are the descendants of *"those who had received the mark of the beast and those who worshiped his image,"* for they came up against the nation of Israel on their way to destroy the Harlot (Rev. 17:16–18). These outsiders are the ones who are alive through the millennium as subjects to the *King of kings* and His Martyred Saints, but they will live outside the holy city. They will teach their child, and their Grand Children, and their Great Grand Children the lie, *"all the peoples walk each in the name of his god,"* and they will again be deceived by Satan once more to wage war against the holy ones (God's people; i.e., Christian and Jew—the One New Man).

Unlike what many Prophecy Buffs teach, this is NOT the Battle of Armageddon. I repeat, this is NOT Armageddon, though Gog and Magog are mentioned. This army derives itself from the descendants of those who took the mark of the beast and who continued to teach their children the lie. These descendants are still found in the geographical area from which the Antichrist came from (ancient Assyria where Gog and Magog were located, which is modern Turkey). That is why they are mentioned here in v. 8, so we know that these are the same people, and come from the same geographical area.

Even Martin Luther in 1519, understood that Gog and Magog in Revelation 20:8, is the biblical designation for the Turks. This was such an important point for him that he published his translation of Ezekiel 38 and 39 as separate treaties with an introduction underscoring the whole connection.[45] Though he was waging war with the Pope and the Catholic Church, he understood from scrip-

---

[45.] *LW 16*, 263.

tures that the Worthless Sheppard (a.k.a. the Antichrist) would arise out of Assyria and be a Turk (a Muslim).[46] This Antichrist would lead an army against Israel, he would then desecrate the temple and declare himself to be god. Thus, this battle of Gog and Magog (a.k.a. Armageddon) where *"the dead did not come to life until the thousand years were completed"* (Rev. 20:5), is obviously prior to the millennium.

The passage from Isaiah ties in with this Gog/Magog invasion (a.k.a. Armageddon) when Christ returns and defeats them. Once they are defeated, those who are left: *"They will hammer their swords into plowshares and their spears into pruning hooks. Nation will not lift up sword against nation, and never again will they learn war"* (Isaiah 2:4b). The prophet Micah picks up on this theme and add more to our understanding of the millennium by letting the reader know that the nations will come up to the temple to be taught by the Lord Himself:

> *"Many nations will come and say, "Come and let us go up to the mountain of the LORD And to the house of the God of Jacob, that He* (Christ) *may teach us about His ways and that we may walk in His paths." For from Zion will go forth the law, even the word of the LORD from Jerusalem. And He* (Christ) *will judge between many peoples and render decisions for mighty, distant nations. Then they will hammer their swords into plowshares and their spears into pruning hooks; Nation will not lift up sword against nation, and never again will they train for war. Each of them will sit under his vine and under his fig tree, with no one to make them afraid, for the mouth of the LORD of hosts has spoken. Though all the peoples walk each in the name of his god, as for us, we will walk in the name of the LORD our God forever and ever."* (Micah 4:2–5)

---

46. Timothy J. Wengert, 248.

Now going back to Revelation 20, and the struggle/war that we are dealing within this chapter. It all takes place after the millennium reign when Satan deceives these same nations once again and causes them to *"proclaim this among the nations: prepare a war; rouse the mighty men! Let all the soldiers draw near, let them come up! Beat your plowshares into swords and your pruning hooks into spears"* (Joel 3:9–10). This can only happen following after the one thousand year reign when there has been no wars and no need for weapons.

However, when they gather together from the four corners of the earth, *"and surrounded the camp of the saints and the beloved city* (remember that Jerusalem is the apple of God's eye), *"* they will be destroyed by God when *"fire came down from heaven and devoured them."* God will finally say enough is enough. Thus putting an end to the rebellion of Satan, for he will be *"thrown into the lake of fire and brimstone, where the beast and the false prophet are also; and they* (all three, the unholy trinity) *will be tormented day and night forever and ever,"* never to deceive mankind again.

Then God will judge all mankind, *"I kept looking until thrones were set up, and the Ancient of Days took His seat…and the books were opened"* (Dan. 7:9–10). This is repeated here in chapter 20: *"Then I saw a great white throne and Him who sat upon it, from whose presence earth and heaven fled away, and no place was found for them"* (Rev. 20:11). This is the Great White Throne of Judgment taking place, which is also known as the second death. *"And they were judged, every one of them according to their deeds"* (Rev. 20:13).

So if this event is not Armageddon, when does the actual war/battle take place? I will submit to you, *"That which has been is that which will be, and that which has been done is that which will be done. So there is nothing new under the sun…Already it has existed for ages which were before us."*

Now the first major event which I will discussing now after the second event (the defeat of Satan) previously discussed (see the chronological order of these chapters at the end of my notes in Revelation 20, part A for a better understanding) is when the nations have come down against the Harlot and have swept through Israel on their way to Arabia for plunder.

"That which has been done is that which will be done" understanding history is important here for it will repeat itself; Israel was caught between the territories of the Seleucids Empire (the kingdom of the North) and the Ptolemaic Empire (the kingdom of the South), subsequently it became the combat zone between these two major kingdoms as detailed in Daniel 11:5–35 from 300–30 BCE. This will happen again when the Antichrist (an archetype of Antiochus IV Epiphanes, the kingdom of the North) comes south to destroy the Harlot (an archetype of Ptolemy VI Philometer, the kingdom of the South).

> *"He* (The Antichrist) *will stir up his strength and courage against the king of the South* (Arabia) *with a large army; so the king of the South* (Arabia) *will mobilize an extremely large and mighty army for war; but he will not stand, for schemes will be devised against him... As for both kings, their hearts will be intent on evil, and they will speak lies to each other...but it will not succeed, for the end is still to come at the appointed time. Then he* (the Antichrist) *will return to his land with much plunder; but his heart will be set against the holy covenant* (Israel)*, and he will take action and then return to his own land... Forces from him* (the Antichrist) *will arise, desecrate the sanctuary fortress* (The Temple in Jerusalem)*, and do away with the regular sacrifice. And they will set up the abomination of desolation..."* (Daniel 11:5–35)

Now I know you are going to ask; why does the kingdom of the North attack the kingdom of the South? Well, because *"the ten horns which you saw, and the beast, these will hate the harlot and will make her desolate and naked, and will eat her flesh and will burn her up with fire"* (Rev. 17:16). The Antichrist together with the other kingdoms (the ten toes/horns) will make war against this one nation (the Harlot) and do away with her, because they are tired of being controlled and manipulated by her because of her influence and power (see Ezekiel 16:37–41). They also want her wealth:

> *"Sheba and Dedan* (Southern Arabia) *and the merchants of Tarshish with all its villages will say to you* (the Antichrist), *'Have you come to capture spoil? Have you assembled your company to seize plunder, to carry away silver and gold, to take away cattle and goods, to capture great spoil?"* (Ezekiel 38:13).

After the northern army takes their spoils they will return north and gather the armies in the valley of Jezreel, this is what is known as Armageddon and it is here when Christ returns, in what is called the *parousia*, the Second Coming, where He pours out the Wrath of God on these nations. This event is recorded in Revelation chapters 16–19 and Ezekiel 38–39. After the nations are defeated then starts Christ's Millennium Reign.

So let's take this step by step and try to figure out what is taking place and why this first event is known as Armageddon. Now, according to Judges 6:33, *"Then all the Midianites and the Amalekites and the sons of the east assembled themselves; and they crossed over and camped in the valley of Jezreel."* This is the valley where Gideon defeated the enemies of the Lord and it is this same exact valley that Christ will defeat His enemies at. *"And he* (the Antichrist) *gathered them together into a place called in the Hebrew tongue Har-Magedon* (Mount Megiddo and the valley of Jezreel)*"* (Rev. 16:16). Thus, there is nothing new under the sun, what was will be again.

> *"And I saw the beast* (the Antichrist) *and the kings of the earth* (the leaders of the ten toes/horns) *and their armies assembled to make war against Him* (Christ) *who sat on the horse and against His army"* (Rev. 19:19). For *"these* (the followers of the Antichrist who gather in the valley) *will wage war against the Lamb, and the Lamb will overcome them, because He is Lord of lords and King of kings,*

and those who are with Him (the 144,000, a.k.a.
the remnant) *are the called and chosen and faithful"* (Rev. 17:14).

Now, if you remember that the 144,000 are to the Lord what
the three hundred were to Gideon in Judges 7:19–8:26. Gideon
is an archetype of Christ who leads his people in victory over the
Midianites, Amalekites, and the kings of the east (the same enemy
that Christ must deal with in the last days) for raiding and terrorizing the people and the land. Gideon does it with a chosen few (only
three hundred men), least Israel boasts that they delivered themselves
and God's hand was not involved. Christ will deliver Israel with His
chosen (144,000 men), for again least anyone should boast that God
was not involved in the victory. Thus, as I have shown before (see my
Notes on Revelation 14) there is a parallel here between Judges and
Revelation, between Gideon and Jesus.

I also submit to you that there are parallels between Ezekiel
and Revelation, between the Battle of Gog/Magog and the Battle
of Armageddon. Thus I content that these are the same prophetic
events seen through different lenses or perspectives and that Gog is
the Antichrist whom Christ defeats *"on that day,"* which is a euphe-
mism for *"The Day of the Lord."*

The prophet Ezekiel makes it clear that Gog, the chief prince of
Meshech and Tubal, is the leader of the forces that will come against
Israel:

> *"Thus says the Lord GOD, "Are you* (Gog) *the one of
> whom I spoke in former days through My servants
> the prophets of Israel, who prophesied in those days
> for many years that I would bring you against them?
> It will come about on that day* (The Day of the
> Lord), *when Gog comes against the land of Israel."*
> (Ezekiel 38:17–18).

It is interesting that the Prophecy Buffs have a tendency to
repeat the false interpretation that the word Rosh, means Russia (any

first-year Hebrew student will tell you different) this is just sloppy and bad exegetical and hermeneutical research, plain and simple. The Hebrew word *Ro'sh*, translates as "chief or head," NOT Russia, so the passage should be read as the chief prince or head prince of Meshech and Tubal, the leader of these two major cities whom will lead the troops against Israel just like Antiochus Epiphanes did after he fought with the king of the south. Remember that Antiochus (a.k.a. Gog) is also an archetype of the Antichrist.

Even the direction from which the Antichrist comes in Daniel 11 (the kingdom of the North) is mentioned here in Ezekiel: *"Behold, I am against you, O Gog, chief prince of Meshech and Tubal; and I will turn you around, drive you on, take you up from the remotest parts of the north and bring you against the mountains of Israel"* (Ezekiel 39:2). The land of Magog has been identified as an area in Turkey along the lower southern coast of the Black Sea, formally part of the land of Assyria (remember that one of the names of the Antichrist, is the Assyrian). Even the prophet Joel prophecies that God will *"remove the northern army far from you"* (Joel 2:20) when he invades the land of Israel.

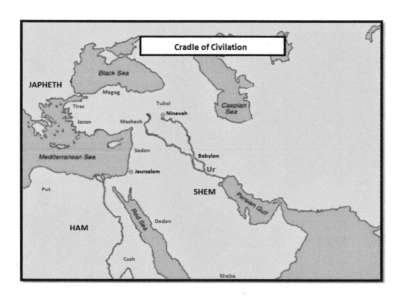

All this will take place after Israel is brought back to life, which I believe took place in 1948 when Israel became a nation:

> *"For I will take you* (the Jews) *from the nations, gather you from all the lands* (the diaspora) *and bring you into your own land* (Israel). *Then I will sprinkle clean water on you, and you will be clean; I will cleanse you from all your filthiness and from all your idols. Moreover, I will give you a new heart and put a new spirit within you; and I will remove the heart of stone from your flesh and give you a heart of flesh. I will put My Spirit within you and cause you to walk in My statutes, and you will be careful to observe My ordinances. You will live in the land* (Israel) *that I gave to your forefathers; so you will be My people, and I will be your God...the nations that are left round about you* (i.e., the ten toes/horns which make up the Islamic Middle East) *will know that I, the LORD, have rebuilt the ruined places and planted that which was desolate; I, the LORD, have spoken and will do it."* (Ezekiel 36:24–36)

God raised the nation of Israel from the dead, so Satan has to raise his counterfeit Satanic Empire from the dead. Thus, we have the symbolism of one of the heads being slain unto death and being resurrected so that the nations would be amazed. *"I saw one of his heads* (the seven headed beast, a.k.a. the seven empires) *as if it had been slain, and his fatal wound was healed. And the whole earth was amazed and followed after the beast* (this raised new eighth empire)*"* (Rev. 13:3). This seventh/eighth empire will rise again and the masses will flock to it thinking that it is something great and wonderful.

> *"In the latter years you* (the Jews) *will come into the land* (Israel) *that is restored from the sword, whose inhabitants* (Jews) *have been gathered from many*

nations to the mountains of Israel which had been a continual waste; but its people were brought out from the nations, and they are living securely, all of them. You (the Antichrist) will go up, you will come like a storm; you will be like a cloud covering the land, you and all your troops, and many peoples (the resurrected seventh/eighth empire) with you." (Ezekiel 38:8–9)

So if we try to put this in perspective, we find that after Israel has been established as a nation (1948) sometime in the future, the Antichrist (a.k.a. Gog, a.k.a. the Assyrian) will scheme an evil scheme with the other ten toes/horns nations and will attack the kingdom of the South (a.k.a. the Harlot, a.k.a. Edom) and Israel just happens to be the stomping grounds. Just like Antiochus Epiphanes did in Daniel 11. They will attack the un-walled villages of the southern kingdom but will also turn aside and attack the waste places, i.e., Israel, which are now inhabited and have wealth.

"It will come about on that day, that thoughts will come into your mind (the Antichrist) and you will devise an evil plan, and you will say, 'I will go up against the land of unwalled villages (Araibia). I will go against those who are at rest, that live securely, all of them living without walls and having no bars or gates, to capture spoil and to seize plunder, to turn your hand against the waste places (Israel) which are now inhabited, and against the people (the Jews) who are gathered from the nations, who have acquired cattle and goods, who live at the center of the world." (Ezekiel 38:10–12)

Why do I claim that this land of un-walled villages is Arabia? Because there are two events going on in this passage. One is dealing with the Southern kingdom and the other is turning a hand against the people who were gathered from the nations. They will attack the un-walled villages of the southern kingdom but will also turn aside and attack the waste places. *"But I will camp around My house because of an army, because of him who passes by and returns,"* Zechariah 9:8-10. Why do they return? Because Israel is inhabited with God's people and there is more wealth to plunder.

> *"And the ten horns* (these ten nations, a.k.a. ten toes/horns) *which you saw, and the beast* (the Antichrist), *these will hate the harlot* (Mecca) *and will make her desolate and naked, and will eat her flesh and will burn her up with fire. For God has put it in their* (this resurrected seventh/eighth empire) *hearts to execute His purpose by having a common purpose* (that of jealousy over her wealth, power and influence), *and by giving their kingdom to the beast* (Antichrist), *until the words of God will be fulfilled. The woman whom you saw is the great city* (Mecca), *which reigns over the kings of the earth* (all the nations). *"* (Rev. 17:16–18)

So like Antiochus, these nations come south to steal the wealth and destroy the power and influence the harlot has over the kings of the earth. Even:

> *"Sheba and Dedan* (Southern Arabia) *and the merchants of Tarshish with all its villages will say to you* (the Antichrist), *'Have you come to capture spoil? Have you assembled your company to seize plunder, to carry away silver and gold, to take away cattle and goods, to capture great spoil?"* (Ezekiel 38:13)

This passage of Sheba and Dedan parallels Revelation 18:15–20 and the wealth and influence which is destroyed when the Antichrist's forces come south to attack Arabia:

"The merchants of these things, who became rich from her (the Harlot), *will stand at a distance because of the fear of her torment, weeping and mourning, saying, 'Woe, woe, the great city* (Mecca), *she who was clothed in fine linen and purple and scarlet, and adorned with gold and precious stones and pearls; for in one hour such great wealth has been laid waste!' And every shipmaster and every passenger and sailor, and as many as make their living by the sea, stood at a distance, and were crying out as they saw the smoke of her burning, saying, 'What city is like the great city* (Mecca)?' *And they threw dust on their heads and were crying out, weeping and mourning, saying, 'Woe, woe, the great city* (Mecca), *in which all who had ships at sea became rich by her wealth, for in one hour she has been laid waste!"*

Now the Antichrist has made a peace treaty or covenant as recorded in Daniel 8:25 and 9:27, which will allow both Israel and the surrounding nations to be at rest and live securely (without walls), meaning that they do not fear attack from each other. This ability to feel safe is the moment when the Antichrist will attack, for in the middle of the covenant he will break the deal and wage war.

Keep in mind 2 Thessalonians 2:2–8, where the Apostle Paul reveals what will take place leading up to Christ's Second Coming:

"Let no one deceive you, for it (the rapture) *will not come unless the apostasy comes first and the man of lawlessness is revealed* (the Antichrist), *the son of destruction, who opposes and exalts himself above every so-called god or object of worship* (just like Antiochus Epiphanes), *so that he takes his seat in the temple of God, displaying himself as being God."*

Now I can hear the Prophecy Buffs disagreeing and saying that Israel is not living in a land of peace and safety, with no walls; the only way this will ever be achieved is during the millennium, but they are wrong. A *"Peace Accord"* between the neighboring countries will achieve this exact scenario. They also interpret the passage incorrectly for the un-wall villages belong to the harlot not Israel, the waste lands which are now inhabited are Israel.

The prophet Isaiah also adds a twist to this when he prophesies that the Harlot will be dwelling securely:

> *"Now, then, hear this, you sensual one* (the Harlot), *who dwells securely, who says in your heart, 'I am, and there is no one besides me. I will not sit as a widow, nor know loss of children.' "But these two things will come on you suddenly in one day: Loss of children and widowhood. They will come on you in full measure In spite of your many sorceries, In spite of the great power of your spells. "You felt secure in your wickedness and said, 'No one sees me,' your wisdom and your knowledge, they have deluded you; for you have said in your heart, 'I am, and there is no one besides me.'"* (Isaiah 47:8–10)

So I ask, who is supposed to be living safely in the land of un-walled villages, Israel or Arabia? And if Israel is the one living in safety, why is the Harlot so upset and why is she mourning?

The Antichrist will establish this Peace Accord between the nations for seven years, but 3.5 years into it he will break it like Daniel prophesied and destroy the Temple in Jerusalem, *"forces from him* (the Antichrist) *will arise, desecrate the sanctuary fortress, and do away with the regular sacrifice. And they will set up the abomination of desolation"* (Daniel 11:31).

As a side note, a unique and not highly known aspect of Islam is their term for peacemaking, a *hudna,* the making of a truce for a fixed duration of time, which is a legal concept dating to the birth of Islam and Mohammad. To understand this we need to look at the historical meaning of the Muslim expression.

Mohammad the founder of Islam struck a legendary seven-year *hudna* (peace treaty) with the Quraysh tribe that controlled Mecca in the seventh century. In the first three and half years of the peace, Mohammad rearmed and built up his forces. He then, at the three ½ year mark, took advantage of a minor Quraysh infraction to break the *hudna* and launch the full scale conquest of Mecca, which became then the holiest city in Islam. Does this sound familiar? Does not the Antichrist make a peace treaty for seven years and in the middle of it will he not desecrate the temple?

Yassir Arafat infamously invoked Mohammad's *hudna* in 1994 to describe his own Oslo commitments "on the road to Jerusalem," and the implication was very clear. Arafat was asserting to his Islamic brethren that he will, "when his circumstances change for the better, take advantage of some technicality to tear up existing accords and launch a military assault on Israel." Indeed, this is precisely what occurred in September 2000 when the Palestinian Authority launched a terror assault upon Israeli citizens.

The Antichrist will follow suit like his Muslim brothers before him and proceed to attack Arabia to displace the harlot's influence and power. This war will last several years in which Israel will be caught in the middle. When everyone felt safe and secure because of this Peace Accord, then sudden destruction comes.

> *"It will come about on that day, when Gog* (Assyria/Turkey*) comes against the land of Israel," declares the Lord* GOD, *"that My fury will mount up in My anger. In My zeal and in My blazing wrath I declare that on that day there will surely be a great earthquake in the land of Israel."* (Ezekiel 38:18–19)

This earthquake parallels the anger and wrath of the seventh bowl judgment, *"and there was a great earthquake, such as there had not been since man came to be upon the earth, so great an earthquake was it, and so mighty"* (Rev. 16:18). It also marks the coming of the

Lord, the *parousia,* because this earthquake is like none before, so that even *the fish of the sea, the birds of the heavens, the beasts of the field, all the creeping things that creep on the earth, and all the men who are on the face of the earth will shake at My* (Christ's) *presence; the mountains also will be thrown down, the steep pathways will collapse and every wall will fall to the ground. I will call for a sword against him* (the Antichrist) *on all My mountains," declares the Lord* GOD. (Ezekiel 38:20–21)

When Christ returns and His presence is upon the face of the earth and the 144,000 gather with Him like Gideon's warriors, the Battle Cry goes forth, *"A sword for the Lord and for Gideon."* And like Gideon: *"Every man's sword will be against his brother. With pestilence and with blood I* (Christ) *will enter into judgment with him* (the Antichrist)*; and I will rain on him and on his troops, and on the many peoples who are with him, a torrential rain, with hailstones, fire and brimstone"* (Ezekiel 38:22).

When the kingdom of the north and the other nations with him come (the text seems to be pointing to a massive regional war against Israel, indicating that many nations are involved which are not necessarily specified), God will then punish all these nations for blaspheming His name (stoning was the punishment for blaspheme in the Old Testament). *"Moreover, the one who blasphemes the name of the* LORD *shall surely be put to death; all the congregation shall certainly stone him. The alien as well as the native, when he blasphemes the Name, shall be put to death"* (Leviticus 24:16).

Here now in Ezekiel, God proclaims that *"My holy name I will make known in the midst of My people Israel; and I will not let My holy name be profaned anymore. And the nations will know that I am the* LORD, *the Holy One in Israel. Behold, it is coming and it shall be done," declares the Lord* GOD. *"That is the day of which I have spoken."* (Ezekiel 39:7–8)

This is *"the Day of the Lord,"* when He returns (the *parousia*) and pours out His wrath on those who have received the mark of the beast. Thus, God will stone the Antichrist and his hordes with His holy hailstones of fire and brimstone. Again we have a parallel found in the seven bowls, *"and huge hailstones, about one hundred pounds each, came down from heaven upon men; and men blasphemed God because of the plague of the hail, because its plague was extremely severe"* (Rev. 16:21).

The Antichrist's forces will then gather *"together into a place called in the Hebrew tongue Har-Magedon* (Mount Megiddo and the valley of Jezreel)*"* (Rev. 16:16), where they will be defeated:

> *Behold, I am against you, O Gog, prince* (and chief) *of Meshech and Tubal; and I will turn you* (the armies of the Antichrist) *around, drive you on, take you up from the remotest parts of the north and bring you against the mountains of Israel. I will strike your bow from your left hand and dash down your arrows from your right hand. You* (the Islamic armies) *will fall on the mountains of Israel, you and all your troops and the peoples* (the Islamic armies) *who are with you; I will give you as food to every kind of predatory bird and beast of the field…thus says the Lord GOD, 'Speak to every kind of bird and to every beast of the field, "Assemble and come, gather from every side to My sacrifice which I* (Christ) *am going to sacrifice* (trampling out the vintage) *for you, as a great sacrifice on the mountains of Israel, that you may eat flesh and drink blood. You will eat the flesh of mighty men and drink the blood of the princes of the earth."* (Ezekiel 39:1–18)

This passage is again a parallel of Revelation 19:17–19:

> *"Then I saw an angel standing in the sun, and he cried out with a loud voice, saying to all the birds which fly in mid-heaven, "Come, assemble for the great supper of God, so that you may eat the flesh of kings* (the Antichrist and the leaders of the 10 toes) *and the flesh of commanders and the flesh of mighty men and the flesh of horses and of those who*

*sit on them and the flesh of all men, both free men
and slaves, and small and great."*

The metaphor is unmistakable, the defeat is final and the victor is the Lord Christ Jesus. *"And the rest were killed with the sword which came from the mouth of Him who sat on the horse, and all the birds were filled with their flesh"* (Rev. 19:21). That sword is the Word of God physically carried out by the 144,000.

It is also interesting that Edom's judgment is carried out personally by Christ during this time frame as well. *"Surely in the fire of My jealousy I have spoken against the rest of the nations* (the ten toes/ horns), *and against all Edom* (Arabia), *who appropriated My land for themselves as a possession"* (Ezekiel 36:5).

Now if we go to the Book of Isaiah, chapter 34 we find a poetic portrayal of Edom being sacrificed by Christ Himself. Hence, the Lord's wrath is executed against all of Edom specifically because of their unjust treatment of Israel which is also part of the Armageddon Campaign:

> *"Draw near, O nations, to hear; and listen, O peoples! Let the earth and all it contains hear, and the world and all that springs from it. For the* Lord's *indignation is against all the nations* (the seventh empire, ten toes/horn), *and His wrath against all their armies; He* (Jesus) *has utterly destroyed them, He has given them over to slaughter. So their slain will be thrown out, and their corpses will give off their stench, and the mountains will be drenched with their blood...For My* (Christ's) *sword is satiated in heaven, behold it shall descend for judgment upon Edom* (Arabia) *and upon the people whom I have devoted to destruction."* (Isaiah 34:1–5)

Now as we look at Revelation 19:13 the reader is given insight into what will come. For *"He is clothed with a robe dipped in blood."* Why are His robes dipped in blood you might ask? Well the prophet

Isaiah tells us that on the *"Day of the Lord,"* God will pour out His vengeance on His enemies.

> *"Who is this who comes from Edom* (Arabia)...?
> *Why is Your apparel red, and Your garments like
> the one who treads in the wine press? "I* (Jesus) *have
> trodden the wine trough... I also trod them in My
> anger and trampled them in My wrath; and their
> lifeblood is sprinkled on My garments, and I stained
> all My raiment. "For the day of vengeance was in
> My heart, and My year of redemption has come...
> I trod down the peoples* (those who received the
> mark of the beast) *in My anger and made them
> drunk in My wrath, and I poured out their life-
> blood on the earth."* (Isaiah 63:1–6)

This passage is a very graphic image of what will happen when Christ returns and pours out His Wrath, which is unlike the poetic portrayal passage above. God is long-suffering, but His patients has come to an end! The battle of Armageddon is over and the Victorious Christ is returning to Jerusalem from Edom and will enter the eastern gate.

When we read the Book of Obadiah, the same conflict is described in great detail. The entire theme of this short prophecy is the ultimate victory of Zion, i.e., Israel over the nations, i.e., the ten toes/horns which has become known as the Battle of Armageddon. *"For the day of the* LORD *draws near on all the nations. As you have done, it will be done to you. Your dealings will return on your own head"* (Obadiah 1:15).

In the Book of Zephaniah, again the same theme of judgment is found:

> *"For Gaza* (Palestine) *will be abandoned and
> Ashkelon* (Palestine) *a desolation; Ashdod*
> (Palestine) *will be driven out at noon and Ekron*
> (Palestine) *will be uprooted. Woe to the inhabi-*

tants of the seacoast, the nation of the Cherethites (Palestinians in Crete)*! The word of the* LORD *is against you, O Canaan, land of the Philistines; and I will destroy you so that there will be no inhabitant...you also, O Ethiopians* (Sudan and Somalia), *will be slain by My* (Christ's) *sword. And He* (Christ) *will stretch out His hand against the north and destroy Assyria* (Turkey), *and He will make Nineveh* (Iraq) *a desolation, parched like the wilderness"* (Zephaniah 2:4–13).

Even in the Book of Amos as well as in all the other Minor Prophets the theme of judgment on the nations (i.e., Armageddon) is carried out. *"So I will send fire upon Moab* (Jordan) *and it will consume the citadels of Kerioth; and Moab* (Jordan) *will die amid tumult, with war cries and the sound of a trumpet. I will also cut off the judge from her midst and slay all her princes with him," says the* LORD*"* (Amos 2:2–3). So as you can see, judgment comes to the nations for what they have done to Israel. This is the chief reason why they are utterly conquered and annihilated by Christ.

Now, however, as with the end of all battles, there will be the cleaning up of the mess: *"For seven months the house of Israel will be burying them in order to cleanse the land. Even all the people of the land will bury them; and it will be to their renown on the day that I* (Christ) *glorify Myself, declares the Lord* GOD*"* (Ezekiel 39:12–13). They will also gather the enemy's weapons and burn them for seven years, according to Ezekiel 39:9–10, and beat them into plowshares.

Now starts the Millennial Reign with Christ in our midst, *"And I* (Christ's) *will set My glory among the nations; and all the nations will see My judgment which I have executed and My hand which I have laid on them. And the house of Israel will know that I am the* LORD *their God from that day onward"* (Ezekiel 39:21–22).

Revelation

CHAPTER 21

New American Standard Bible (NASB)

The New Heaven and Earth

²¹ Then I saw a new heaven and a new earth; for the first heaven and the first earth passed away, and there is no longer any sea. ² And I saw the holy city, new Jerusalem, coming down out of heaven from God, made ready as a bride adorned for her husband. ³ And I heard a loud voice from the throne, saying, "Behold, the tabernacle of God is among men, and He will dwell among them, and they shall be His people, and God Himself will be among them, ⁴ and He will wipe away every tear from their eyes; and there will no longer be any death; there will no longer be any mourning, or crying, or pain; the first things have passed away."

⁵ And He who sits on the throne said, "Behold, I am making all things new." And He *said, "Write, for these words are faithful and true." ⁶ Then He said to me, "It is done. I am the Alpha and the Omega, the beginning and the end. I will give to the one who thirsts from the spring of the water of life without cost. ⁷ He who overcomes will inherit these things, and I will be his God and he will be My son. ⁸ But for the cowardly and unbelieving and abominable and murderers and immoral persons and sorcerers and idolaters and all liars, their part will be in the lake that burns with fire and brimstone, which is the second death."

⁹ Then one of the seven angels who had the seven bowls full of the seven last plagues came and spoke with me, saying, "Come here, I will show you the bride, the wife of the Lamb."

The New Jerusalem

¹⁰ And he carried me away in the Spirit to a great and high mountain, and showed me the holy city, Jerusalem, coming down out of heaven from God, ¹¹ having the glory of God. Her brilliance was like a very costly stone, as a stone of crystal-clear jasper. ¹² It had a great and high wall, with twelve gates, and at the gates twelve angels; and names were written on them, which are the names of the twelve tribes of the sons of Israel. ¹³ There were three gates on the east and three gates on the north and three gates on the south and three gates on the west. ¹⁴ And the wall of the city had twelve foundation stones, and on them were the twelve names of the twelve apostles of the Lamb.

¹⁵ The one who spoke with me had a gold measuring rod to measure the city, and its gates and its wall. ¹⁶ The city is laid out as a square, and its length is as great as the width; and he measured the city with the rod, fifteen hundred miles; its length and width and height are equal. ¹⁷ And he measured its wall, seventy-two yards, according to human measurements, which are also angelic measurements. ¹⁸ The material of the wall was jasper; and the city was pure gold, like clear glass. ¹⁹ The foundation stones of the city wall were adorned with every kind of precious stone. The first foundation stone was jasper; the second, sapphire; the third, chalcedony; the fourth, emerald; ²⁰ the fifth, sardonyx; the sixth, sardius; the seventh, chrysolite; the eighth, beryl; the ninth, topaz; the tenth, chrysoprase; the eleventh, jacinth; the twelfth, amethyst. ²¹ And the twelve gates were twelve pearls; each one of the gates was a single pearl. And the street of the city was pure gold, like transparent glass.

²² I saw no temple in it, for the Lord God the Almighty and the Lamb are its temple. ²³ And the city has no need of the sun or of the moon to shine on it, for the glory of God has illumined it, and its lamp is the Lamb. ²⁴ The nations will walk by its light, and the kings of the earth will bring their glory into it. [25] In the daytime (for there will be no night there) its gates will never be closed; [26] and they will bring the glory and the honor of the nations into it; [27] and nothing unclean, and no one who practices abomination and lying, shall ever come into it, but only those whose names are written in the Lamb's book of life.

Notes on Revelation 21

The New Heaven and Earth

Again Revelation 21:1, starts off with a scene change *kai eidon, "and I saw,"* only now John beholds a *"new heaven and a new earth; for the first heaven and the first earth passed away."* The questions which arise are; how does the Disciple John know this is a new heaven and earth and how does he know that the first heaven and earth has passed away? Nowhere in our scriptures do they tells us that heaven and earth will be annihilated or destroyed to the point of oblivion and then be recreated all over again. This doctrine that the earth will be destroyed is a fallacy which has been propagated throughout recent history do to many Prophecy Buffs misinterpretation of scripture; they take this passage to be literal and not metaphorical like most of the Book of Revelation as we have already discussed.

The newness of the "New Heaven and Earth" begins with regeneration. The prophet Isaiah tells us that: *"For behold, I* (God) *create new heavens and a new earth; and the former things shall not be remembered or come to mind"* (Isaiah 65:17). If it is new and the old are now gone, why would it be remembered? Unless this passage like the above passage is a metaphor. The Psalmist David informs us that God: *"established the earth upon its foundations, So that it will not move out of place forever and ever"* (Psalm 104:5). Not being moved out of it place forever and ever can only mean that the earth will remain as it is for eternity. However, the face of the earth and what is on it may change.

The Apostle Peter also adds to this metaphor when he wrote *"But the day of the Lord will come like a thief, in which the heavens will pass away with a roar and the elements will be destroyed with intense heat, and the earth and its works will be burned up*" (2 Peter 3:10). What happens to the forest once a fire passes through the wooded area? You get new life emerging from the ground, thus the cycle of life starts all over again. Peter's metaphor does not equate to the total destruction of the earth to the point of non-existence, but to the point where new life may emerge. Hence, the regeneration of those who follow after the Lord. For as Peter continues: *"but according to His promise we are looking for new heavens and a new earth, in which righteousness dwells"* (2 Peter 3:13).

Thus, it is not a new creation created out of nothing, *ex nihilo*, like that of Genesis 1; rather the newness of heaven and earth shall be like our own. For we shall be the same person and have the same body and the same soul, but we will be an entirely new creation in Christ. The Apostle Paul explains it this way: *"Therefore if any man is in Christ, he is a new creature; the old things passed away; behold, new things have come"* (2 Cor. 5:17). So to be regenerated, we must according to Paul: *"put on the new self, which in the likeness of God has been create in righteousness and holiness of the truth"* (Eph. 4:24).

Even Jesus tried to explain it to Nicodemus: *"Truly, truly, I say to you, we speak of what we know and testify of what we have seen, and you do not accept our testimony. If I told you earthly things and you do not believe, how will you believe if I tell you heavenly things?"* (John 3:11–12). So just except it that this passage is a metaphor and does not mean the complete destruction of the planet.

Even the mention of the sea no longer existing is metaphorical like the new heavens and new earth. Remember water symbolizes *"peoples and multitudes and nations and tongues"* (Rev. 17:15). And the sea is synonymous with the sea of humanity, which envelopes all the unbelievers of *"every tribe, tongue, people, and nation"* (Rev. 13:1). Thus the term *"no longer any sea"* is an analogy of the turbulent, tossing of the unrighteous nations of the earth, which have now been dealt with and judged by Christ Himself during the "Judgment of the Nations" (Rev. 20:4–6), which takes place in the Valley of Jehoshaphat as we find recorded in Joel 3:2 and 12.

So this does not mean that all the wicked and unrighteous people are gone from the face of the earth and that only the righteous are left, for the Great White Throne Judgment has not yet taken place. The Great White Throne Judgment will take place after the millennium is over and after Satan has been defeated for the last time when all mankind will be judged and held accountable for their deeds and if their names are not found in the Book of Life, they will then be thrown into the lake of fire. However, now there are still unrighteous people living in the nations during the millennial reign whom the martyred believers will rule over (see notes on chapter 20).

Our picture of this event is now made complete in verse 2 and 3, because the Lord now tabernacles among us in this "new heaven and new earth" where righteousness now dwells for eternity. There will no longer be any deception, nor any corruption, and no mourning, verses 3–7, but only rejoicing for those living in the very presences of God. Those who are admitted into the holy city, the New Jerusalem, and drink from the spring of the "Water of Life" flowing out of the city toward the east and west *will bring the glory and the honor of the nations into it."*

However, *"Outside the city* (the New Jerusalem) *are the dogs and the sorcerer's and the immoral persons and the murderers and the idolaters, and everyone who loves and practices lying"* (Rev. 22:15). When the New Jerusalem comes down from heaven, only the Bride of Christ will be allowed inside, for there is a stipulation as to who can enter the New Jerusalem: *"Nothing unclean and no one who practices abomination and lying, shall ever come into it"* (Rev. 21:27).

These outsiders are the descendants of *"those who had received the mark of the beast and those who worshiped his image"* (Rev. 17:16–18). These outsiders are the ones who are alive through the millennium as subjects to the *King of kings* and His Martyred Saints, but they will live outside the holy city. They will teach their child, and their grandchildren, and their great-grandchildren the lie, *"all the peoples walk each in the name of his god,"* and they will again be deceived by Satan once more to wage war against the holy ones (God's people; i.e., the one new man). These descendants are still found in the geographical area from which the Antichrist will come from (ancient Assyria, which is modern Turkey).

However, verse 2 starts another scene change *"and I saw,"* kai *eidon*, which taken together with verses 9–27 should be considered as a whole, for they reveal to us new insights into the identity of the holy city: *"And I saw the holy city, new Jerusalem, coming down out of heaven from God, made ready as a bride adorned for her husband."* Hence, Jerusalem is a metaphor for Israel like Babylon is a metaphor for the Beast and she is in contrast to the harlot of chapter 17 who is the seductress of mankind and the dwellers of the earth.

Israel is the Bride, the wife of the Lamb who is adorned in splendor in all her heavenly robes and jewels which is composed of all the glorified saints. In chapter 17 we find the harlot increasing in her seductions of men and kings before the *parousia*, the Second Coming; and here in chapter 21 the Bride is shown after the *parousia*, in all her glory which is synonymous with all that is pure, lovely, beautiful, and righteous.

Our Prophecy Buffs will tell you that this New Jerusalem is a metaphor representing only the Christian Church, but this heresy was created with John Nelson Darby in the mid-1800s with his doctrines of Dispensationalism and Replacement Theology, which states that the Church replaces Israel. Darby taught that the Jews rejected Christ, so God has rejected them and replaces the Old Covenant and the Jews with the New Covenant and the followers of Jesus.

However, Israel (the Jews) did not reject Christ, a few may have been bribed to cry out "crucify him," but as a nation they did not reject the Lord. They as a nation missed His first coming, because they were looking for their Messiah (the anointed one, Greek equivalent is Christ) to arrive on a white charger with all his armies with him as described throughout the Old Testament Books to defeat the nations and establish God's reign on earth. They have been looking for what we call the second coming, the *parousia*, where Christ comes riding a white horse in all His Glory to defeat the nations. They totally missed His first coming as a child: *"The kingdom of God is not coming with signs to be observed; nor will they say, 'Look, here it is!' or, 'There it is!' For behold, the kingdom of God is in your midst"* (Luke 17:20).

It is important to remember that God has NEVER rejected His chosen people, He may have chastised them for disobedience, but he has always loved them:

> *"For God so loved the world, that He gave His only begotten Son, that whoever believes in Him shall not perish, but have eternal life. For God did not send the Son into the world to judge the world, but that the world might be saved through Him."* (John 3:16–17)

Verse 5 changes thing up for in the midst of the New Jerusalem sits Christ on His Throne. "And He who sits on the throne said, "Behold, I am making all things new." Again we are dealing with the idea of regeneration of becoming a new creature (a joint heir) in Christ which comes at no cost to the ones who long for it. *"I will give to the one who thirsts from the spring of the water of life without cost. He who overcomes will inherit these things, and I will be his God and he will be My son"* (Rev. 21:6b–7). What a wonderful symbolic picture we have displayed here, Christ in the midst of His Bride pouring out His love and salvation to Israel and the surrounding nations. This water of life will heal the nations, but yet there will still be a great number who will reject this salvation and who will experience the "second death" once the millennium is over during the Great White Throne Judgment.

Now let us look at the New Jerusalem verses 10–27. Scripture describes the New Jerusalem as a cube coming down from Heaven. The angel *"measured the city with the rod and found it to be twelve thousand stadia* (about 1,400 miles) *in length, and as wide and high as it is long..."* (Rev. 21:16). This cube represents perfection, for the Cross of Christ is the perfect gift that God can give and bestow upon mankind. Thus, when it descends from Heaven it comes in the form of a gift box which then is opened displaying the Cross of Christ to the entire world.

If we look back at the Book of Numbers we find in chapter 2 the arrangement of the camp of the Israelites around the Tabernacle of the Lord while they were wondering in the wilderness. The Twelve Tribes are arranged with three tribes on each side with Levites in the center with the Tabernacle. The eastern side with the Tribes of Judah, Issachar and Zebulan form the longest side of the Cross. Hence, God had a cross shining in the wilderness when he lead his people out of bondage, as he will have a Cross shining to the world when he establishes his kingdom on the earth. There is nothing new under the sun.

Follow the directions below for cutting out the New Jerusalem:
Cut out the cross with all the tabs and slots attached. Then slots need to be cut along the border line of the cube for the tabs to be inserted into. Once it is together it makes a perfect cube, thus the New Jerusalem.

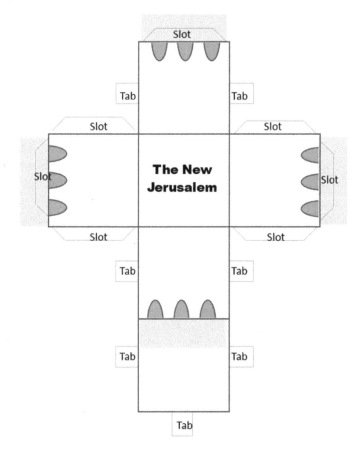

Revelation

CHAPTER 22

New American Standard Bible (NASB)

The River and the Tree of Life

²² Then he showed me a river of the water of life, clear as crystal, coming from the throne of God and of the Lamb, ² in the middle of its street. On either side of the river was the tree of life, bearing twelve kinds of fruit, yielding its fruit every month; and the leaves of the tree were for the healing of the nations. ³ There will no longer be any curse; and the throne of God and of the Lamb will be in it, and His bond-servants will serve Him; ⁴ they will see His face, and His name will be on their foreheads. ⁵ And there will no longer be any night; and they will not have need of the light of a lamp nor the light of the sun, because the Lord God will illumine them; and they will reign forever and ever.

⁶ And he said to me, "These words are faithful and true"; and the Lord, the God of the spirits of the prophets, sent His angel to show to His bond-servants the things which must soon take place.

⁷ "And behold, I am coming quickly. Blessed is he who heeds the words of the prophecy of this book."

⁸ I, John, am the one who heard and saw these things. And when I heard and saw, I fell down to worship at the feet of the angel who showed

me these things. ⁹ But he *said to me, "Do not do that. I am a fellow servant of yours and of your brethren the prophets and of those who heed the words of this book. Worship God."

The Final Message

¹⁰ And he *said to me, "Do not seal up the words of the prophecy of this book, for the time is near. ¹¹ Let the one who does wrong, still do wrong; and the one who is filthy, still be filthy; and let the one who is righteous, still practice righteousness; and the one who is holy, still keep himself holy."

¹² "Behold, I am coming quickly, and My reward is with Me, to render to every man according to what he has done. ¹³ I am the Alpha and the Omega, the first and the last, the beginning and the end."

¹⁴ Blessed are those who wash their robes, so that they may have the right to the tree of life, and may enter by the gates into the city. ¹⁵ Outside are the dogs and the sorcerers and the immoral persons and the murderers and the idolaters, and everyone who loves and practices lying.

¹⁶ "I, Jesus, have sent My angel to testify to you these things for the churches. I am the root and the descendant of David, the bright morning star."

¹⁷ The Spirit and the bride say, "Come." And let the one who hears say, "Come." And let the one who is thirsty come; let the one who wishes take the water of life without cost.

¹⁸ I testify to everyone who hears the words of the prophecy of this book: if anyone adds to them, God will add to him the plagues which are written in this book; ¹⁹ and if anyone takes away from the words of the book of this prophecy, God will take away his part from the tree of life and from the holy city, which are written in this book.

[20] He who testifies to these things says, "Yes, I am coming quickly." Amen. Come, Lord Jesus.

[21] The grace of the Lord Jesus be with all. Amen.

Notes on Revelation 22

The Final Message

Revelation 22:1–5 starts off with an allusion to the Paradise lost, the Garden of Eden, which is now Paradise regained with the Water of Life flowing out from the throne of God here in the center of New Jerusalem. However, the image of this Paradise regained applies to the millennium and the thousand year reign of Christ and not eternity. For the nations are healed by the fruit of the tree of life and living water of life within the city for anyone who is able to enter through the gates. Thus the gates are open to all who bow their knee and confess that Jesus Christ is Lord and who wash their robes in righteousness, for their names are written in the Lamb's Book of Life in Revelation 21:27.

However, there is a stipulation as to who can enter the New Jerusalem, for God makes it clear that *"Nothing unclean and no one who practices abomination and lying, shall ever come into it"* (Rev. 21:27). For *"Outside the city are the dogs and the sorcerer's and the immoral persons and the murderers and the idolaters, and everyone who loves and practices lying"* (Rev. 22:15).

These are the ones whom the martyred saints will reign over during the millennium (Rev. 22:5b). These subjugated *"outsiders"* will be the ones deceived when Satan is released from his prison. For he *"will come out to deceive the nations which are in the four corners of the earth, Gog and Magog, to gather them together for war…and they came up on the broad plan of the earth and surrounded the camp of the saints and the beloved city"* (Rev. 20:7–9).

This takes us back, by contrast to the multitudes of the beast whom bear the mark of his name on their foreheads, they come up against the nation of Israel and overtake the holy city of Jerusalem and are defeated (Rev. 19:20–21). Their descendants now will live through the millennium as subjects to the *King of Kings* and His saints. But they will live outside the holy city; they will teach their child, and their Grand Children, and their Great Grand Children the lie, and they will again be deceived by Satan once more to wage war against the saints and Christ.

These are the ones whom the angel with the seventh bowl of plagues is referring to when he says *"Let the one who does wrong, still do wrong; and the one who is filthy, still be filthy"* (Rev. 22:11a). Which is what Ezekiel was communicating to us when he states *"He who hears, let him hear; and he who refuses, let him refuse; for they are a rebellious house"* (Ez. 3:27b). For they will reap their own rewards when Christ comes, *"Behold...My reward is with Me, to render to every man according to what he has done"* (Rev. 22:12).

The main point, however, which must not be overlooked, is that Jesus himself utters this final testimony, *marturo ego, "I myself testify!"* Not only will all who hears these words of prophecy and adds or changes them will receive their just rewards, just like those outside the holy city here at the end, but all those, from the time this book was written until the end, which are unwilling to change their wicked ways and repent; will no longer receive God's Mercy. For *"evil men and impostors will proceed from bad to worse, deceiving and being deceived. You, however, continue in the things you have learned...which are able to give you the wisdom that leads to salvation through faith which is in Christ Jesus"* (2 Tim. 3:13–15).

The testimony of at least two witnesses is required to properly and legally settle any matter, John 8:17, 2 Corinthians 13:1, Hebrews 10:28. So here we have both the attested witness of the angel of the Lord (the one holding the seventh bowl) and Christ Jesus Himself confirming the fact that the revelation given to John is faithful and true and will come about as foretold. Of this we are assured, there can be no doubt.

About the Author

Patrick Basal is a Retired US Army Chaplain and decorated combat veteran of Kuwait, Kosovo, and Iraqi Campaigns. In his twenty-four years of active federal service he has served as a Battalion Chaplain, Brigade Chaplain, Resource Manager, Ethics Instructor, and as a Garrison Command Chaplain throughout Central America, Europe, the Middle East, and in the Pacific Area of Operations. He holds four earned degrees from Augsburg College, Minneapolis; Gordon-Conwell Theological Seminary, Boston; and Lutheran Theological Seminary, Philadelphia. Currently, he works and minsters to International Military Officers from around the world who are here attending advanced US Military education. He has been married for over thirty-seven years and has three surviving children.

CPSIA information can be obtained
at www.ICGtesting.com
Printed in the USA
LVHW052349100720
660358LV00008B/371